THE ABUSE OF POWER

The Abuse of Power

*The War between Downing Street and the
Media from Lloyd George to Callaghan*

by

James Margach

W. H. ALLEN · LONDON
A Howard & Wyndham Company
1978

For RONA, as ever

Printed and bound in Great Britain by
The Garden City Press Limited
Letchworth, Hertfordshire SG6 1JS

for the Publisher, W. H. Allen & Co. Ltd,
44 Hill Street, London W1X 8LB

ISBN 0 491 02044 9

Contents

Illustrations

INTRODUCTION

No. 10's Secret Power Battles

"Public opinion could not be ignored, it had to be fooled. The power of Government to deceive is so immense..." No. 10 Downing Street official spokesman.*

This is an eye-witness story of the tempestuous and never-ending war between Downing Street and Fleet Street, Whitehall and the Press. For forty-four years as a political correspondent I was a front-line observer of the battles between the two empires and have seen at first hand the complex and fascinating exercise of real power in a war which has been neglected to an astonishing extent in histories, biographies and memoirs. Its very existence is the unmentionable secret of politics.

To win this war has been the first priority of nearly all the dozen Prime Ministers I have known. With almost obsessional ruthlessness the majority sought to dominate and influence the Press, TV and Radio, as the vital precondition to their domination of Parliament, parties and public opinion. They desired to enrol and exploit the media as an arm of government. Two objectives possessed them. First, to establish and fortify their personal power; and secondly to reinforce the conspiracy of secrecy, to preserve the sanctity of Government behind the walls of Whitehall's forbidden city.

The twelve Prime Ministers I have known, in many cases in terms of personal friendship, were: Stanley Baldwin, Ramsay MacDonald, Neville Chamberlain, Winston Churchill, Clement Attlee, Anthony Eden, Harold Macmillan, Alec Douglas-Home, Harold Wilson, Edward Heath and James Callaghan. Lloyd George I claim as a bonus. Although he ceased to rule before I became a

* William Clark, Press and Broadcasting Adviser to Sir Anthony Eden during the Suez crisis (*Secrecy*, OUP, New York); now international director of the World Bank.

political correspondent, he remained by far the most commanding national and international figure of the inter-war years.

My purpose is not to present a series of potted biographies of these Premiers or to recapture the main events in which they were the central characters; it is to portray them in front-line action, when the pressures were on. How they appeared to me in my ring-side seat will conflict in many cases with the pictures they preferred to present of themselves in the memoirs and diaries which they dashed off to meet publishers' deadlines and the demands of serialised extracts—"the new cannibalism" as Baldwin described the process of protecting your own reputation and destroying the reputation of others. Nor am I concerned, in this book, with the passing show of party politics and the small-print of long-forgotten policies. What is so much more exciting and revealing is politics from which the parties and the policies have been scraped away. Then, only power and personalities remain.

For close on half a century I have witnessed a revolution inexorably taking place. Parliament has gone into decline, with its powers shifting to a menacing extent to No. 10 Downing Street. The resulting influence of "the Executive"—that cross-breed created by incestuous relations between the Government and Whitehall—has produced, as Lord Hailsham has said, an "elective dictatorship". The political reality is that we live in a society controlled to a degree undreamed-of when I began in this business. As Whitehall has accumulated more and more power from Westminster, the techniques of news-management and centralised control have become more complete while secrecy is more widespread and ruthlessly organised, sustaining the mystique of power which in turn sustains all Prime Ministers. In my early days Ministers, Permanent Secretaries and the Ministers' private offices within Departments were always accessible to political correspondents, ready to answer questions and explain policies. Since then, although the number of newspapers and of overseas correspondents has declined, a battalion of 1,500 Press and information officers has been created to man the front-line trenches. Moreover, the jungle of the Official Secrets Act remains as impenetrable as ever, despite many modern promises of reform. In an allegedly free and open society, the public's right to know what is being decided in its name is treated as high treason.

Much is sometimes made of the superiority of the openness of Washington. There is a deep irony here, for the Washington practice was actually based on the success of the pre-war Westminster–Whitehall methods. Indeed, as the eminent authority, Douglass

Cater, points out in his classic study of the Press in Washington*, the famous Presidential Press conference was introduced by President Wilson to provide the American equivalent of the Prime Minister's question-time. But while Downing Street now increasingly controls output, sources and access in Britain, the focus of attention in the USA, as Cater points out, is moving strongly from the White House to the network of Congressional Committees which make the head-lines as their scrutiny tightens their control of the Government. Furthermore, Washington's top civil servants are trained and expected to cope with Press inquiries and to be accessible to individual correspondents—a far cry from the mandarins of Whitehall, Britain's Silent Service.

Unlike civil servants, however, Prime Ministers are men who may be in a job one day and out the next. And so, having pursued power and seized it, they proceed to use and abuse it in order to dominate the Press in an apparently paranoid pursuance of survival. Each has his own style. Some are blatantly wooing and anxious to please, others play hard to get; a few are full of bluster, others ooze flattery. But they all have the same repertoire: Royal Commissions, tribunals, threats of the Official Secrets Act and the might of the law, inquiries and writs galore or peerages and other honours in abundance. With two exceptions, my Downing Street dozen dis-played a remarkable degree of ruthlessness and in certain instances were even prepared to try to get journalists of high integrity sacked or even moved from the political scene. Downing Street deploys its own array of "dirty tricks" when the heat in the kitchen is at its most intense. But for preference the mailed fist is kept firmly inside the velvet glove. Premiers who are increasingly put across to the electors in the manner of a can of beer or a packet of soap powder, pay court to the upper echelons of the Fourth Estate as an integral part of the PR machinery of advertising, packaging and image-building. Their attentions are frequently devoted. One Premier spent each Wednesday for five weeks in newspaper boardrooms and during that time seldom attended meetings of his own party M.P.s.

But as they go a-wooing there is "rape" in their hearts. Their approaches are ostensibly part of the process of open government, extending the frontiers of freedom of the Press, co-opting proprietors, editors and journalists into the mystique of decision-making and secret-sharing, opening the doors of Whitehall, liberal-ising the laws of secrecy. But this is a grand illusion. The reality is that they are manipulating the Press, using all the arts of statecraft. For example, I have several times heard Prime Ministers reinforce the totality of the Official Secrets Act by the simple expedient of

* *The Fourth Branch of Government*, Random House, New York.

appearing to lift it by sharing secrets with Fleet Street board members under cover of the "off the record" formula. It runs something like this: "I'm glad you've raised this crucial policy problem. I want you to understand the issues which were before the Cabinet yesterday. I want to be frank. May I speak freely, in confidence?" But of course; not a word will ever be repeated outside the boardroom, let alone published! Having secured this pledge of secrecy and confidentiality in a calculated exercise in flattery which did not pass unappreciated, committing the highest powers in Fleet Street to sealed lips, they proceed to recite highly selective versions of inside history, confident that they have enmeshed everybody present in the Official Secrets Act and that not a single word will leak out despite the primary aim of newspapers to disclose and expose. It is the new confidence trick. The Press, by satisfying its own right to know, at the same time guarantees that secrecy remains total by gagging itself.

In this tightly balanced Premier–Press, relationship, responsible journalists must be guided by the counsel of Thomas Barnes, famous editor of *The Times* (1817–41), that the "newspaper is not an organ through which Government can influence people, but through which people can influence the Government". In the ceaseless power battles most, if not all, Prime Ministers subscribe to a rather different dictum, the rule-of-thumb favoured by Lloyd George and Churchill, that "what you can't square you squash, and what you can't squash you square".

In the power vacuum created by the retreat of Parliament it has never been more vital for there to be tough scrutiny by the media as a counterbalance to the increasing despotism of Downing Street and Whitehall. Yet such surveillance is eroded when newspapermen are treated as buddies, an arm of government manning an outstation in Fleet Street. In this intricate power game, communicators, whose basic interests must be in conflict with those of Prime Ministers, face the dilemma of where precisely to draw the line.

Without accepting the extreme judgment of Hazlitt, who advised editors to stay in their garrets and avoid exposing themselves to the subtleties of power, Walter Lippmann, one of the most famous American newspapermen of all time, made broadly the same point to the International Press Institute some years ago. He said that the danger to the independence and integrity of journalists did not come from the pressures that might be put upon them; it was that they might be captured and captivated by the company they keep. In the same vein, the distinguished former doyen of Washington correspondents, Arthur Krock, said after six decades in the business: "It is true that in most cases the price of friendship with a politician is

4

too great for any newspaperman to pay". Nearer home, A. P. Wadsworth, the great editor of the *Manchester Guardian*, said that no editor should ever be on personal terms with our leaders for fear of creating a false sense of relation of confidence. Speaking from my own experience, I believe that it is when leading media figures see too much rather than too little of Prime Ministers that the freedom of the Press is endangered. When Premiers go courting in Fleet Street, and follow with pressing invitations to cosy little chats at No. 10, or even Chequers, then the alarm bells should start ringing.

One notable example to support the Lippmann–Krock–Wadsworth warnings is the occasion when Sir Gerald Barry, editor of the *News Chronicle*, and all his senior editorial staff, joined in unprecedented (and successful) strike action when their chairman, Lord Layton, decreed that the celebrated Vernon Bartlett's report from Munich on the night of the Munich agreement between Hitler and Chamberlain, should not be published because it was too depressing. At the time Layton's attitude was incomprehensible. He was a great Liberal in the classic tradition; a fighter for freedom. Then years later (as I discuss in Chapter 4) I learnt of the intimidation of Layton by Chamberlain himself: he summoned the *News Chronicle* chairman to Downing Street to rebuke him for his paper's reports about the appeasement of Mussolini, and, as the Cabinet secret files report, Layton "apologised". The dangers are surely self-evident when Premiers feel they can demand personal apologies from the topmost perches in Fleet Street.

It also follows that the occupation of a political correspondent in the lobbies and corridors of power at Westminster may be a hazardous one, particularly when it arouses the fury of Prime Ministers, other Ministers and the Whitehall dynasty. Political correspondents, also known as Lobby correspondents, should be distinguished from Parliamentary and Gallery correspondents who are concerned mainly with what goes on on the floor of both Houses. The Lobbymen are permitted, under the so-called "Lobby system", to mix freely with Ministers and M.P.s in the Members' Lobby and elsewhere at Westminster. They are primarily concerned with what takes place, mostly under cover, in Cabinet, Government Departments, Parliament and the political parties. When too successful in their role as investigative journalists they provoke violent reactions, especially when they ferret out and publish information which the Executive consider to belong exclusively to them, regardless of the fact that the policies at the heart of the trouble may affect every man, woman and child in the country. A few representative instances demonstrate how Prime Ministers, the Executive, and even party establishments, try to get such Lobbymen blackballed or gagged and even, in some astonishing cases demanding their removal from the centre of power.

In late 1966 when Lord Thomson was awaiting the results of the deliberations of the Monopolies Commission on his proposed take-over of *The Times* he was invited to Chequers for dinner with Harold Wilson. I was present. When, over coffee, Roy Thomson asked the Prime Minister what his first action should be to improve the paper's prospects if the takeover went through, the Prime Minister's immediate reply was that he should sack the paper's political correspondent, David Wood.

A diatribe followed. At the same dinner were Denis Hamilton, who became editor-in-chief of Times Newspapers Ltd., and William Rees-Mogg, who was appointed editor of *The Times*. Later they demonstrated what they thought of such interference by a Prime Minister in the independence and integrity of the paper: they promoted Wood to political editor. (In his time Wilson demanded of proprietors and editors that at least three Lobby correspondents should be removed. David Wood was no newcomer to such tactics. Some years earlier he was the target of the Conservatives' 1922 Committee who despatched a powerful delegation to the then chief proprietor of *The Times*, Gavin Astor, demanding that Wood should be removed from Westminster because they classed him as *persona non grata* following what they regarded as "unfriendly" reports about the party and the Prime Minister, Harold Macmillan. They complained not because his reports were inaccurate but because they were too true, revealing facts about their internal leadership crises that they wished to be suppressed as an official secret. Sir William Haley, the then editor (with Gavin Astor's full support) stood firm and demanded an apology, which he got.

A similar incident centred on Noyes Thomas of the *News of the World* who confidently forecast in his paper that Marcia Williams, political secretary to the Prime Minister, Harold Wilson, was about to be created a life peer and made a Minister in the Wilson Government. Wilson was so incensed that he immediately demanded that his Press secretary, Joe Haines, should denounce the report as a lie and then instructed Haines not to give Press briefings to Lobby meetings attended by Thomas. This attempt to blackball Thomas, if successful, would have prevented him from earning his living (though Haines told Wilson he could not stop his attending Lobby meetings as demanded). The Lobby repudiated the implication that it should blacklist a colleague in response to a *diktat* from Downing Street and in due course Thomas's forecast was vindicated. He still awaits an apology from Harold Wilson.

6

Having read the full record of Cabinet minutes since they were introduced by Lloyd George in 1916, during the First World War (and with the gap created by the thirty-year rule plugged by the diaries of Richard Crossman, Barbara Castle and others as well as the Churchill, Eden, Macmillan and Wilson memoirs) I am struck by the obsession with secrecy which gripped all Prime Ministers and their Governments. Every other week complaints were raised about leaks. Indeed, they became such a formality that successive Cabinet Secretaries used a standard reference in their minutes: "LEAKS— Unauthorised Disclosure of Information". Yet with rare exceptions these regular and endless entries in the minutes had nothing remotely to do with the Official Secrets Act and the categories of State secrets envisaged by the original legislation: espionage, intelligence, services, spies, the security of the State, defence secrets.

Little of this sort disturbed the serenity of Cabinet meetings. What angered Prime Ministers were reports in newspapers about Government decisions, taken or pending, on policies of major importance and interest for the general public.

Indeed, from the frequency of references to newspapers' titles in these hallowed tomes, one can pick out the go-ahead papers in Fleet Street's competitive world. If pressed, I could compile a league table of the most successful editors and Lobby correspondents, defence and diplomatic correspondents, from the points awarded for honourable mentions in the Cabinet files. Lobby newsmen in particular have been far more successful in breaching Whitehall's secrets than their detractors would ever care to admit. According to the evidence of the Cabinet's form-book, political correspondents succeeded in advancing the frontiers of freedom of the Press with astonishing regularity.

The secrecy phobia has affected all Prime Ministers of all parties; they fall victim to the power drug when they fear their authority is being challenged by the Press. The all-time greats, Lloyd George and Winston Churchill, could be as extreme and ruthless as any. Apart from Lloyd George's cynical use of mass honours of all shapes, sizes and prices to keep the new generation of Press lords sweet, he went in for character assassination of journalists whose loyalty to himself he suspected.

Similarly, during the Second World War, Churchill had to be resisted by his own Cabinet in his zeal to suppress the Mirror newspapers, and reacted by treating the papers' directors, editors, writers and cartoonists as "quislings", harbouring secret sympathies for the enemy and a negotiated peace.

In more modern times the most astonishing and melodramatic

instance of Prime Ministerial mania was provided when Harold Wilson boasted to the *Observer*'s editor-proprietor, David Astor, that he had had his paper's political correspondent, Nora Beloff, shadowed in order to discover her sources. He accurately named six or seven Ministers and prominent M.P.s she had seen on one day to confirm that the exercise was mounted in great detail—a scenario one would more readily associate with the K.G.B's surveillance in the Kremlin or the C.I.A's trailing of suspects in Washington.

Because they control the levers and the timing, Prime Ministers are ruthless in striking back whenever newspapers can be exposed before public opinion as irresponsible and dangerous, especially in cases where they can be accused of abusing people's privacy. Where there have been excesses by a few, the Press as a whole has always been compelled to retreat. And each retreat in my experience has made it that much easier for the Executive to increase the Whitehall barriers of secrecy. In each of the four major Government–Press power crises during my time at Westminster and Whitehall the Press has been routed and discredited by the Prime Minister of the day, losing much ground painfully won. Most significant of all, the Executive skilfully succeeded in persuading public opinion to take a cynical view of the standards set by Fleet Street. And each time, when this happened, the ideal of an increased freedom of the Press in a free society receded yet further.

Let me summarise the four crises when the conduct of a few meant that the Press, in effect, connived at turning its own flank. The first concerned the original generation of Press lords, made vastly rich by the mass readerships created by compulsory education. In the 1930s they acted as though they were more powerful than the elected Governments. Two of them, Beaverbrook and Rothermere, actually formed their own political party on a national basis, complete with candidates, in order to destroy the then Prime Minister, Stanley Baldwin. He finished them off in his famous phrase: "Power without responsibility, the prerogative of the harlot throughout the ages." The Press lords were never the same again.

Twenty years later, in the Attlee era, the Press celebrated its post-war release from controls and newsprint rationing by an unbridled campaign of screaming irresponsibility, in my experience the worst period for the reputation and standards of journalism. I am in good company. Sir Hartley (later Lord) Shawcross, Attlee's Attorney-General and afterwards Chairman of the Press Council, vigorously attacked the ruling Press lords—the final generation of personal and family proprietors—for their reckless "campaign of calumny which the Tory party and the Tory stooge Press" had pursued against the Attlee Government. There had never been a time, he claimed, when certain sections of the Press "had more seriously abused the freedom of the Press" which did not give "freedom to tell lies . . . or cook the news . . . distorting news, suppressing facts". Shawcross spelled out a moral which is just as relevant today as then: that the freedom of the Press must be preserved by the Press itself in insisting on the highest standards, because "there would be nothing more dangerous to democratic freedom in this country than that the Press should be gagged". It was in this same period that Aneurin Bevan attacked "the most prostituted Press in the world". The Press had to pay a severe price for having so many prostitutes, pimps and sadists in its midst. The first Royal Commission was imposed as a penalty, leading to the formation of the first Press Council in the hope of maintaining self-discipline and standards in the ranks.

The third occasion when Fleet Street excesses played into the hands of the Executive, when once again the Press was discredited in the public eye, came in the Macmillan age. Following the Vassall and Profumo scandals—the first dealing with spies, the second with prostitutes in high places—the Prime Minister and his Ministers were the victims of the most unbridled series of attacks and smears, with countless innuendoes about secret scandals and cover-ups. Harold Macmillan shrewdly timed his counter-strike. He appointed Lord Radcliffe, a famous law lord, to chair a judicial inquiry into all the newspapers' allegations. On the conduct of Fleet Street, the inquiry's report was so devastating that not even a whimper of protest was heard in the land when two reporters were imprisoned for refusing to disclose their sources. The Radcliffe Tribunal reported that they had investigated over 250 separate newspaper reports linked with the Vassall affair and that there was not a word of truth in any of them—not even after editors, news executives and reporters had been offered the protection of privilege under which to give evidence.

The Radcliffe exposures stoked the anti-Press feelings in Parliament and in the country, and helped to push back overdue reforms by a generation. But the most significant aspect of the whole affair passed unnoticed. The appointment of the Tribunal proved a master-stroke in the hate-hate relations between Downing Street and Fleet Street. Harold Macmillan, as ever a shrewd and subtle pastmaster in the exercise of power, succeeded nobly in turning the inquiry into a show trial of the Press and its methods, with the Press humiliated in the dock. As a result, scant attention was ever given in public to Whitehall's responsibility for allowing a foreign spy service to operate with ease at the heart of Britain's defence system.

The fourth occasion when the overall reputation of the Press was discredited by a single misjudgment came in 1977 when the *Daily Mail*'s strident campaign on alleged bribery and corruption at British Leyland provoked bitter reactions and criticism when it was discovered within hours that it was based on a forged letter. The Prime Minister, James Callaghan, did not miss the opportunity to deride the judgment, credibility and responsibility of the Press. Once again newspapers as a whole surrendered ground and reputation painfully won.

Even when the Press appears to win it can still lose. In 1970 the Official Secrets Act was invoked for the prosecution of the *Sunday Telegraph* which, during the Biafran war, published a secret report on the Nigerian Army by a British military expert. Brian Roberts, the editor, and three co-defenders were acquitted, the judge commenting that the controversially wide-ranging Section Two of the Act, nigh on sixty years old, should be pensioned off and a more modern section inserted. Eighteen months later a committee chaired by Lord Franks recommended that Section Two should be repealed and replaced by something more realistic, dealing only with defence, security and foreign affairs. But despite friendly noises by several Ministers, promising that reform was imminent, nothing has yet happened. The reason for the delay is the powerful resistance by the high priests of Whitehall to any reforms which would encourage open government and disclosure.

An even more bizarre use of the Official Secrets Act took place a year after the *Sunday Telegraph* case when the *Sunday Times* published a railway policy document, drafted inside the Transport Ministry, proposing major closures of railway lines as part of wide-ranging reorganisation. Scotland Yard raided the offices of the *Railway Gazette*, suspected as the initial channel of the leak, and then attempted to intimidate Harold Evans, editor of the *Sunday Times*, and Richard Hope, editor of the *Railway Gazette*, in the hope of discovering how the document reached them. The fact that the subject had nothing remotely to do with State security, foreign spies or military secrets, confirms the eccentric uses for which the Act can be invoked. Evans and Hope were not scared by the display of police and departmental power, and refused to reveal their sources.

This experience also illustrates how little Government and Whitehall obsessions with secrecy have changed in almost half a century. In 1931, in a case now enshrined in Lobby history, the Special Branch grilled an old friend of mine for five hours trying to discover the source of a Cabinet leak. The Attorney-General, Sir William Jowitt, tried to justify such blatant pressure by stating in Parliament: "I should certainly desire to uphold the freedom of the Press in every possible way, but I would point out that there is no question of this journalist either being guilty or innocent. He was merely asked to comply with the duty which the State imposes upon him, namely, to give the source of his information." The identical pressure was exerted on Evans and Hope. The Act remains the Executive's toy; not to protect what defence secrets remain, but to discover the source of leaks of matters essential to informed public opinion.

Evans also made a substantial breakthrough of the Executive's defences-in-depth when he defied the Government and Civil Service pressures exerted by Cabinet Secretary Sir John Hunt, to censor the diaries of Richard Crossman which revealed secrets about the way in which Cabinets operate and reach decisions. Evans won his right to publish by successfully resisting a gagging action in the courts by Sam Silkin, Attorney-General.

Yet, however successful such challenges prove to be on particular sectors of a very long battlefront determinedly manned by the Executive, the fact remains that the laws which prevent movement towards greater freedoms of disclosure and exposure remain in force. There exists a formidable catalogue of major reforms and minor changes proposed by a series of committees and inquiries over many years: Caulfield and Franks on Official Secrets; Younger on Privacy; Faulks on libel and slander; Phillimore on contempt. No action has yet been taken. Harold Wilson and Roy Jenkins made most encouraging noises about their determination to modernise official secrets, balanced in a package which included privacy. But the caravan has moved on; Wilson and Jenkins are no longer at the Cabinet table. When this volume was being prepared for publication the promised White Papers proposing changes in Section II of the Secrets Act were still pending. Legal reforms, therefore, still lie far ahead. When they finally appear they are likely to prove minimal, far removed from the ambitious idea of a Freedom of Information Act.

The moral is clear. Access to information will be no greater, there will be no more disclosure as of right; no new dialogue in a free society with the Press and Media providing the two-way communication link. Secretiveness is more firmly entrenched than ever it was; it has become the way of life. Even physical access to the centres of power is more difficult.

My firm belief is that the Press will never make any significant penetration of the Executive's defences unless and until a revitalised

Parliament is able to claw back some of its power and authority, for Parliament and Press in the new situation now share objectives: more disclosure, more access to sources of information, wider decision-sharing, reform of secrecy and so forth. When I started at Westminster great controversy was raging over the revelations in *The New Despotism* by Lord Chief Justice Hewart about the growth in the 'twenties of the new autocracy. Now the infant has grown into a frightening giant, Lord Hailsham's "elective dictatorship", but Hewart's definition of tyranny has stood the test of time: "the accumulation of despotic power in the hands of anonymous officials".

There are many excellent ideas around to restore to Westminster some of its lost power. But they are never seriously debated or investigated. They include a written constitution, a Bill of Rights, more select committees on American lines with power to question Ministers and senior officials on details of policies, a major monitoring committee of senior status, as suggested by Edward du Cann, with sub-committees to mark every major department, and more open consultation with M.P.s and Press before legislation is introduced.

Even the most promising initiatives are frustrated. As Leader of the Commons, Richard Crossman introduced the Select Committee system to keep watch and ward on Whitehall. Yet when a key Committee asked Cabinet member and Paymaster-General Harold Lever to appear before it and give evidence about a Government decision, he refused on the authority of the Prime Minister, Harold Wilson. Faced with such resistance to the traditional majesty of Parliament, what hope has Fleet Street ever to break through the secrecy barriers which prevent access to information, disclosure, decision-sharing, and other reforms for open government in a free society?

This is not always the fault of Whitehall's top brass. It is still an "in" Secret in Whitehall's network that in the late 'sixties Sir William Armstrong, in a courageous move towards more 'Open Government', minuted all his Permanent Secretaries suggesting that they should make themselves more accessible to the Media. Some of them acted on his advice and took tuition at the Central Office of Information's studios to get accustomed to TV cameras and equipment moving around them. After some successful appearances the plan was dropped, mainly for two reasons. TV interviewers tried to entice the Permanent Secretaries on to political minefields: and one or two Ministers showed jealousy streaks over the TV star potential of their topmost advisers! The problem was to draw the dividing line between Departmental policies and Government initiatives stemming from partisan manifesto pledges.

I

LLOYD GEORGE

December 1916–October 1922

"The Press? What you can't square you squash, what you can't squash you square." LLOYD GEORGE

Lloyd George was the first Prime Minister to discover Fleet Street. His period of supreme power coincided with the first mass reader-ship produced by the compulsory State education of which he had been a great protagonist. The power potential of the first literate national electorate fascinated him. As Britain's most dynamic Prime Minister and an imaginative genius he seized at once on the prospect of running Downing Street and Fleet Street in tandem. So he proceeded deliberately and cynically to establish his personal ascendancy over the Press, to control as his personal possession the vast new power offered by Fleet Street, and to pioneer methods of news-management and opinion-forming to reinforce his personal power.

There has never been any mystery as to how he did it. He dangled baubles before the moguls of Fleet Street and so entranced were they that they not only handed over power they handed over real money as well. To save time and effort the transactions were conducted wholesale. Seven members of the pioneering Harmsworth family variously became Viscounts, Barons, Baronets and Knights, and other family dynasties were founded with the creation of Lord Beaverbrook of the *Daily Express*, Lord Burham of the *Daily Telegraph*, Lord Dalzeil of *Reynolds News* and Lord Riddell of the *News of the World*. On all sides, Lloyd George sprayed honours with a hose pipe; it was a golden era for the Press. A dazzling variety of prized awards and medals were showered on cousins, brothers and nephews; even the offspring of mistresses were included among the ranks of the remittance men. As double insurance of personal loyalty Lloyd George lavished high office on the pillars of the Press: at one time six of Fleet Street's families were in his

Government. He also distributed public service posts—thus beginning a vast patronage business which today covers some forty thousand jobs at national, regional and local level, with the fortunate ones sharing the contents of the gravy train, or the port barrel.

From his commercial exploitation of the honours system Lloyd George is estimated to have amassed a £3 million Lloyd George Fund or War Chest (valued at the sterling rates of the period) and of this the newly ennobled Press lords must have contributed a handsome proportion. When I arrived at Westminster in the early 'thirties my elderly colleagues used to quote me from the course the starting prices in the ermine race (the Central Statistical Office tells me to multiply by ten for the equivalent value today). A viscountcy was anything from £120,000 (£1.2 million today) down to £80,000 according to the state of your bank account and your anxiety to beget a new aristocracy for Debretts; baronies were a knock-down at £30,000 to £50,000; baronetcies, if you had a son ready to continue the line, were £25,000, perhaps a little more to encourage you to renewed effort if no heir was yet available; for run-of-the-mill knighthoods at £15,000, supply obligingly kept pace with demand. Medals were graded according to the attractive ribbon colours for wear on full evening dress.

In this way, without a party to sustain his post-war Government in any semblancy of unity, and the prisoner of the Conservatives, Lloyd George bought the allegiance of Fleet Street as his power base. It was an effort to be repeated often by subsequent Prime Ministers but never in quite the same bizarre style.

It was only when Lloyd George's racket became too objectionable for normal nostrils that his world started to fall to pieces around him. George V himself frequently protested about the way in which Press owners were being fed like a pack of hungry wolves. He objected vigorously to the viscountcy for Rothermere, and successfully delayed it: "The King would like to remind the Prime Minister that in less than six years Mr Harold Harmsworth has become a Baronet in 1910; a Peer 1914; a Privy Councillor 1917...". It was a year later that the King gave his approval—"but with much reluctance". The King also opposed Beaverbrook's ennoblement, the promotion of Russell of the *Liverpool Post*, and put up a last-ditch fight against Dalzeil's peerage. His most violent objections were against the peerage for Lord Riddell of the *News of the World*, the Press ally to whom Lloyd George owed most and who had given him most in kind, such as a country home. And it was not only the Palace which was shocked by the swift presumption of nobility for Fleet Street and the frantic bidding to found new empires. The Duke of Northumberland did his sums and told the House of Lords: "Only two or three honours were conferred on journalists every year, but you will find that the number of this profession who have been appointed Privy Councillors, peers, baronets and knights since amounts to no fewer than forty-nine, and that number does not include CMGs and other unconsidered trifles of that kind."

In the light of the widespread resentment engendered by these excesses between Lloyd George and the Press world it is as well to bear in mind that the Prime Minister did not actually start the trade in honours; he simply took it down into the market place, striking the final bargain between eager buyer and willing seller. Before him the business remained part of the accepted code of conduct between gentlemen; both Conservatives and Liberals regarding honours as a marketable commodity to provide regular income for their parties.

In the words of Alfred Harmsworth, himself created Lord Northcliffe by the Tories ten years before the heyday of Lloyd George's system: "When I want a peerage I will pay for it like an honest man". The bitter political row over Lloyd George's twice-yearly auction did not, therefore, stem from considerations of ethics or morality but from the fact that Lloyd George was gaining an advantage regarded by his opponents as being unfair. As the Tory party chairman of the day put it: "Lloyd George's whips were gathering corn in Tory fields and poaching for rare birds in Conservative preserves".

In the early 'twenties, this did not bring any dividends. As his political position weakened his Press barons deserted him. Like other worldly creations, newspaper owners do not feel grateful or loyal for long; they soon convinced themselves that they had achieved their ermine as of right without any outside assistance. Moreover, after Lloyd George lost power in 1922 they pursued him vindictively in a most violent campaign of persecution. Even Riddell deserted the stricken warrior; only Beaverbrook remained a loyal friend to the end. Arguably, this whole squalid era in relations between Downing Street and Fleet Street might have been averted if only the two sides had remained on a love-hate footing, each keeping to its own empire. But they did not. In the excesses of mutual infatuation, Lloyd George tried to run the whole of Fleet Street by putting owners under debts of honour while, in return, the new breed of newspaper owners imagined they had a divine right to run the Government, manage Whitehall, and pick and choose their Ministries. Such an affair could not last.

The pattern for the lovers' quarrel was set over the Versailles Peace Conference in 1919. Northcliffe assumed and expected that his importance in public life would be recognised by the Prime Minister's inviting him to be a member of the British delegation, a mistaken impression which was perhaps encouraged when Lloyd George suggested that the magnate should take a house in Paris during the Conference in which to entertain world figures. When Northcliffe discovered that he was not actually to be included in the British delegation he over-reacted by launching the most vindictive campaign against the Prime Minister, accusing him and the British team of betrayal, of failing to stand up for Britain. This shrill propaganda campaign at home and abroad threatened to undermine Lloyd George's position, especially in Parliament, so he decided to return at once to defend himself. How he did it provided the perfect illustration of what the Earl of Birkenhead (F. E. Smith), one of the century's most brilliant figures, had in mind when he said: "The man who enters into real and fierce controversy with Mr Lloyd George must think clearly, think deeply and think ahead. Otherwise he will think too late." Northcliffe thought too late. In one speech Lloyd George finally destroyed the original popular Press baron and, along with him, Fleet Street pretensions to dictate Government policy. This was how he set about the execution:

> When a man is labouring under a deep sense of disappointment, however unjustified and however ridiculous the expectations may have been, he is always apt to think the world is badly run. When a man has deluded himself that he is the only man who can win the war, and he is waiting for the clamour of the multitude that is going to demand his presence there to direct the destinies of the world, and there is not a whisper, not a sound, it is rather disappointing, it is unnerving, it is upsetting. But let me say this, that when that kind of diseased vanity is carried to the point of sowing dissention between great Allies, then I say that not even that kind of disease is a justification for so black a crime against humanity.

Crucially, as he spoke his final sentence, Lloyd George tapped his forehead, indicating that Northcliffe had become a victim of madness—and, indeed, he died of a brain illness two years later. By deciding, on such an occasion, to go for the throat—or rather the head—Lloyd George was acting on his own advice on how to deal with difficult Press figures: "When you can't square them, squash them".

It was a carefully thought-out formula, successfully followed, among others, by Baldwin and Bevan who respectively identified owners and editors as harlots and prostitutes. Sir Geoffrey Shakespeare, Lloyd George's private secretary and personal aide at the time, told me that this was how Lloyd George saw the strategy: "If the Press are constantly attacking, you go for them in a big way, in public of course. Hit them as hard as you possibly can, because proprietors and editors don't like being attacked; they're not accustomed to it and start squealing like stuck pigs. Then they howl that you're attacking the freedom of the Press—but that doesn't help them, because the people are naturally anti-Press anyway. Attack them on a major issue in a major speech. They're easily scared and readers are naturally sympathetic to you. They say to themselves: 'So that's why the Daily Whatnot keeps boring away about the PM'."

Lloyd George's relations with the Press were nothing if not multi-faceted. Proceeding on the theory that as well as beating 'em you could also then join 'em, Lloyd George himself became a newspaper proprietor in 1918, buying the *Daily Chronicle*, then a powerful organ of the old Liberal cause, from funds acquired through his early honours deal. Fascinated by the revolutionary expansion of the new popular Press, merging a new source of great private wealth with vast public power, he planned to use the paper as a platform for his own type of radicalism. However, he soon tired of being a Press magnate, and in 1926 disposed of the paper on Lord Beaverbrook's advice. His £1 million investment proved rewarding, for he realised £3 million on the sale, the proceeds going to the Lloyd George War Chest. In the subsequent controversies over the sources of this fund he always argued that most of it came from the *Chronicle* sale, and not from hawking honours.

His most ambitious attempt to join the select band of Press proprietors was launched immediately after the death of Lord Northcliffe in 1922 when a syndicate of his very rich friends were prepared to put up the money and buy *The Times* on his behalf. He was still Prime Minister but sensed that the Conservatives were plotting to overthrow him and under the deal he was to become editor. The myth that the editor of *The Times*, as the mouthpiece of the Establishment, often exercises more influence than the Prime Minister, has been carefully nourished by journalists, but Lloyd George was the first Prime Minister to demonstrate his willingness to move from Downing Street to the editor's chair in Printing House Square. The plan came to nothing. Because Establishment leaders were shocked by the fear that he might get *The Times*, the paper was bought by the Walter and Astor families; and, in any case, Lloyd George's millionaire friends, suspecting that his days of power were drawing to a close, prudently failed to produce their cheque books. Nevertheless, the idea of becoming editor of *The Times* stirred his imagination and he made great play of appearing serious.

According to his personal secretary, Frances Stevenson, later Countess Lloyd George, he told her: "I would not mind resigning as Prime Minister if I could become editor of *The Times* at a salary with a decent contract*." However, she was in the best position to judge his moods and real intentions, and she considered that he never had any real intention of entering Fleet Street; it was simply that he liked to toy with an idea without ever being committed. A. J. P. Taylor, the eminent historian, who edited the Stevenson Diaries, added as a footnote: "Apparently Lloyd George made a determined attempt to become editor of *The Times*". Like many Prime Ministers after him, he found book publishers' and newspaper offers irresistible (notably in the rush to get memoirs out quickly). Even so, one can imagine the fuss today if James Callaghan or Margaret Thatcher, while still in Downing Street, were to own a morning paper or to be a member of a syndicate negotiating to take over *The Times*.

But neither his role as a proprietor nor his patronage throughout Fleet Street accounted for the continuous silence about the irregularities of his private life. I recall being told, as the "baby" of the Lobby, that High Church Conservative and Nonconformist Labour M.P.s shared a mutual understanding not to mention the Welsh Wizard's prowess as a lover but that this was not inspired by any respect for privacy; it was simply that they feared he would sweep the country if the electorate discovered how vigorous he was. His womanising exploits, even as an old man, were discussed on the Westminster–Whitehall circuit with wonderment and admiration.

He lived dangerously yet he was never given away. Nobody wrote poisoned paragraphs, even during the worst Press excesses after his fall from power. Behind all this, I am sure, is the curious revolution in standards of public morality which has taken place in my Westminster life-span. Fifty years ago, before anyone had dreamed up the need for a Press Council to advise on standards of conduct and to curb intrusions into privacy, newspapers instinctively drew their own dividing line between public standards and private lives. It is ironic that today, when one might expect a greater tolerance, the private "morals" of Ministers have become fair game for Press exposure; consider how, in recent Governments, John Profumo, Lord Lambton and Earl Jellicoe, for example, were compelled to sacrifice public careers, having been hounded for private diversions. Certainly no Prime Minister today could hope to run two rival

* *A Diary* by Frances Stevenson, Hutchinson.

domestic establishments, as Lloyd George did, without being pilloried by gossip writers.

Lloyd George was easily the greatest creative genius among all Prime Ministers, the last great natural orator and, in my experience, a man with the most electrifying presence. He was also an enthusiastic innovator and in 1917 introduced a measure which it was feared might destroy the authority and mystique of Government: he ordered that all Cabinet discussions and decisions should be minuted. It is an innovation for which historians and biographers remain forever in his debt (despite the still-delayed disclosure of these documents); until his decision the only records available were the Premier's daily policy despatch to the Sovereign.

The student of these minutes does not have to wait long before coming across the heading "Leakage of Information", nor to realise that the frenzied Government methods used to discover sources follow a pattern which today continues unchanged and which doubtless existed before the minutes began. In particular, the record reveals the way in which, all too often, Official Secrets have been invoked over the years on small-time political problems totally unconnected with the security of the State; and that where top-secret issues have genuinely been involved they have been frequently transferred from the legal into the political-party sector for Cabinet discussions. One controversial case will demonstrate how, in such circumstances, relations with the Press can get dangerously out of hand.

It concerns Lt. Col. Repington, Military Correspondent of the *Morning Post*, a strongly Conservative and pro-services paper later merged with the *Daily Telegraph*. He was prosecuted for publishing military secrets in an article which went into considerable detail about the new strategical plans reached at a meeting of the Allied High Command at Versailles. In his article Repington wrote: "Newspapers have been strictly enjoined not to refer to one of the chief results of the Council. In this way it is hoped that criticism will be burked. But there are times when we must take courage in both hands and risk consequences. . . ." Although his French sources were excellent, much of the most damaging information affecting Lloyd George and his Inner Cabinet was suspected to have been fed to him by Field Marshals Haig and Robertson, who were in continuous conflict with Lloyd George about the balance to be struck between political and military control.

What is interesting to note is the way in which the case, which began in purely legal terms as a breach of the Official Secrets Act, increasingly became a political prosecution with the War Cabinet devoting several sessions to the issues raised. The following extract from the Cabinet minutes of 11 February 1918 reveals that Lloyd George and his Ministers knew how to inflict the maximum injury on a newspaper, without the formality of prosecution in the courts; namely, by use of the Defence of the Realm regulations:

It was pointed out that the most effective way of dealing with newspapers which published matters which gave information to the enemy was by seizure of the printing presses rather than by prosecution, which was dilatory. Press machinery had been seized in the case of the *Glasgow Forward* and the *Globe*, and this policy could be put into effect by any competent military authority. The War Cabinet requested the Solicitor-General to consult with the Director of Public Prosecutions and to submit recommendations at a special meeting of the War Cabinet to be held this afternoon at 5 pm.

After talks with the Home Secretary and other legal experts the Prime Minister himself later that night suspended the decision to seize the plant, a decision which would so easily have brought the sudden death of the *Morning Post*. In the end Repington and his editor were each fined £1,000 (£10,000 at today's value) at Bow Street.

The case illustrates the extent to which a Government is prepared to go in order to crush critical reporters and newspapers. Prime Ministers seldom forgive and never forget. Years later, when writing his memoirs, Lloyd George returned to the old battle and wrote that he knew "nothing comparable to this betrayal in the whole of our history". He asserted that Germany, following the Repington story, immediately "appreciated" the situation of the Allies and that Professor Dulbruck, the famous German authority on military strategy, expressed his thanks for the leak. "Repington's betrayal," wrote Lloyd George, "might and ought to have decided the war."

The case of the *Daily Herald* of the day also serves to highlight the hysteria of Government in the face of Press forces identified as hostile.

It is perhaps difficult to conceive now of the extent to which the Russian Revolution terrified the Government and the great mass of people in Britain and elsewhere in the West. Time after time the post-war Cabinet minutes conjure up the nightmare of bloody re-volution and political massacre sweeping from Europe across the Channel. It was Britain's first taste of Reds under the beds. The Cabinet minutes contain all the ingredients for a drama of interna-tional conspiracy, including plots to kill the king and overthrow the

Government, played against a blackcloth of red gold, Russian roubles and jewellery looted from the murdered Tzar's princesses.

As mass unemployment led to riots on the Clyde and Mersey, mutinies in the Army and the birth in 1920 of the British Communist Party, the *Daily Herald*, then struggling for survival as the organ of the Labour Party under the editorship of George Lansbury, became identified by the Cabinet as the advocate of massacres and arson, insurrection and anarchy. The Intelligence Service investigated many executives and journalists on the paper but their reports, though containing many smears and impugning the loyalty of the journalists, proved nothing.

This is not an isolated instance of Government hysteria; in the Second World War the Churchill Government ordered a secret inquiry into whether foreigners and enemies of the State were shareholders in the *Daily Mirror*, suspecting that sinister pro-Nazi sympathisers were exercising influence through nominee shareholdings.

The Government–Press relations over the generations never change in character. Who knows what secret intelligence reports are being compiled today about the suspected loyalties of political writers on the far right and left? Thirty years from now the next generation of Fleet Street and Lobby journalists may discover some shocking revelations about us in the Public Records Office just as I have come across secret files and comments about established journalists whom I knew well when I started at Westminster. They were "probed" not because they were ever disloyal but because they insisted on their independence and the freedom of the Press.

The final significance of Lloyd George in the evolution of Government–Press relations lies in the fact that he pioneered the modern Lobby system at Westminster. In the techniques of news-management and in the more subtle manipulation of opinion-writers he was a superb performer. However, he never operated the political correspondents as a group; he preferred to work with Liberal writers who had been his friends for years. In his final period as Premier, No. 10 Downing Street kept open door to selected newsmen. Eventually, Sir Geoffrey Shakespeare became the first official spokesman, but before him Lloyd George left the job of manipulating Fleet Street to an astonishing character, Sir William Sutherland, the go-between in the honours racket and a man who knew nothing about journalism and less about what was going on inside the Government. His main role, as he saw it, was to invent the most outrageous rumours about Lloyd George's opponents and to manufacture news events which never happened. He would deny himself several times each day. Press relations he saw as a vast circus act with himself, under his own title of "Bronco Bill", as the ringmaster.

To the end the Press retained its fascination for Lloyd George. Like Churchill he was compulsively interested in making big money, and drove hard bargains with newspapers and publishers. Lloyd George sold his memoirs to the *Daily Telegraph* for £90,000 and even in 1934, twelve years after ceasing to be Premier, he was paid £1 per word for thousand-word articles given world syndication. That's £10,000 an article by today's standards, making modern ex-Prime Ministers mere bargain-basement scribblers.

2

STANLEY BALDWIN

May 1923–January 1924
November 1924–June 1929
June 1935–May 1937

"He always won—he always beat me—the toughest and most unscrupulous politician you could find—cold, merciless in his dislike." LORD BEAVERBROOK

"The Press? I would as soon have ink squirted over me by a cuttlefish, as their praise has no more effect than their blame." STANLEY BALDWIN

The war between Government and Press was never so ferocious as in the 'twenties and 'thirties; the quotations above capture the mood. For most of Baldwin's fifteen years as Tory leader, more than half that time being spent in Downing Street, Beaverbrook and Rothermere campaigned mercilessly to overthrow him and in 1930 formed the New Empire Party, with ready-made policies and candidates. Had their endeavour succeeded the Press would have emerged as the supreme national political force with Downing Street reduced to the status of a Fleet Street outpost. As it was, they failed calamitously. By the time Baldwin had finished with them they were relieved to retire, humiliated, from the field.

In fact, the demolishing of the Press barons was a mere side-show for Baldwin. During his three administrations he held the all-comers' record in winning every decisive power battle: the General Strike, the Abdication, the India reforms which marked the beginning of de-colonisation, the National Government, "peace in our time" in reconciling industrial strife, modernising the Tory Party, preparing Labour for office and rescuing Britain from Red Revolution. In addition, he proved the political master of both Lloyd George and Churchill—no mean feat in itself. And never once did he court Fleet Street! I am confident that he will stand out in history as the most substantial and successful peace-time Premier of the century. Beaverbrook and Rothermere should have known better.

But their lordships were drunk with power. This was the golden age of journalism, with the buoyant circulations of the popular papers producing high salaries for all and vast riches for the owners. Subsequently, competition from radio and television started the great decline but for two decades the Press barons held immense power—and this power fed the appetite for yet more power. Although it is hard for later generations to sense or share the intensity of their conviction, Beaverbrook and Rothermere really did believe that they were more powerful than the elected Baldwin. Rothermere in particular convinced himself that he could dictate terms about policies and even hold the right of veto over the Ministers the Prime Minister should have in his Government.

So how exactly did Baldwin survive? First, he was a great Parliamentarian in the classic tradition. The Imperial Parliament was still supreme; it had not yet been undermined by Whitehall. He therefore remained totally safe so long as he controlled Parliament. Secondly, as a very adroit political operator, he deployed the well-tried formula of divide and rule: he isolated the Press lords from the rest of journalism. The great provincial and Scottish papers of those days became disillusioned by the antics of the *Daily Express* and *Daily Mail* empires. In no time, leading articles were referring to "Beavermere and Rotherbrook" as though they were a double turn at the music hall. This was where Baldwin was much cleverer than later Prime Ministers, such as Macmillan, Heath and Wilson, in handling relations between Downing Street and Fleet Street. When these Premiers fell out with Fleet Street they did it wholesale: with proprietors, editors and journalists. Baldwin kept the mass-circulation lords isolated in tandem, always timing his attacks on them when he could distinguish them from the rest of the newspaper world.

He adopted a similar approach to his relations with the Lobby; he encouraged Neville Chamberlain to have regular group or selective meetings, and yet remained personally friendly with and accessible to quite a number of us. As a cub reporter in my home town of Elgin, in the north-east of Scotland, I had interviewed him on local problems when he was holidaying on Speyside and ever afterwards he was unfailingly helpful in my job at Westminster. He sympathised with the role of the Lobby, but never tried to news-manage his contacts; he would answer questions, but never try to sell a line.

I recall one occasion when Baldwin was the guest of honour at a private luncheon given in his honour by Lobby correspondents.

Encouraged by the chairman's pledge that anything he cared to say would be treated as completely "off the record", never to be mentioned, he took a wry pleasure in revealing facts about Government policies and major decisions. It was the perfect example of "open Government", with the Press, to Baldwin's sardonic delight, gagging itself with its own conditions of confidentiality. It placed editors and correspondents in professional conflict with conscience. One editor resolved his dilemma with great ingenuity: the following Sunday, his astrology feature "What the Stars Foretell" set out in detail Baldwin's revelations about policies in the pipeline. Subsequent proof of the accuracy of this mystical reading of the stars in their courses, provided a striking circulation boost and increased the craze for star-gazing in the popular Press.

On the whole, however, Baldwin kept Fleet Street at arm's length, his attitude being coloured by the way in which journalists' skills were debased in the Beaverbrook–Rothermere campaign and by two unfortunate occasions when he considered that journalists had abused his courtesy and friendship. His son wrote that "he found it difficult to sympathise with the vulgar and improper tasks that some journalists are forced to perform in the course of their job, having himself the feeling that it would be better to do the humblest job in the land than to sell one's pen".

Baldwin never recovered from his first experience of meeting the Press in 1922—at least that is my impression based on a comment of his one evening. As Chancellor of the Exchequer in Bonar Law's Government he met a group of journalists at Southampton on his return from New York after negotiating with the US Government the terms for the American debt settlement after the First World War. In those days there were no public relations advisers at No. 10, no ground rules for off-the-record and background chats for non-attributable guidance. Baldwin told the correspondents that he considered the debt repayment terms satisfactory, as good as he could expect, and that the decision rested with Congress, indicating that the terms must satisfy the mid-Western states.

Baldwin learned the hard way. His views, when quoted and interpreted, caused major crises in Britain and America. In London, Bonar Law threatened to resign in protest against Baldwin's terms and received a rebuke in robust naval terms from King George V for allowing his Chancellor to announce British policy before the Cabinet had approved and the Monarch had been informed. In America, the reaction was even more explosive, Baldwin being quoted as describing American Senators as "hicks from the way back", pastoral types who did not understand international finance.

The second occasion on which he felt let down occurred in 1924, in the run-up to the general election when he gave an interview to a reporter from the *People*, then a right-wing popular weekly, to discuss his recent series of policy speeches on the "New Conservatism". His views were of the usual bromide character for such set-pieces, though even then he started pointing the party towards more progressive ideals:

> Every future Government must be socialistic, in the sense in which our grandfathers used the words. . . . I do know that if the Tory party is to exist we must have a vital democratic creed and must be prepared to tackle the evils, social and economic, of our over-populated, over-industrialised country.

Good radical stuff but hardly the material of which history's footnotes are made. It was the second part of the article which was sensational, containing frank and inflammatory opinions on many of his prominent colleagues and on national figures including Churchill, Birkenhead, Beaverbrook and Rothermere, Why had he broken up the Coalition Government at the famous Carlton Club meeting?

> I spoke because I was determined that never again should the sinister and cynical combination of the chief three of the Coalition—Mr Lloyd George, Mr Churchill and Lord Birkenhead—come together again.

There followed even more startling comments: he had welcomed Austen Chamberlain back into the party and

> with Austen came Birkenhead, who had attached himself to the strings of Austen's apron the year before very cleverly. And Austen is one of those loyal men who could not see disloyalty or intrigue even if it was at his elbow. But I am under no illusions about Lord Birkenhead. If his health does not give way, he will be a liability to the party.

And the attacks by Beaverbrook and Rothermere?

> As for myself I do not mind. I care not what they say or think. They are both men I would not have in my house. I do not respect them. Who are they? As for Beaverbrook: He contracted a curious friendship with Bonar Law [Baldwin's predecessor as Tory leader and Prime Minister] and had got his finger into the pie where it had no business to be. He got hold of much information which he used in ways in which it was not intended. When I came in, that stopped. I know I could get his support if I were to send for him and talk things over with him. But I prefer not. That sort of thing does not

26

1. Ramsay MacDonald (seated left) with the young, Cagney-hatted, smoking reporter, James Margach, in 1929. The speaker is the Lord Provost of Elgin

2. Lloyd George with his wife (*left*) and Mrs Asquith, wife of the earlier Liberal Prime Minister

3. Stanley Baldwin broadcasting in 1937

4. Lord Northcliffe, the father of modern popular journalism, with Winston Churchill in 1922

5. Neville Chamberlain with his wife, September 1938

6. Winston Churchill campaigning during the 1950 general election

7. Clement Attlee, Deputy Premier in the war-time Government and Labour Prime Minister 1945-51

appeal to me. . . . I often wonder if my silent contempt irritates them more than if I were to speak out. Churchill is a problem. What do these intriguers want? Simply to go back to the old dirty kind of politics.

Even after fifty years such views have a riveting freshness. If only James Callaghan and Margaret Thatcher would use such provocative language and express such home truths! It is no wonder that the Conservative Party was rocked, as confirmed by the private papers of the men involved. But Baldwin, as ever, rode out the storm, keeping his head down and paying no attention to the uproar—an attitude so different from the instant Government by instant reaction which became the fashion in the 'sixties and 'seventies.

But how did Baldwin's astonishing comments come to be published? Certainly it was not his intention that they should be. I remember him explaining one evening that after the set interview was over, and he and the *People*'s political correspondent were relaxing and gossiping, the newsman asked about his colleagues. He spoke his mind, as privately to a friend over a cup of tea. In seeing them published he felt betrayed. The truth, however, is seldom so simple. The other side of the picture I learned years later from the correspondent concerned. After the formal question-and-answer session the notebook was put away and Baldwin, in relaxed mood, called for tea. During the informal gossip Baldwin dropped his guard and spoke with such unbelievable frankness that when the journalist returned to the *People* office he mentioned the fact to his editor. "Forget the set interview," commanded the editor, "let's have the real story, all the dirt, about what he thinks of the others." The correspondent protested: "But he meant his words to be completely off the record. He was talking to me in confidence; and in any case I didn't and couldn't take a note of what he said." The editor was unmoved. "Never mind that," he said, "do it from memory." Never again did Baldwin give a formal interview or speak to groups of journalists whether on the record or for Lobby guidance.

However, with individual political correspondents whom he trusted, he continued to talk frankly—though never in formal question-and-answer sessions. Indeed he always showed a warmth and cordiality which extended to personal loyalty in protecting us from the hazards of the business. I can best illustrate this by the case of Francis Sulley, of the *Sheffield Telegraph*. In 1936 Sulley, then about the most experienced and senior figure among the political correspondents outside Fleet Street, wrote a detailed

27

forecast of a Defence White Paper, due to be published shortly afterwards. His report was of major national and international importance since at the time Britain's rearmament programme was being rapidly expanded to combat the mounting menace of the Nazi and Fascist dictatorships. (Sulley's special regional concern was, of course, the impact of an enlarged programme upon Sheffield and the steel industry.) When the White Paper itself was published it was discovered that Sulley's forecast was exceptionally accurate in all major facts and policy decisions, so accurate, in fact, as to be a blatant breach of the Official Secrets Act—and Baldwin was so advised. Inevitably, a Parliamentary question was inspired by the Opposition, demanding an explanation from the Prime Minister about the revelation of military secrets involving a clear breach of State security. The reply, I think, perfectly illustrates the Baldwin style. Instead of being stampeded into setting up a judicial inquiry under, say, the Lord Radcliffe of the period, and asserting his determination to defend the sanctity of the Official Secrets Act against the challenge of the Press, Baldwin defused the situation by blandly congratulating the correspondent on his political acumen and perspicacity. This is his Parliamentary reply, turning his back on excited demands for an official investigation into the leak:

> I have looked at it carefully—and I have had a good deal of experience in looking at articles in the Press which have been based on intelligent anticipation—and I see nothing in the article to lead me to believe that it could not have been compiled by an intelligent journalist, with such knowledge as would naturally have been in his possession. The Right Honourable Gentleman [A. V. Alexander, First Lord of the Admirality in Labour's 1929 Cabinet] has, of course, been a member of a Government and he knows as well as I do that occasions do arise in which anxiety is caused to members of a Government by what are obviously leakages. In this particular case, I have examined the article and, speaking with some experience, I say that I do not believe that I could not have written it myself, with the knowledge that I would have possessed, had I the position and, may I add, the intelligence, of the ordinary journalist.

I happened to be standing with Francis Sulley in the Members' Lobby immediately after question hour as Baldwin strode from the Chamber to the Library. As he passed a few feet from us he turned in our direction, smiled broadly, and gave us a prodigiously long wink, as if to say: "I thought I did that rather well. I didn't let you down, did I?"

28

The Baldwin touch has many lessons for all Prime Ministers. If only Harold Wilson, for instance, thirty years later, had similarly kept his head and his temper over the *Daily Express* D-Notice affair his relations with Fleet Street might never have become as embittered as they did. But then Wilson would never seek the advice of experience; he always knew best! As Baldwin proved, there are few problems in relations between Government and Press that cannot be handled with judgment and timing.

These were the skills which finally gave him victory over Beaverbrook and Rothermere. Although their campaign was sustained almost daily it was only occasionally that Baldwin counter-attacked. But when he did, he was deadly. While Baldwin was preparing public opinion and the Tory party for the first major constitutional reforms for India, the *Daily Mail* reported at length what purported to be the critical views of the Viceroy. This provoked the Prime Minister's first major assault and it set the tone and style of much that was to follow:

> It is sufficient for me at the moment to say that every statement of fact and every implication of fact contained in that article is untrue and in my opinion gravely injurious to the public interest, not only in this country but throughout the Empire. . . . A friend of mine has told me that the article was only a journalistic stunt. . . . I agree. I am glad to think that the word "stunt" is as little English in its derivation and origin and character as the whole of that article.

When Beaverbrook and Rothermere finally decided to form the New Empire Party in 1930, it was Fleet Street's biggest challenge of all time, with the ultimate, and astonishing objective of taking over No. 10 Downing Street and forming their own Government. The real and more immediate objective was to split the Conservative Party, thus terrifying Tory M.P.s and constituencies and creating a desperate situation in which Baldwin would have to be sacrificed. It was a massive launching, strongly backed every morning by the "two engines of propaganda". If the gamble had succeeded Fleet Street would have been in the political business permanently. Yet within a matter of months of its birth, the Press political party was shattered—and again it was largely because of Baldwin's sense of timing. Two paragraphs in a speech at a party meeting in May 1930 largely did the trick:

> The desire to dictate the policy to a big Party, to choose a leader, to impose Ministers on the Crown; the only parallel to that was the action of the TUC in 1926. We are told that

unless we make peace with these noblemen, candidates are to be run all over the country. The Lloyd George candidates at the last election smelt; these will stink. The challenge has been issued. I accept, as I accepted the challenge of the TUC. I am all for peace. I like the other man to begin the fight and then I am ready. When I fight, I go on to the end, as I did in 1926.

Here is a letter from Lord Rothermere which I have permission to read: "I cannot make it too abundantly clear that, under no circumstances whatsoever, will I support Mr Baldwin unless I know exactly what his policy is going to be, unless I have complete guarantees that such policy will be carried out if his party achieves office, and unless I am acquainted with the names of at least eight or ten of his most prominent colleagues in the next ministry." Now these are the terms which your leader would have to accept and when sent for by the King would have to say: "Sire, these names are not necessarily my choice, but they have the support of Lord Rothermere." A more preposterous and insolent demand was never made on the leader of any political party. I repudiate it with contempt and I will fight that attempt at domination to the end.

Editors became personally involved as they rallied to the support of the beleagured proprietors. When Baldwin used the phrase "insolent plutocracy" to describe the pretensions of Fleet Street, the *Daily Mail* was provoked to launch yet another attack, this time signed as by "The Editor". He wrote: "These expressions come ill from Mr Baldwin, whose father left him an immense fortune which, so far as may be learned from his own speeches, has almost disappeared. It is difficult to see how the leader of a party who has lost his own fortune can hope to restore that of anyone else, or his country." By comparison, modern Fleet Street editors lead a sheltered existence.

But Baldwin swallowed such insults whole. He replied again at a by-election speech in St George's, London:

I have no idea of the name of that gentleman. I would only observe that he is well qualified for the post which he holds. The first part of that statement is a lie and the second part of the statement, by its implication, is untrue. The paragraph itself could only have been written by a cad. I have consulted a very high legal authority and I am advised that an action for libel would lie. [Shouts of "Take it"] I shall not move in the matter, and for this reason. I should get an apology and heavy damages. The first is of no value and the second I would not touch with a barge pole. What the proprietorship of these papers is aiming at is power, and power without responsibility —the prerogative of the harlot throughout the ages.

That was the knock-out. The editor of the *Daily Express* was himself sitting at the Press table preparing to launch another attack next morning. When he heard Baldwin's words (the celebrated last sentence being supplied by Rudyard Kipling, Baldwin's cousin) he threw down his pen, saying: "That's the finish. There can be no answer to that." He was right. It was all over. The Press attacks spluttered on but all the old fire was gone. Finally a phoney peace settlement was patched up and friendly comments of reconciliation appeared in leading articles. Fleet Street never again repeated such a stridently orchestrated campaign for paper power.

While the great battles between Baldwin and the Press barons were being waged in public, equally crucial power battles between Government and Fleet Street were taking place far from the public gaze. They were all about secrecy, confidentiality, the sanctity of Cabinet discussions and decisions and the need to resist disclosure and Press intrusion.

The scene was set for Baldwin's three Premierships as far back as 11 March 1925: "Leakage of Information: The attention of the Cabinet was drawn to *several* [my emphasis] recent instances of premature disclosure in the Press of decisions taken by the Cabinet ... the Prime Minister made an appeal for the utmost reticence in revealing outside the discussions which had taken place in Cabinet." It is one exhortation among many hundreds in Cabinet minutes under all Prime Ministers. When too many secrets were leaking the Cabinet Secretaries often used the anti-spy device of withholding items from Cabinet papers for a few days, and from selected people, to see if the leakers might fall into the trap. But apart from two or three cases when minor officials talked out of turn, the records confirm that out of all the complaints about Cabinet leaks not one source was ever identified. Any experienced journalist could have provided the answer. All the leaks, then and now, came from Ministers: the higher up the barrel, the bigger the leak.

In the 'thirties, with the menace of Hitler, Mussolini and Franco mounting alarmingly, Baldwin's Cabinet minutes reveal a great many strange and ominous devices whereby top Ministers attempted to influence and curb the freedom of the Press and prevent honest reporting of the dangers to civilisation inherent in the rise of the dictators. The most alarming feature was the extent to which senior Ministers, with Neville Chamberlain as the driving force, were prepared to exert pressures on proprietors, editors and writers to doctor news and soften editorials in order to avoid giving offence to the dictators. Two examples from the Cabinet minutes indicate the methods used and illustrate the Cabinet's obsession with the inconvenient democratic expression of news and opinion.

On 25 November 1936 "the First Lord of the Admiralty (Sir Samuel Hoare) directed the attention of the Cabinet to the alarmist atmosphere of the Press in matters connected with the Spanish civil war". He proceeded to quote recent examples and asked that something should be taken "to stop such reports and rumours". Then the Foreign Secretary (Anthony Eden) took up the running by stating "that the Press department of the Foreign Office was always trying to check these objectionable practices". On recent occasions Reuters Agency had been the cause of trouble. After some discussion the Cabinet agreed:

> (a) That the Secretary of State for Foreign Affairs should arrange for a private notice question to be addressed to him on both points mentioned by the First Lord, and that in denying the accuracy of the Press rumours he should draw attention to the harm that was done by raising these scares.
> (b) That Reuters Agency should not be mentioned by name in the answer to the private notice question proposed, but that the Secretary of State for Foreign Affairs should see the head of Reuters Agency and warn him that on a future occasion he would not undertake to omit a reference if that agency continued to offend.

The perfect example of how power really works at the top: the owner or top executive to be summoned for a confrontation; then the complaint and the warning; finally the blackmail threat of future action if the offences are repeated. This technique of intimidation did not apply to Reuters only; dozens of other extracts from Cabinet minutes spell out the same story. This Minister asked to have a word with that proprietor; on another complaint another Minister with appropriate links would have a word of counsel with the editor; the law officers or some other Minister would make inquiries to discover the sources of particular Lobby correspondents' leaks about Cabinet decisions and discussions. But they all harmonised on the same theme: intimidate, pressurise, persuade, advise, warn and court Fleet Street.

The second example is from the minutes of 24 March 1937:

> The Secretary of State for Foreign Affairs said that the difficulties of the present situation were being very much increased by the attitude of the Press and Parliament. For

example, that afternoon no less than twenty-five questions had been addressed to him, and some of them were calculated to irritate Signor Mussolini. In spite of his efforts, in which he had the co-operation of the Prime Minister, to avoid a debate on Foreign Affairs tomorrow, the question of the massacre at Addis Ababa was to be raised on the motion for the adjournment for the Easter recess.

He had been considering whether any such action could be taken with a view to obtaining assistance from the leaders of the Opposition parties in modifying the attitude of some of their supporters. He himself was prepared to see the leaders of the Opposition in any numbers that were necessary.

In the course of a short discussion the Cabinet were reminded that the British Broadcasting Corporation published daily bulletins in regard to Spain, as well as weekly talks, and that these had a widespread effect resulting in pressure being put by constituents on Members of Parliament. If the British Broadcasting Corporation could be induced to drop their nightly statement it was suggested that it would have a quietening effect.

Much sympathy was expressed with the difficulties raised for the Secretary of State for Foreign Affairs by ill-timed publicity methods.

The Cabinet agreed that the Secretary of State for Foreign Affairs should confer with the Prime Minister immediately after the meeting with a view to opposing the raising of the Abyssinian massacres in the House of Commons the following day.

Another extract from the minutes of the same meeting serves to underline the hyper-sensitivity of the Cabinet if a dictator frowned and made formal protests about reports and comments by a free and independent Press—so unlike the regimented newspapers of their own regimes:

The Secretary of State for Foreign Affairs informed the Cabinet that the Italian Ambassador [Signor Grandhi] had spoken to the Parliamentary Under-Secretary of State for Foreign Affairs [R. A. Butler] about the British Press reports of the recent Italian reverses north-east of Madrid and had stated that Signor Mussolini was annoyed with their tenor. He had indicated that the point might be brought up later on, not in the non-intervention committee but through diplomatic channels.

So the Duce was "annoyed" with Fleet Street!

Fortunately, these attempts to muzzle the Press, news agencies and even the House of Commons came to nothing. Nor did Baldwin fare any better with that rapidly developing new sector of the communications world—sound radio. The minutes above indicate the level of the Cabinet's concern with the BBC's nightly bulletins on Spain, and this applied equally to Italian and German affairs. The dictators must hear no uncomplimentary remarks over the airwaves. And on the home front, too, the BBC had to fight hard for its independence. During the Budget leak crisis of 1936—when J. H. Thomas, a member of the Cabinet, was driven from public life for leaking Budget secrets to friends who made vast profits in the city by gambling on his disclosures—complaint was made to the BBC over a news bulletin which reported that the Cabinet had considered the findings of the judicial tribunal investigating the case. The minutes demonstrate how the Government tried to keep the BBC under its surveillance:

> The Cabinet were reminded that some of the newspapers gave accounts of what had happened at the Cabinet with some accuracy, but it was suggested that there was some difference between a statement in political notes and one contained in the BBC news . . . the Cabinet agreed that the rule should be definitely laid down that no reference should be made in news bulletins to what is supposed to have passed at a Cabinet meeting unless special and direct authority for the statement had been obtained by the British Broadcasting Corporation from No. 10 Downing Street.

The covering letter from the Cabinet secretary conveying the Cabinet's demand made the additional point that the initial report must have been either a leak or an invention!

The reply from the BBC chairman, R. C. Norman, accepted the command but in such a way that the next Cabinet commented that "the tone of the reply was criticised as harsh and almost offensive". Then comes the hint of the ultimate pressure kept in reserve: "A note however, it was suggested, might be taken of this letter for consideration, in conjunction with other relevant information, when the composition of the Board of Governors came up for reconsideration." The moral: one squeak and you're out. Co-operate like a good fellow, otherwise there will be no re-appointment. That's how the twin pressures of power and patronage are exploited. In the long run, however, the happy circumstances that the Government and Whitehall had inherited the redoubtable director-general John Reith when the privately-owned British Broadcasting Company became a State-owned corporation made it certain that their ambitions to have the BBC organised and disciplined as an arm of the Administration would be frustrated.

Baldwin had one lasting, and not insignificant, influence on the links between Government and Press: he created the guidelines which to this day govern the practice of Ministers writing for newspapers. But it was not until half a century later that the curious details of their birth were brought to light.

The issue came to a head over the writings of Lord Birkenhead, a man whose brilliance was matched only by his luxurious tastes. When he was in the Cabinet variously as Lord Chancellor and, later, Secretary for India, he earned fabulous sums by writing pot-boiling books and articles. His *Famous Trials* and *Law, Life and Letters* won enormous sales and he pioneered the newspaper serialisation seams, since mined with even more enthusiasm and for ever richer rewards (*pace* Lloyd George) by succeeding generations of Cabinet Ministers and generals. In the end, however, the daily sight of a London evening newspaper contents bill screaming "Famous Murder Trials—by the Lord Chancellor" proved too much for some stomachs. There were complaints by fellow Ministers, either alarmed by the affront to Ministerial solemnity of such catchpenny tactics or envious of such vast earnings. These complaints, when reinforced with protests in Parliament, finally compelled Baldwin to act. He decreed that for Ministers to write articles explaining Government and Departmental policies was permissible, without fee, but that all other forms of journalism must cease forthwith.

Birkenhead, according to his son, "yielded with an ill grace and nourished an abiding grievance. He sincerely believed that an injustice had been done to him. He had given up a great practice at the Bar to discharge public work and he saw no reason why he should not supplement his salary by journalism*"—a sentiment which conveniently ignored the fact that he had gone into public life to satisfy an ambition: to capture the "glittering prizes" of the highest political and judicial offices of all. Nevertheless, in order to keep Birkenhead in the Cabinet, Baldwin agreed that £10,000 should be paid to him out of Conservative Party funds (about £100,000 today) as compensation for loss of earnings and for the "loss" of the £5,000-a-year pension to which he would have been entitled if he had instead decided to retire as Lord Chancellor. As revealed in the papers of the late Lord Davidson†, Baldwin's closest

* *F. E. The Life of F. E. Smith*, by his son, Eyre and Spottiswoode.
† *Memoirs of a Conservative*, by Robert Rhodes James, Weidenfeld and Nicolson.

friend, Baldwin confirmed the deal on 21 May 1926 in a note to
F. S. Jackson, the party chairman. He wrote:

> My dear Jacker,
> You remember a very private matter I discussed with you
> some time ago, on which you have just had a word with the
> Chancellor [Churchill]. The time is come now for you to go
> ahead, so will you take the necessary steps.
> Yours ever,
> SB

And the Davidson record continues: "On June 14 a sum of £3,500
was paid into Birkenhead's account at the Midland Bank, Liverpool;
on November 9 a further cheque for £6,500 was paid. In this
manner the political services of Lord Birkenhead, and his silence
in the Press, were secured for another two years."

But only for two years; in the spring of 1928 he suddenly resumed his writings, without warning, with an article, "The
Intrusion of Women", which bitterly attacked any further extension
of female suffrage. This was meant as a controversial challenge to
Baldwin who was committed to electoral reform by introducing
"the flappers' vote". Birkenhead then resigned from the Cabinet
without much argument and at once collected an imposing list of
City directorships. Thus enormous income to meet enormous
expenditure was once more assured.

But since Birkenhead's day Ministers, restrained from supple-
menting their official salaries while in office, have perfected a new
formula. By writing up their diaries faithfully every night, or by
Richard Crossman's labour-saving device of using tape-recorders,
they prepare for generous book and serialisation royalties to keep
them in their old age. The more pungent the poison per paragraph
the higher the commercial reward. A perfect example of how to lay
up great treasure for tomorrow by a little exercise in instant history
tonight.

3

RAMSAY MACDONALD

January 1924–November 1924
June 1929–June 1935

"In one case, namely, the decision of the Cabinet to approve the Government of India's proposal to arrest Mr Gandhi, the possible consequence of the leakage had been so serious that steps had been taken, under the threat of prosecution, to ascertain the source from which certain newspapers had derived the information." CABINET MINUTES, 7 May 1930

According to the form book Ramsay MacDonald's relations with the Press ought to have been better than those of any other Prime Minister. He knew his way around Fleet Street as a professional, having derived most of his income from a prolific flow of feature and leading articles for the national papers and commentaries for the regionals. Even after becoming Premier he was a regular and welcome visitor to the Press Club. He was regarded by journalists as one of themselves and when he took office he already had the kind of relaxed rapport which other Premiers had specially to acquire under tuition. In short, he appeared perfectly equipped to reconcile the conflicting demands of Government and Press. So what went wrong?

Basically, I think, it was that when he first came to power in 1924 the papers were very much under the one-man rule of the lordly dynasties founded by Lloyd George; it was many years before shares were marketed in the City. And these Press lords saw MacDonald, Britain's first Labour Premier, as the apostle of Red revolution and the bringer of civil war, the man who shattered the old cosy rhythm of power between Liberals and Conservatives. Quite simply, they were out to get him and, when the gloves were off, his cordial relations with humble working journalists availed him little. He was hounded, in campaigns of personal venom, more widely than any other Premier.

Even before he became Prime Minister he experienced the bitter anguish of so-called Press exposure at the hands of Horatio Bottomley, Fleet Street proprietor and M.P., the greatest demagogue and charlatan who ever tried by fraud to dominate Parliament and Press simultaneously. He sought to destroy MacDonald by publishing his birth certificate in his jingoistic *John Bull*, thus revealing to the world that the Labour leader was illegitimate.

This may appear trifling to a modern society in which young women announce the birth of babies with the rider that they have no intention of marrying the father. But in the social climate of sixty years ago anyone born illegitimate had to carry the secret cross of shame for the rest of his life. For someone of MacDonald's excessive ensitivity the Bottomley revelation brought much private agony, the more so since he himself was unaware of the circumstances of his birth until he read *John Bull*. This assault on his baby's cot left wounds that never healed. Nor was Bottomley concerned only with MacDonald's birth; he was interested in his death as well. *John Bull* campaigned for the Labour leader to be tried as a traitor and shot because of his anti-war campaign.

MacDonald's first Government lasted only nine months. It was marked by the curious affair of the Prime Minister's Daimler, in which the *Daily Mail*, identifying itself as the propaganda arm of the Tory party, acted as chief MacDonald-baiter and it ended with the case of the *Workers' Weekly* in which MacDonald acted with singular ineptitude to embrace Parliamentary defeat. Subsequent disaster at the polls, putting Labour out of office for five years, resulted largely from the *Daily Mail*'s publication of the Zinoviev letter which again MacDonald mishandled. But one thing at a time.

First, the case of MacDonald's Daimler. Perhaps it needs explaining that MacDonald was the first genuinely poor man ever to reach Downing Street—the British equivalent of the American dream: log cabin to White House. He had never owned a car. In his early months as Prime Minister he moved to and from appointments by tram, bus or Underground and when really pressed for time he stood on the corner of Downing Street to hail one of the old taxi-cabs. To reach Chequers, where he might be weekend host to the world's leaders, he went by Underground to Baker Street, and then by Metropolitan Railway to a station several miles from Chequers where he would take a hired car. It was therefore particularly noticeable when he suddenly began riding around in a chauffeur-driven Daimler, a car available only to the very rich.

Gossip soon reached Fleet Street that there was a secret patron in the background and poison paragraphs appeared in many gossip columns about the penniless Premier who had miraculously acquired a Daimler. The atmosphere of the time was favourable to any hint of bribery; in the immediate post-war years people were sickened by the widespread scandals constantly revealed about the sale of honours under Lloyd George. Thus when MacDonald eschewed the tram which was felt appropriate for a working-class leader, Fleet Street assumed it had stumbled on a new form of corruption.

The hunt was on. Who was the shadowy figure prepared to provide luxury transport for the poor man at No. 10 who had never been able to acquire any capital of his own? The *Daily Mail* found out. By searching through the company's share records it discovered that some 300,000 shares in the Edinburgh biscuit firm of McVitie and Price had been transferred to MacDonald from Sir Alexander Grant, the chairman, and an old friend. The Prime Minister's reputation suffered grievously from the smear campaign which followed the disclosure of this information. At public meetings his speeches were interrupted with frequent cries of "Biscuits!" That Grant had been recently knighted stimulated gossip about the car being the price of the honour—which ignored the proven fact that Grant had been on the list of the outgoing Conservative Government for his generosity in providing and endowing the magnificent Scottish National Library in Edinburgh.

In September 1924, after six months as the victim of such taunts, MacDonald gave an interview at his Lossiemouth cottage, The Hillocks, explaining why he had accepted the use of the car. He and Grant had been brought up in poor circumstances in Morayshire, the families knew each other, MacDonald's uncle and Grant's father were fellow guards on the old Highland Railway. At the same time, a detailed statement by Grant on the arrangement about the car and the shares (which were to revert to the Grant family when MacDonald ceased being Prime Minister) demonstrated to the public the genuine transport problems which faced a man without resources who became Prime Minister. The explanations successfully cleared the air and the affair did have one practical outcome: the provision of official cars and drivers for Ministers. At the last count there were over 400 cars in the official transport pool, 72 of which are specifically reserved for Ministers. The list includes relatively unimportant mid-tier Ministers, who have cars on call at all times, former Prime Ministers and Opposition leaders. All of which is doubtless more congenial than standing on the Embankment waiting for a bus.

I add a postscript to this story to show how at least one Premier remained loyal in friendship to an old newspaperman when he reached the top. The MacDonald statement followed a conference between himself and Grant at The Hillocks (which became as well known to British and American journalists as Chequers and Camp David are today). All Fleet Street and the American papers, sensing that the car crisis had reached its crunch, had sent their political writers to Lossiemouth for the expected kill, but after MacDonald and Grant had agreed on the wording of the statement and interview, the Prime Minister did not summon the anticipated conference. Instead, he sent Grant's car to Elgin, six miles distant, to pick up a veteran journalist, A. G. Wilken, then over seventy years old. MacDonald remembered that Wilken, who represented the radical-liberal *Aberdeen Free Press*, was the only reporter who never deserted him during the dark days of war and who faithfully reported the actual speeches without commenting or editorialising to suit the jingoistic anti-MacDonald temper of the time. So Wilken was invited into The Hillocks, while the top correspondents of the world clamoured outside, and was given the official statement and interview exclusively.

This typical loyalty by MacDonald to an old friend brought a financial windfall to Wilken (who was my journalistic mentor in my home town of Elgin); he became a relatively rich man overnight. He was driven back to Elgin and from his office he wired individual stories to the scores of papers he represented as a freelance correspondent. Furthermore, to MacDonald's abiding pleasure, the high-powered Fleet Street men crowding the tiny village were left in ignorance that the Prime Minister had issued a personal statement and given a long interview! They were stunned to receive telephone calls from their editors demanding to know how they had been "scooped" by a small-town freelance on the biggest political story of the time. The answer was simple. He had observed one of the basic rules of journalism: always keep your friendships and contacts in good repair.

In parallel to this affair was the case of the *Workers' Weekly* which fed MacDonald's growing Press persecution complex and, a month later, proved fatal to his first Administration. In July the official Communist paper published a controversial appeal to the armed forces urging them not to use their arms against the workers but against the bosses and capitalists; and for good measure soldiers, sailors and airmen were encouraged to form committees in every barracks, aerodrome and ship to help the workers smash capitalism. This was seen as an open incitement to mutiny and to be exhorting the armed forces to refuse to allow themselves to be used in strikes. This view appeared to be endorsed by the heading on the article: "The Army and Industrial Disputes: An Open Letter to the Fighting Forces".

Because of its seditious and mutinous terms, the article was five days later referred by the Director of Public Prosecutions to Labour's Attorney-General, Sir Patrick Hastings, the famous criminal lawyer. Hastings decided that the article did amount to an incitement to mutiny and authorised prosecution. The acting editor, J. R. Campbell, was duly arrested and the Opposition began firing off Parliamentary questions about the "Communist challenge" to law and order. Labour M.P.s wondered what all the fuss was about, because the article was in tune with much of the current Labour rhetoric about working class solidarity.

If the law officers had only kept the case to themselves, the Government might possibly have survived long enough to reshape politics. Instead, the lawyers moved the case into the political arena. They had discovered that Campbell had an exceptionally good war record, having been badly wounded in frontline action and decorated for gallantry. Moreover, Campbell was not editor (actually he was assistant editor under R. Palme Dutt) and was only temporarily in charge. For both these reasons the lawyers sensed that they might not win a conviction from a jury and decided to consult MacDonald. His opinion was that a court case would do more harm than good and could only serve to publicise the Communists as the true champions of the workers. Hastings told his Prime Minister that he also had come to the conclusion that the prosecution should be withdrawn. So far, so good.

But, unfortunately for them, the issue was raised at Cabinet. Here is the official minute which serves as a permanent warning to Governments of all colour of the dangers which arise when political arguments become entangled in the administration of justice:

August 6: The *Workers' Weekly*—Prosecution of Editor. 6 p.m. The attention of the Cabinet was called to a prosecution which had been instituted against John Ross Campbell, Editor of the *Workers' Weekly*, the official organ of the Communist Party of Great Britain, under the Incitement to Mutiny Act, for attempting to seduce from loyalty to the King members of the Navy, Army and Air Force who might read the articles in the *Workers' Weekly* entitled "The Army and Industrial Disputes".

The Home Secretary stated that a letter of apology had been received from the printers, who are giving notice to terminate their printing contract, and he understood that the Attorney-General had given instructions that the printers should not be proceeded against.

The Attorney-General said he took full responsibility for

proceeding with the case, which disclosed a bad criminal offence, but in as much as it transpired that the person charged was only acting temporarily as Editor and was prepared to write a letter to the effect, steps could be taken not to press the prosecution in the circumstances against this particular offender, if the Cabinet so desired.

After considerable discussion of the procedure which led to action being taken in the courts without the knowledge of the Cabinet or the Prime Minister, the Cabinet agreed: (a) that no public prosecution of a political character should be undertaken without the prior sanction of the Cabinet being obtained. (b) That in the particular case under review the course indicated by the Attorney-General should be adopted (i.e. withdrawal of the prosecution).

Leading Conservative and Liberal figures, more experienced in Government than Labour Ministers still trying to find their feet, were suspicious. This was clearly spelled out in a carefully fused Conservative question which asked the Prime Minister whether any directions were given to the Director of Public Prosecutions by him, or with his sanction, to withdraw the case against Campbell. The reply:

I was not consulted regarding either the institution or the subsequent withdrawal of these proceedings. The first notice of the prosecution which came to my knowledge was in the Press. I never advised its withdrawal, but left the whole matter to the discretion of the Law Officers, where that discretion properly rests.

The conflict between the MacDonald statement and the Cabinet minute explains why Tom Jones, number two to Hankey in the Cabinet Secretariat, subsequently described the Prime Minister's statement as "a bloody lie" (although a Hankey minute later excused MacDonald by explaining that too many papers were pushed before him when he was already seriously overworking in his dual roles as Prime Minister and Foreign Secretary).

Unimpressive explanations from the Government fuelled Opposition suspicions that the Cabinet had behaved improperly. The Tories, under Baldwin, moved a vote of censure on the Government; the Liberals under Asquith moved an amendment asking for a Select Committee inquiry. Yet, instead of accepting the Liberal compromise, MacDonald opposed it as unacceptable—an astonishing error for such an adroit Parliamentary tactitian. Baldwin was thus allowed to move in with speed, promising Conservative support for the Liberal motion and late on 9 October, MacDonald crashed to defeat by a combined Conservative-Liberal vote of 364 to 198.

Any lingering prospects that Labour might win the ensuing general election were demolished four days before polling day when, with explosive effect, the *Daily Mail* unleashed the Zinoviev "Red Letter" scare upon the country. Other papers joyously joined in. The letter purported to be from Zinoviev, President of the Communist International, to the British Communist Party, and contained detailed instructions on how to set about all forms of seditious and revolutionary schemes, how to foment rebellion in the armed forces, and how they should prepare to take over the country by well-planned military insurrection.

For almost fifty years the Zinoviev letter remained one of the great unsolved mysteries of British politics: was it, or was it not, a fake? The oddest feature of the affair was that nobody really tried by independent inquiry to find out. But in 1967 three *Sunday Times* colleagues—Lewis Chester, Stephen Fay and Hugo Young—wrote a book which showed that it was forged by a group of reckless Russian emigrés in Berlin and planted on the international intelligence network to reach the Foreign Office as authentic, with copies forwarded to the *Daily Mail* and the Tory Central Office to ensure the maximum impact.

MacDonald's first knowledge of the letter was when the Foreign Office forwarded it to him during his election tour. He was immediately suspicious and minuted his comment that special inquiries should be made to check its authenticity before an official note of protest was despatched to Russia about her apparent interference in Britain's internal affairs. But he did nothing else; he was slow in publicly denouncing the letter as a hoax, and this omission enabled the *Daily Mail* and other papers to step in and make hay. Their strident campaign had a decisive impact on the result of the election.

I like to think—despite some recent indications to the contrary —that no newspaper today would have published without first establishing the letter's authority. But in those days papers of Right, Left and Centre saw their role primarily as propagandists. Even the fact that the Central Office was deeply involved in promoting publicity for the letter did not suggest to the papers that they were being used. On the contrary, most of them insisted on getting the maximum mileage out of the affair so as to make doubly sure, as their editorials saw it, that the country would be saved from another dose of Socialism now that the Labour Government had been shown to be the dupes and accomplices of the murderous Red revolutionaries in the Kremlin. Fear is always a potent vote-catcher.

Since the Zinoviev letter served to confirm MacDonald's theory of Press persecution perhaps it was not surprising that his next Government, 1929–31, should produce one of the gravest of Government assaults on the freedom of the Press. As I am the only person still around who is familiar with the details I feel I should chronicle the incident in some detail, as a warning of the dangers to Downing Street and Fleet Street alike when Whitehall loses its head in an obsessive concern about official secrets.

The drama centres on the five-hour grilling of a Lobby correspondent by Special Branch detectives, invoking the Official Secrets Act. Their aim: to intimidate him into disclosing the source of his story about a Cabinet decision to approve the Viceroy of India's proposal to arrest Gandhi for his civil disobedience campaign. MacDonald suspected the loyalty of his Cabinet Ministers or the presence of undercover spies working inside Downing Street. The true, and much less fevered, explanation lay, as it so often does, with some first-class Lobby work by experienced political correspondents. Their crime was only that they had been proved too accurate and well-informed. Yet no protest was made by Fleet Street proprietors, editors and journalists against the Government's subsequent use of dictatorial powers and their threats of arrest and prosecution in order to trace the leak.

What happened was this. Late on the evening of 30 April 1930 Frederick Truelove of the Kemsley group learned from a Parliamentary Private Secretary that earlier in the day the Cabinet had given its approval to Gandhi's arrest. On this uncorroborated hint Truelove hesitated to send in a report but he later saw J. R. Clynes, the Home Secretary and an old close friend. The Minister broadly "assented" to Truelove's subtle questioning, suggesting that Gandhi could not expect to be free much longer because of his civil disobedience campaign aimed at wrecking administration in India. Enough was said to confirm Truelove's judgment that the arrest was imminent and he shared the news report with Jack Kirk of the *News Chronicle* and William Forse of the *Daily Telegraph*.

The next morning broadly similar reports appeared in their papers. It is interesting to note the economy of words. Today we would be treated to two whole pages of unnecessary detail, including the colour of the Viceroy's pyjamas. This is Kirk's report in its entirety:

> The Government of India is preparing, I understand, to take decisive action against Gandhi.

44

His arrest is to be expected at any time.

The matter is entirely within the province of the Government of India.

Nevertheless, the latter has taken the precaution of ascertaining the views of the Home Government before moving.

The British Government has decided to support the Viceroy and his advisers.

The matter was reviewed at some length at yesterday's meeting of the Cabinet, and the conclusion was reached, with natural regret.

The whole story in eighty-five words.

The Lobbymen did not have to wait long for confirmation of the accuracy of their reports. Within hours of publication senior Scotland Yard officers appeared at the *News Chronicle*, *Telegraph* and *Sketch* offices and, under the Official Secrets Act, demanded from the editors an explanation of the reports, their sources, and the names and addresses of the political correspondents concerned. The *Telegraph* and *Sketch* editors refused to give any information, as they were not prepared to accept that there had been any breach of the Act, but the editor of the *News Chronicle* was not available and his deputy, alarmed by the display of official might, disclosed Kirk's name and address.

Shortly afterwards three Special Branch officers arrived at Kirk's home brandishing the Secrets Act and again demanding to know the source of his story. Their "interview" lasted five hours, at the end of which the Chief Inspector in charge informed Kirk that he would have to take him to Scotland Yard for further inquiries. On hearing this clear threat of arrest, Mrs Kirk had a fainting fit, which alarmed both Kirk and the Special Branch posse, so Kirk decided to telephone Truelove, his only informant, to tell him the situation. My old colleague Truelove, convinced that both Government and police were behaving with unbelievable stupidity, decided to return the ball from Fleet Street to Downing Street. He told the Chief Inspector to cease the exhausting and pointless interrogation of Kirk, to return to the Yard and to tell the Commissioner that the story arose out of a conversation he had had with the Home Secretary—who was also head of Scotland Yard. Truelove then went immediately to see Clynes in his room, reported what was happening over the Gandhi leak and said that he had mentioned the Home Secretary's name to Scotland Yard. Clynes was unaware of what had been going on, inquiries having been initiated by the Attorney-General on a complaint from No. 10. He was very understanding of the correspondents' problems and informed the Prime Minister that he, as Home Secretary, had been the original Cabinet contact. The hunt was called off without further delay.

But that was not the end of the story. Still bristling with annoyance a week later, the Prime Minister read a lecture to his colleagues. The Cabinet minutes of 7 May read:

> The attention of the Cabinet was drawn to several cases that had occurred recently of leakage to the Press of Cabinet decisions or of the contents of secret documents communicated to the Cabinet, some of which had been circulated under the same precautions as are taken in the case of Cabinet minutes.
>
> In one case, namely, the decision of the Cabinet to approve the Government of India's proposal to arrest Mr Gandhi, the possible consequences of the leakage had been so serious that steps had been taken, under the threat of prosecution, to ascertain the source from which certain newspapers had derived the information. The investigation indicated the desirability that all persons in possession of Cabinet secrets should avoid answering any questions whatsoever, whether apparently innocent or not, by Pressmen and others in regard to Cabinet business.
>
> The Prime Minister appealed to his colleagues to observe this rule.

Such troubled political waters proved irresistible to zealous anglers on the Opposition benches and questions inevitably appeared on the Parliamentary papers. On 12 May it was asked: What action had been taken against the person who had disclosed a Cabinet secret to a Lobby correspondent? Why had Scotland Yard officers severely questioned and threatened a newspaperman about his source? Who authorised the questioning? Was further action pending?

Sir William Jowitt, then Attorney-General and later Lord Chancellor, paraded the full majesty of the Official Secrets Act before the Commons, with great stress on the section laying down that any person must give information about his source, and that refusal to do so constitutes an offence. He went on, in an astonishing passage, to admit that the Home Secretary had made a statement "that the home Government would not dissociate itself from any action which the Viceroy might find it necessary to take"—a unique example of one Minister publicly identifying another Minister as the source of a serious leak. And he then proceeded to contradict himself by denying reports that a Cabinet Minister had "disclosed information relating to the intention of the Indian Government to arrest Gandhi or disclosed information that there had been consultation between the two Governments. These statements are completely untrue."

The real saga behind this incredible exercise—involving the Prime Minister, the Home Secretary, the Attorney-General, the Director of Public Prosecutions and the Special Branch specialising in counter-espionage in Whitehall—was told me years later by an excellent Downing Street source. According to this authoritative version, King George V, who always insisted on constitutional protocol being observed in requiring the Crown to be informed of all Government decisions, read the news of the Cabinet's authority for Gandhi's arrest and at once demanded to speak to his Prime Minister on the telephone. MacDonald admitted to him that the newspaper stories were true, and apologised for an official oversight which had delayed the Palace's being informed. The King, who was vigorous in using lurid naval language when displeased, "blew his top". Was he not still Emperor of all India? How was it that newspapers were informed of a Cabinet decision which had been withheld from the King?

After this royal roasting it seems that MacDonald over-reacted: there must be spies within Downing Street itself! He at once called in his Attorney-General—it was a pity he did not have a word with the more relaxed Clynes—and told him that a most disastrous leak had occurred, suggesting that the source could only have been from inside the Downing Street machine. From that moment the hunt was on.

There is an important moral in all this for both Downing Street and Fleet Street. It is that pledges and statements by Ministers have no legal validity. Only a decade earlier, well within the memory of the central figures in the Gandhi case, when the Official Secrets Act was going through Parliament a perspicacious back-bencher suggested that it might be used against the Press. The then Attorney-General, Sir Gordon Hewart, pooh-poohed the suggestion. The Act's powers, he firmly declared, were to be used only in cases of espionage and for national security.

And Gandhi? He was arrested just seven days after publication of the newspaper stories.

As for my old Lobby friends and colleagues, they were quick to do battle in the cause of Press freedom, even though their proprietors and editors had deserted the field. Lobby representatives held talks with MacDonald, Jowitt and Clynes, after which they received written pledges that in any future situation in which Scotland Yard and the legal authorities wished to interview a Lobbyman the chairman and secretary of the Lobby would first be informed and would have the right to be present to see that the interests of journalism and of the journalist would be protected against any abuse of the Official Secrets Act. That pledge is still in force.

Even without such assurances I am happy to think that the re-sounding Press silence of the time would not be repeated today; that if a political correspondent were interrogated for five solid hours and then threatened implicitly with detention, the whole of the media would join in a mighty protest against such KGB tactics. This thought may not be conclusive proof of progress towards more Press freedom but at least it signifies that some signs of life may still be detected fifty years on!

Of all the Prime Ministers in this gallery MacDonald has had the rawest deal from history. He has received inadequate recognition as one of the powerful influences in shaping the twentieth century largely because he was the earliest victim of the vogue for "instant history", being used then as the ready-made peg on which to hang myths and legends now sanctified in Labour's folklore. He was that odd combination of realist and idealist, one moment a mob orator and spellbinder, the next the organisation man. His achievements were substantial: he welded together an astonishing collection of groups, movements, splinters and committees into the Labour Party, and then became Prime Minister three times. As Harold Macmillan said of his old adversary*: "The first Labour Govern-ment was a remarkable achievement. MacDonald had brought a party to power in a single generation and himself to the highest office.... His life must be judged whole." The verdict of A. J. P. Taylor†: "He had, in some undefined way, the national stature which other Labour men lacked. He was maybe vain, solitary; yet, as Shinwell has said, in presence a prince among men. He was the last beautiful speaker of the Gladstone school, with a ravishing voice and turn of phrase ... he dominated that movement as long as he led it."

It has been said that he was a man possessed with pride over the trappings and rewards of power. As someone who knew him from my days as a cub reporter I can discount this. One brief story illustrates the point. I was with him in his private sitting-room at No. 10 in 1935 when he returned from the Palace on resigning as Prime Minister. In answer to my query, he replied: "Yes, the King pressed me to accept an earldom. But I refused. Me an Earl? How ridiculous." Or the Garter? "Certainly not. When my time comes I'll be buried with my ain folk in the Spynie kirkyard as

* *The Pastmasters*, by Harold Macmillan, Macmillan.
† *English History 1914–45*, by A. J. P. Taylor, O.U.P.

plain Jamie MacDonald, as I started, with no nonsense about titles."
Not the response one would expect from someone supposedly con-
sumed with pride and, without naming names, one can think of no
other Labour leaders who showed any hesitation in laying their
hands on an earl's ermine and a knight's garter. As he said a few
hours later to the wife of his elder son Alister: "I know you'd have
made a lovely Countess, my dear, but it's something I couldn't do,
even for you."

4

NEVILLE CHAMBERLAIN

May 1937–May 1940

"The Prime Minister said he had sent for the chairman of the *News Chronicle* and had protested in the strongest possible terms as to the attitude which his paper had adopted in this matter. The chairman had given an apology." CABINET MINUTES, 13 April 1939

"The Cabinet agreed . . . the Prime Minister to consider the best method of approaching the proprietors with a view to securing a cessation of the present Press campaign against the Government." CABINET MINUTES, 3 November 1939

Neville Chamberlain was the first Prime Minister to employ news management on a grand scale. His aim had nothing remotely to do with open Government, access to information and the strengthening of the democratic process; it had everything to do with the exploitation of the Press to espouse and defend Government thinking. From the moment he entered No. 10 in 1937 he sought to manipulate the Press into supporting his policy of appeasing the dictators. As he became increasingly passionate over appeasement and the more it came under attack from the media, the more he abandoned persuasion, turning instead to the use of threats and suppression to coerce the Press into co-operation. The two extracts from Cabinet minutes at the head of this chapter—never before published—give the game away. Finally, in order to cling to power Chamberlain was prepared to abuse truth itself. He made the most misleading and inaccurate statements which he was determined to see published so as to make his policies appear credible and successful. Quite simply, he told lies.

Had Chamberlain been a charlatan, a cad, a demagogue, a trickster, his performance might have been written off as an inevitable defect of character. On the contrary, however, he was a man of the utmost integrity, dedicated to the highest standards of rectitude in public and private life—a worthy son of that great Tory radical Joe Chamberlain, and half-brother of Sir Austen Chamberlain (who always struck me as too much a gentleman for the greasy pole when I knew him as a distinguished back-bencher in his later years).

Neville Chamberlain vividly demonstrated what power can really do to a man, transforming his character and temperament. When I knew him first, long before he became Prime Minister, he was the most shy, kindly, generous-minded and warm-hearted of men, always friendly and understanding although by nature cold, indrawn and lonely. But when he became Prime Minister and his appeasement policy first overwhelmed and finally destroyed him he became the most authoritarian, intolerant and arrogant of all the Premiers I have known. I am in no doubt that but for his obsession with Hitler and Mussolini he would have proved the most radical, modern and reforming of all Tory Premiers this century; he was really happiest when dealing with human problems such as housing, health, child welfare and the depressed groups.

His news management began quite ruthlessly while he was still Chancellor of the Exchequer and Crown Prince to Baldwin. He saw it as the best way of advancing personal ambition and power alike and he became increasingly obsessed with the necessity of keeping all the Press levers in his own hands; Fleet Street was his exclusive preserve. In the biography of Chamberlain by Iain Macleod* the story is told of Chamberlain confiding to his Cabinet colleague Kingsley Wood his private fears lest Baldwin "should muscle in on his regular briefings of Lobby correspondents" and when he became Prime Minister, in turn, he made quite sure that no other Minister met the Lobby.

He was assiduous in courting some fifty to sixty UK Lobbymen but he paid special attention to private meetings with three or four from true-blue Conservative papers. I was included in this magic circle because I happened to represent the loyalist Kemsley group of the time. We would meet regularly for lunch at the St Stephens Club opposite Westminster Bridge, the safest of venues since only Tory M.P.s and leading party figures were members. The host was usually Sir Robert Topping, the director-general of the Conservative Central Office, thus ensuring that Chamberlain's simultaneous control over Government and party networks remained tight. It was the closest Government–Press exercise I have known. When, many years and Premiers later, Harold Wilson invited a few hand-picked Lobbymen to meet him privately and regularly at No. 10 and Chequers—we became known as the "White Commonwealth"

* *Chamberlain*, by Iain Macleod, Muller.

group—it was denounced as a dangerous and sinister new departure in news manipulation. New? It was a method fifty years old—and it still flourishes under wraps.

In journalistic terms, the Chamberlain era was by far the most exhausting of my life. Scarcely a day passed without its own international crisis as the dictators became more reckless and war-like, their acts of aggression stretching across the world: the Spanish Civil War; Hitler's succession of invasions from the Rhineland right through to Austria, Czechoslovakia and Poland; Mussolini's invasion of Abyssinia and Albania; while in the Far East Japan's invasion of Manchuria split and distorted British and American priorities. And as the war-clouds grew so did Chamberlain's obsession with the media. His own personality and the character of his news management underwent a startling transformation. The old cosy relaxed atmosphere with Lobbymen was replaced by a cold arrogance and intolerance. His news-management became assertive and commanding, not friendly and subtle. Privately he exhibited a deep fear of Communism. (How far his decision to appease the Nazi and Fascist dictators derived from this fear is an aspect of the pre-war years which has never been seriously probed by the analysts and historians.)

In consequence, the critical questions which he was inevitably asked at meetings with the Westminster Press corps made him fear that what he was saying in confidence would be leaked through the Left to Moscow. Indeed, he bitterly resented any critical—or even probing—questions whatever; he always felt they were inspired by opponents. Sometimes he would reply with a haughty sneer. Then he developed a more intimidating style. When he sensed critical undertones he would pause deliberately and ask the correspondent if he would identify the name of the newspaper he represented— the implied blackmail being that the editor and proprietor would not take kindly to their Westminster man proving unfriendly and unpatriotic. He made no attempt to conceal his anger on such occasions. Alternatively, when asked a question which he resented he would attempt to snub a correspondent with frozen silence; after an eloquent pause, staring contemptuously at the questioner without saying a word in reply, he would turn aside, look in a different direction, and snap: "Next question, please". He was the only Prime Minister in my experience who could use this weapon of the total freeze. He was completely immobile, not merely for a fleeting second but for a long pause: an extraordinary show of silent intimidation.

Nor were we select few immune. He had dealt with us for many years yet when we met in his room privately before the final out-break of war he became more and more overbearing. Any question put across the table about, say, reports of the persecution of the Jews, Hitler's broken pledges or Mussolini's ambitions, would receive a res-ponse on well-established lines: he was surprised that such an experi-enced journalist was susceptible to Jewish–Communist propaganda.

Having initially "organised" the Lobby to his satisfaction Chamberlain moved with even greater success into Fleet Street itself where he courted proprietors, leader writers, opinion formers and editors with unabashed zeal, suiting his advances to the style of the men concerned. For instance, every Friday afternoon at 3.30 W. W. Hadley, editor of the *Sunday Times*, went on a pilgrimage to Downing Street to hear Chamberlain's views on the latest twists in the crises which engulfed Europe. And every Sunday morning the paper's leading articles and reports faithfully reflected the Prime Minister's appeasement projects. The *Sunday Times* was not alone. Chamberlain's regular socialising with proprietors ensured, as the yellowing newspaper files confirm, that the top direction of Fleet Street was always sympathetic to himself and his policies.

There were only two exceptions: the *Daily Telegraph* under the first Lord Camrose, who successfully resisted all blandishments and kept the paper on a course often more in harmony with the Churchill and Eden critiques of appeasement; and the *Yorkshire Post*, then closely linked with Eden, which maintained a robust independence. The remarkable feature about this whole period was, again, that Chamberlain handled these many and varied contacts personally. It is true that he appointed the first official Press Officer to No. 10, William Steward, but he was essentially a career civil servant (he was transferred from the Forestry Commission) and confined himself to handing out official statements and com-muniques. Certainly he never attempted to answer investigative questions about the news behind the scenes. In fact he seldom answered any questions at all. I remember as a young Lobbyman asking him when the Prime Minister would be going north. "Don't ask me that," he lectured. "That's an official secret." Five minutes later I met Chamberlain and he gave me the information without fuss. That Downing Street attitude died hard. Some years later my colleague, E. P. Stacpoole, that wonderful Press Association correspondent, discovered that Sir Kingsley Wood, Chancellor of the Exchequer, had collapsed and died a few minutes earlier. He sent an instant news-flash over the agency wires. The PA newsdesk naturally phoned Downing Street, saying that "Staccie has just wired the news" and seeking more details. "You mustn't report that on any account," demanded the news department, "it's not for publication yet." At No. 10 even death is off the record and not for immediate release.

Chamberlain's closest confidant among the upper echelons of Fleet Street was unquestionably the editor of *The Times*, Geoffrey Dawson, a man who needed no persuasion for he was the patron saint of appeasement. The conduct of Dawson and *The Times* is a reflection of events across Fleet Street, but in magnified form. Not only did Dawson excise vital pieces from foreign correspondents' despatches, especially from Berlin, lest they give offence to Hitler, he even slipped in comments of his own, completely distorting the balance of the reports in the hope of comforting and currying favour with the Nazi leaders. Dawson's actions constitute a frightful warning to everybody, at whatever level, in the media: the integrity and independence of journalism is in grave jeopardy when the media become active participants in the affairs of Government and Whitehall.

Despite the careful sub-editing of the despatches from Berlin Dawson could not prevent his exceptionally able correspondent, Norman Ebbutt, from being expelled by the Nazis. Dawson was so astounded that he wrote to *The Times* man in Switzerland to find out why and how *The Times* had offended the Nazis, because, he explained in his letter, he had been doing his "utmost, night after night, to keep out of the paper anything that might hurt their susceptibilities". And not only keeping out; for as he wrote to Lord Lothian in another confessional of 23 May 1937: "I spend my nights dropping in little things which are intended to soothe them".

But the most alarming example of an editor becoming hypnotised by too close contact with political power concerned Dawson and Anthony Winn, promoted at an early age to be Parliamentary correspondent of *The Times*. When, with conspicuous and characteristic political courage, Duff Cooper resigned as Chamberlain's First Lord of the Admiralty within twenty-four hours of Munich he made a powerful and moving resignation speech which, like other writers, I described in my own despatches as eloquent and impressive. Winn duly reported the speech for *The Times*, with political comment, interpreting the considerable effect it had on the House of Commons. These views of the Gallery correspondents were not isolated or distorted; within minutes of sitting down Duff Cooper received a note of congratulations from Winston Churchill, the soundest of judges of great Parliamentary orations, who wrote: "Your speech was one of the finest Parliamentary performances I have ever heard. It was admirable in form, massive in argument and shone with courage and public spirit." Anthony Winn's report was not only killed; Dawson substituted a version of his own, allegedly

54

"From our Lobby Correspondent", which dismissed Duff Cooper's speech as a "damp squib", in the hope of softening the impact on Hitler next morning. Let me elaborate, for the story confirms that the challenge to the freedom and integrity of the Press can come from editorial chairs just as much as from militant trade unionists. One of the phrases Dawson concocted was that "emotional gourmets had expected a tasty morsel but it had proved rather unappetising", and he added for good measure that Duff Cooper must have been "consoled by the thought that his resignation had been accepted with relief". Alas, a total fabrication and misrepresentation by a *Times* editor.

This, in my experience, is about the worst example of editorial distortion deliberately engineered to give comfort and support to a Prime Minister. To his honour, Anthony Winn resigned in protest from *The Times* the same day and all-too-soon afterwards gave his life in battle. His resignation was certainly the most heroic in my memory, the more so because its reasons were known to only a few of us close colleagues. They don't breed them like that any more.

From Chamberlain's point of view Dawson's excesses were Press manipulation by proxy. A far more serious charge against Chamberlain is that he himself constantly attempted to mislead Political correspondents in the most calculated fashion, by telling us what later proved to be the most grotesque version of the truth. He persisted in giving optimistic forecasts of international prospects which were lies. In all situations and in all crises, however menacing, he always claimed that the outlook was most encouraging, with not a cloud in the sky; he claimed his contacts with Hitler and Mussolini were very good and that the dictators were responding with understanding and promise, and if only Left-wing newspapers would stop writing critical and insulting things about them, he was confident that Herr Hitler and Signor Mussolini (he was always punctilious in using the Herr and Signor as a mark of respect, and frowned on any offhand reference to Hitler) would co-operate with him in his peace initiative.

So forget your worries, he would tell us; the world situation has never been more promising; all these war-mongering stories are got up by Communists, Jewish propagandists and their sympathisers, and printed by the yellow liberal papers and periodicals just to annoy Herr Hitler and Signor Mussolini. Have a good holiday, he would say to us at the end of a session or at Easter or Whitsun; things are getting better and better all the while. Alas, all too often we were caught napping. We would report Chamberlain's assessment in good faith, and write news reports and articles reflecting a strong mood of Government optimism on the eve of this or that recess. All too often we would be compelled to come rushing back within twenty-four or forty-eight hours as some new outrage by one or other of the dictators created a war threat which made nonsense of the Premier's dearest hopes. Many journalists' reputations were severely injured in the process.

Chamberlain genuinely believed that by inventing and getting published good news he might contrive to relieve sinister threats and receive as a reward a morsel of comfort from Berlin and Rome. The most notable example of his deliberate deceptions came on 9 March 1939, when Chamberlain met a few of us for one of his seances at a time of very great danger and gloom. This was on the very eve of Hitler's invasion of Czechoslovakia and only six months before the outbreak of war. Yet, Chamberlain averred, the situation had never been better; he was actually working towards halting the armaments race, he claimed, perhaps leading to an agreement later in the year; his relations with Herr Hitler were most cordial; the Spanish crisis was on the point of being solved and this would make Signor Mussolini much happier; he was on the point of bringing about improved relations between France and Italy. And so on and so on; everything going well in the best of all possible worlds.

This attempt to keep from the country the truth about the growing menace to the free world is particularly important because unexpected new sources prove that at the very moment when we were being deceived, another pen was describing—not for the Press but in a diary of secret history—the shock and feeling of incredulity inside the Government and Whitehall about the optimistic Press stories inspired by Chamberlain.

In the diaries of Lord Harvey*, a top Foreign Office adviser to Anthony Eden and later to Lord Halifax, there appears a long and telling entry for March 10:

> *Times* and other papers today all contained identical and rosy accounts of present position in foreign affairs which were obviously inspired. It was said that the Spanish affair would soon be over and after that Franco–Italian difficulties would remain to be tackled. But they did not warrant any undue pessimism. Then the next step would be halt in the armaments race. It was felt that if, in the course of the present year, we could achieve some agreement, it would do much to restore confidence: much depended on Anglo–German relations. but here too the position was more promising.

* *The Diplomatic Diaries of Oliver Harvey 1937–40*, edited by John Harvey, Collins.

When H. [Lord Halifax then Foreign Secretary] came to the office he asked where this had come from, believing it was the News Department. It was then found on inquiry that the P.M. yesterday had received all the lobby correspondents and given them a discourse on foreign affairs. He had never even told H. that he intended to do so or discussed what he should say. No. 10 had not even warned the News Department that it was being done—so that at least they could pretend that the F.O. were in on it; and Horace Wilson [Chamberlain's personal adviser] had not even mentioned it to Cadogan [Permanent Head of the Foreign Office] though he saw him at four yesterday.

H., although he did not show it, was annoyed, and asked to see the P.M. We then heard that he had left for Chequers last evening! H. therefore wrote to him and had it sent down by pouch.

Alec Cadogan feels it particularly unwise to speak now of arms limitation, anyway a very difficult subject which needs most careful preparation, and mention of it will only make Germany think we are feeling the strain. Similarly, to speak glibly of settling Franco–Italian relations will cause suspicion in France, where it will be thought we are preparing to do a deal, and will make Italy think so too and encourage her to stiffen her demands. . . .

But what is one to think of the P.M.'s behaviour in not even speaking to H. before he gave such an important interview? Is it mere obtuseness to decent behaviour; is it jealousy again and determination to do everything himself? Is it a reply to H.'s recent "Halt, Major Road Ahead" speech which No. 10 thought too stiff? Of course the rumour has started that H. and the P.M. no longer see eye-to-eye.

A further extract from Harvey's diaries neatly rounds off the incident:

March 13: P.M. has written a contrite letter to H. about the interview with lobby correspondents, saying it was entirely his fault, he had never thought the Press would take it so literally, he had been under the impression that the F.O. had been consulted and he would not do it again!

H. amused and [?] half-convinced.

As a humble seeker after truth at the time, and having been present at the Chamberlain meeting with the Lobby, I need only add that it is Lord Harvey's diaries which tell the true history, not

Chamberlain's explanation. The Prime Minister deliberately fostered artificial optimism, and his views, tenor and spirit were very accurately reported. Just how much Chamberlain deceived himself and, through the Press, the country, may be judged from this entry in the Harvey diary of the following day, after Hitler's final assault on Czechoslovakia:

> March 14: Fresh Czech crisis—a nice comment on the P.M.'s interview. Slovakia declares herself independent with German support, Czechs reported to have acquiesced before German threats (we know German troops are on the march towards the Czech frontiers), Czech Minister of Foreign Affairs on the way to see Hitler, reports that Germany is appointing two *Staathalters* for Prague and Bratislava and troops move in tonight.

The Nazi invaders occupied Prague itself on 15 March. So much for Chamberlain's guidance to us. From British intelligence reports, he must have been fully aware that Hitler was preparing to smash Czechoslovakia, yet he persisted in living in his world of make-believe, telling the people untruths which he must have known to be untruths, because he was more concerned with pacifying Hitler and Mussolini than with alerting public opinion to the grim dangers.

He would never do it again, he said contritely in his note to Halifax quoted above. A sanguine hope, too easily confounded! In a matter of weeks he was at it again. It was on the eve of the Easter recess that he met a group of us for yet another of his sunshine tours. Reassure public opinion, he urged us; the worst was over and there would be no more shocks or surprise coups by the dictators—he was convinced of their good intentions. Have a good holiday, he advised us, free from worry and care. He was, he added for good measure, acting on his own advice and was leaving that night on the Aberdeen express for a salmon-fishing holiday on the Dee.

In all the major crises of the period—and they were many—Chamberlain showed an unfailing flair for misjudging the gravity of the situation. So it proved on this occasion; once more the Press were taken in by a man who believed that by making rosy forecasts he could somehow change the political climate. For within twenty-four hours of his briefing, on the morning of Good Friday and even as the Prime Minister was preparing to cast his first fly, Mussolini invaded Albania.

Clearly, Chamberlain's game was not one which could be played with impunity for ever. Editors began complaining to Lobbymen that their papers were being made to appear irresponsible and ridiculous by publishing cheery stories being peddled by the Premier only to be confounded within hours by the dictators. A few of us therefore had a private lunch with Chamberlain during which the point was firmly made that editors were becoming sceptical of our sources, Prime Ministerial or not. Chamberlain pronounced himself astounded that journalists should be so short-sighted as to take such a self-centred view of their national responsibilities. Did we not realise how Herr Hitler and Signor Mussolini objected to the constant attacks upon them in the British Press. He had reason to believe, he added plaintively, that Herr Hitler and Signor Mussolini appreciated his efforts to improve the atmosphere and to correct the mischievous criticisms in the British newspapers—all too often, he feared, inspired by Communist sympathisers in Britain in order to frustrate his efforts to find peace. Didn't we realise, too, that the real threat to European civilisation came from Russian Communism? If only we would be patient and help him in his endeavours, he was confident that Herr Hitler and Signor Mussolini would reach agreement with him to satisfy their demands and ambitions. In any case, he added, with a knowing look, he had reason to believe that Hitler's hold on the loyalty of the German people and of powerful figures in the German High Command, was most insecure. He could not understand how and why any of us were having any difficulties with our proprietors and editors; he was seeing them regularly and he found them most understanding and co-operative, unlike the critics among M.P.s and certain hostile Lobby correspondents.

But the overwhelming pressure of events was beginning to tell. Chamberlain frequently reached the point of exhaustion and in this delicate state he became hypersensitive, even emotionally so, to any attack or criticism. He was particularly angry whenever writers referred to the dictatorial manner which he exhibited alike in the Commons, in private meetings and on the public platform. On one such occasion he urgently summoned a few of us to Downing Street where we found him in the Cabinet room, trembling and white with fury. He thumped the table many, many times as he snarled out his protest: "I tell you that I'm not dictatorial, I'm not autocratic, I'm not intolerant, I'm not overpowering. You're all wrong, wrong, wrong, I tell you. I'm the most relaxed and understanding of people. None of you, I insist, must ever say I'm dictatorial again. I tell you." It was a saddening performance. In this angry outburst, which must have seriously depleted his sorely sapped nervous and physical resources, he looked and acted himself as the complete dictator.

I am in no doubt that Chamberlain's dictatorial personal influence on newspaper proprietors, editors and writers made his Premiership, in my experience, the most inglorious period in the history of the British Press. I am in good company. Wickham Steed, the celebrated journalist and Dawson's predecessor as editor of *The Times*, recounted in his book on the Press* how views were "confidentially" expressed to papers so that they would tone down their reports and withhold frank comment. And he added: "No newspaper, as far as I am aware, has denounced in public this impertinent meddling with the freedom of responsible journalism"— a shrewd blow at the unbelievably partisan stance of his successor at *The Times*.

The dictatorial approach is classically illustrated by the case of Vernon Bartlett of the *News Chronicle*. On the night of the Munich settlement between Hitler and Chamberlain, Bartlett—truly one of the most distinguished journalists and communicators in my experience—filed a critical despatch from Munich interpreting the gravity of the settlement for Britain and demolishing the euphoria and make-believe of the night. Just as the paper was ready to go to press, displaying Bartlett's analysis with great prominence, the chairman, Lord Layton, ordered that the article must not be printed "because it was too depressing". Sir Gerald Barry, one of the finest editors in the old tradition of independence and courage, at once reacted vigorously to his boss's assault on his editorial freedom. He announced that he would not bring the paper out because he had total trust in Bartlett's judgment and was determined to stand by his man on the spot. Barry was supported by the senior members of the staff—a unique example of an editor heading a strike to prevent his own paper being published and in defiance of his own chairman. Faced with this powerful revolution, Layton was forced to withdraw his veto on Bartlett's interpretation of the Munich agreement—and, indeed, his prophecies were all too accurately and tragically confirmed by history.

I have discovered evidence which may account for the chief proprietor's astonishing interference, which at the time seemed to be so out of character with his impressive record on liberal, radical and progressive causes. The reason lies, I think, in the fact that he had been successfully cowed by Chamberlain over another article, concerning Mussolini, published some months earlier. As ever, Chamberlain believed in going for the man at the top. The turning of the Downing Street thumbscrews is drily summarised in the Cabinet minutes of 13 April 1939, little more than four months

* *The Press*, Henry Wickham Steed, Penguin.

before the outbreak of war. The record is significant because it shows how an enraged Prime Minister summons the head of a great news-paper organisation to his carpet at No. 10, administers a stern rebuke with no nonsense about the freedom of the Press, and is then graciously pleased to accept an apology:

> The Prime Minister referred to an article which had appeared in the *News Chronicle* on Wednesday 12 April to the effect that he (the Prime Minister) had received assurances from Signor Mussolini through a very private source and was now contemplating some new Mediterranean agreements, to which Italy would be a party. On the strength of this supposed message, the *News Chronicle* had carried a leading article which contained a bitter attack on the Government.
>
> From inquiries, the Prime Minister had ascertained that the Press Officer of the Foreign Office had been aware of this rumour and had assured the Press both on the authority of the Foreign Office and of the Prime Minister that there was no truth in it. The correspondent of the *News Chronicle* had, however, maintained that he had obtained this information from a Cabinet Minister and had insisted on publishing it.
>
> The Prime Minister said he had sent for the Chairman of the *News Chronicle* and had protested in the strongest possible terms as to the attitude which his paper had adopted in this matter. The Chairman had given an apology. An article in that morning's *News Chronicle*, however, stated that reports of such a communication had received very wide circulation in the past two days in well-informed pro-Government as well as in Opposition newspapers, and that reports of this kind are not given publicity in reputable newspapers unless received from authoritative and well-informed sources. He had looked through a number of these papers but had found in them no reference to this rumour.

The author of the offending article, so strongly defended by Barry, was the paper's Political correspondent, David Keir, a friend and contemporary of mine whom I first knew many years before in Scotland. He was never in any doubt about the accuracy of his report. He confided to me that his information came from two Cabinet Ministers who were critical of Chamberlain's policy and appalled at his parleying with Mussolini only a few days after Italy's invasion of Albania. The Cabinet minutes, with their message between the lines, clearly confirm Keir's report. The Prime Minister was advised and pressed by Ministers to deny the report in the Commons on the day of publication; it may have been an oversight, but he made no denial at Westminster. Even so, he felt able to carpet the paper's chairman! Prime Ministers never vary in character. They are always most annoyed by leaks that are too accurate; the inaccurate ones deny themselves in time.

Fairness demands that I should leave the final word with Chamberlain. Despite, or because of, his ruthless Press manipulation over at least six years, he experienced a disastrously bad Press when his appeasement policies collapsed in ruins on the outbreak of war. Newspapers started campaigning for him to go because they could not understand how the Man of Munich could become the Man of Victory. But he fought on. The Cabinet minutes of 3 November reveal his anguish of heart over hostile newspaper proprietors (oddly enough, after all his travail, he did not seem to be worried overmuch about the lesser breeds such as editors and Lobby correspondents). This is how he sought to savage Fleet Street which had given him more than a fair deal long after the demands of national survival allowed:

> [Newspaper criticism] amounted to a mass-produced and artificial agitation which bore no relation to any spontaneous feeling of indignation in the country. The explanation of so unpatriotic a course of conduct on the part of newspaper proprietors lay in the degeneration of our Press. We have now a very different Press from that which, in past ages, had been a bulwark of the liberty of the subject. A free Press today meant a commercial Press out for money and not interested in principles or ideals. This commercial Press was not, for the most part, losing money. In these circumstances its aim was to sell papers, if necessary, by unscrupulous attacks on the Government.
>
> Steps must be taken at once to call a halt to this. The only means by which the Government could deal with the situation were, first, that the charges made by the Press must be demonstrated to be false or exaggerated and, secondly, a patriotic appeal must be made to newspaper proprietors. While this would probably have some immediate effect, he doubted whether it would last long.
>
> The Prime Minister added he thought that the Press campaign against the Government was purely commercial and had no party origin.
>
> The Cabinet agreed to invite the Prime Minister to consider the best method of approaching the newspaper proprietors with a view to securing a cessation of the present Press cam-

paign against the Government, bearing in mind the harmful effect of this campaign upon opinion abroad.

But the end could not be long delayed. Six months later, in May 1940, Churchill became Prime Minister with Chamberlain as Lord President. By the end of the year he was dead. He had been offered an earldom or the Garter but declined both (as did MacDonald and Macmillan). He preferred, he said, "to die plain Mr Chamberlain, like my father before me." His own good-bye to the newspapers is in one of the last entries in his diaries: "Not one shows the slightest sign of sympathy for the man, or even any comprehension that there may be a human tragedy in the background." *Vale.*

5

WINSTON CHURCHILL

May 1940–July 1945
October 1951–April 1955

> "Most of the papers infuriate me. They exasperate. The *News Chronicle*: all over the place. Geese, geese. But the paper I can't stand, the worst of all, is the *Daily Mirror*. Yes, the *Daily Mirror*. It makes me spit." WINSTON CHURCHILL

Winston Churchill was proud to record "journalist" as his profession on his passport. He began as a war correspondent and later became a prolific writer, earning immense sums of money both as a commentator and historian and hack writer of pot-boilers. Fleet Street was the foundation of his fortunes and, during his long years in the political wilderness, it sustained him as a national figure. Yet when he became Prime Minister he became authoritarian and repressive, incapable of tolerating any form of criticism in the Press. Criticism he viewed as treasonable. He had to be restrained by Cabinet colleagues not only from censoring comment but also from suppressing altogether newspapers which he considered hostile. He ordered security inquiries to discover whether there were sinister links between the enemy and leading shareholders in the Mirror group and whether there were alien influences behind writers and cartoonists with unusual names. He was even prepared to have critical Parliamentary speeches blacked out by censors.

Lloyd George's simple motto for resolving battles between Fleet Street and Downing Street was: "What you can't square you squash; what you can't squash you square." Churchill concurred wholeheartedly. But whereas Lloyd George was by nature a squarer, baiting his hooks with honours to land the big Fleet Street fish, Churchill was a squasher. He used the majesty of office to steam-roller Fleet Street. To him power was absolute and it was personal. It was not to be shared.

Churchill was only twenty, a subaltern in the Hussars, when he had his first writing contract, from the *Daily Graphic*: he was to send a series of letter-despatches from the civil war in Cuba and was given Army permission to undertake the assignment. His letters, for which he received £5 each, early showed the rolling periods and grandiloquent style which later characterised his speeches and all his serious historical writings. This, for instance, was the style of the young officer reporting from the front line: ". . . a Cuba free and prosperous, sending her ponies to Hurlingham and her cricketers to Lords, exchanging the cigars of Havana for the cottons of Lancashire . . ." That was the world he knew and loved. For a long time he combined his career as a serving soldier with that of a journalist—until the then Prince of Wales came on the scene. He objected to an officer serving in a campaign and simultaneously writing for newspapers strong criticism of the commanders' conduct of the fighting. After this rebuke, the War Office banned serving soldiers from writing for the Press on military affairs. But Churchill had discovered his flair. He went out to cover the South African war for the *Morning Post* on a four months' contract of £1,000 (say £15,000 today).

Throughout his frequent periods out of office, notably in the 'thirties, Churchill always turned to journalism for his bread and butter—or rather his toast and caviar—while at the same time continuing his major historical books, such as *Marlborough*, *Great Contemporaries* and, of course, *The World Crisis*. His journalistic writings, mainly for the "popular Sundays" which paid him the highest fees and provided the largest market, he regarded as hack work. But he was a brilliant and extremely speedy practitioner, always ready to write on bright ideas put up to him by an enterprising features editor. For instance, he made a very substantial income out of re-writing the world's great popular stories from *Uncle Tom's Cabin* to *Westward Ho!* These slick catchpenny enterprises revealed an astonishing ability in adapting his literary style to the demands of the "pop" market place.

He drove hard bargains for massive fees, a habit which never deserted him. Even after his greatest hour, when he was back in Opposition, rich publishers' contracts maintained their fascination. One afternoon he called E. P. Stacpoole, of the Press Association, to his home at Hyde Park Gate, and there confided the information that he had just sold the copyright of all his wartime secret-session speeches to the American Time-Life group—"because I want to make some dollars". What did Mr Stacpoole think of the project? What would the British Press say? Would Fleet Street feel "aggrieved"?

Churchill was stunned by the response. Stacpoole, normally the mildest and most courteous of men, reacted powerfully. The British nation had paid Winston a very high salary for being Prime Minister; part of the duty of being P.M. was to deliver to Parliament speeches on British Government policies and the future and survival of the British people. Now he was proposing to sell those speeches, which really belonged to the House of Commons and the British people, to the American magazine empire so that the Americans would have the chance to read them first. All for the sake of dollars for his private bank account! Shouldn't they be published in Britain, as a State document if necessary, so that all papers could report the speeches as they wished, without paying copyright fees?

The row continued for much of the afternoon. In the end he accepted the force of Stacpoole's protest but he was unaccustomed to such spirited reaction from any journalist or to having his judgment questioned by a skilled Lobbyman reminding him of the demands of an informed public opinion.

The reason for this was perfectly simple: during his astonishingly long career at Westminster he never had any direct personal contact with the Press in general or with political correspondents in particular. He was a journalist who loved journalism but who never mixed with journalists and who had no understanding or sympathy with the job they were doing. He had close personal ties with Beaverbrook and Camrose and with one or two editors, but never with the mass of newspapermen. He never once met the Lobby correspondents, he never gave a background briefing on or off the record at Westminster or elsewhere. When he was well over seventy years of age he confessed that he did not know anything about the Parliamentary Press. He believed totally in the power and majesty of the spoken word, especially when his was the voice of revelation. He also believed passionately in the power and influence of the written word, especially when he was the author of the compelling prose. His rule was simple. When he had anything to say he said it direct to "the people", either in the House of Commons or on the platform. There was no nonsense about guidance for journalists on what they might write off the record—"compulsory plagiarism" as an American contemporary described the "backgrounders" given by American Presidents. This was not for Churchill.

One curious aspect of his attitude towards the Press was that whenever he visited the USA he always met newspapermen at Press conferences or Press Club lunches in accordance with the American tradition for visiting statesmen. It was during one such trip that a piqued Fleet Street made representations to Downing Street to the effect that the British Press, for a change, would also like to meet their own Prime Minister for a similar session. Churchill, on his way back from the States, agreed. So Fleet Street, represented by a mixed group of political and general writers, rushed to Southampton for a Press conference on board the pride of the Cunard line. Things got off to a bad start. First of all, Churchill kept the Press waiting for about half an hour, sending messages that he was suffering from a severe cold. When he finally appeared he destroyed the atmosphere of the great occasion by announcing that, of course, the journalists must please understand that he could not be expected to answer any questions bearing on his American visit, the subjects discussed with the President, the decisions reached, or what he would be saying to the British Parliament: in short, all the subjects about which the reporters wanted to ask.

This was how the meeting proceeded, with the Prime Minister's straight bat never letting one past. "I'm very sorry, I can't say anything on that until I have reported to Parliament"; "I must inform my Cabinet colleagues first"; "Anything on that subject I propose to say in my next broadcast to the British people"; "You must forgive me if I refuse to say anything in reply to that particular question"; "As I am certain to be asked questions in the House I had better postpone anything I have to say until then"; "On that, Parliament must be told the facts first". And so on. It is impossible to imagine any Prime Minister today, brought up in the discipline of the bromide set-pieces before the cameras, trying to get away with such Churchillian replies. Yet stripped of their style, their courteous responses are probably no more informative than Churchill's.

The great man had seen and heard Roosevelt's Washington Press conferences, with the President making a special point of identifying correspondents by their first names, as proof of the camaraderie between old buddies, and never forgetting to ask about the wife, also by her first name, if she had been ill. But Churchill could not bring himself to attempt anything similar. So far as I know, Southampton was his first and last Press conference. It was regarded by both sides as something best forgotten. Yet again, Churchill had demonstrated his total lack of rapport with the toilers of Fleet Street.

There was only one working journalist whose judgment he valued—that of Harry Boardman, the distinguished Parliamentary correspondent of the *Manchester Guardian*. After every major speech in the House of Commons, Sir Fyfe Clarke, Press Secretary at No. 10, would seek out Boardman to ask him what he thought of the Prime Minister's oration. Churchill was always anxious for his frank view—but he still used an intermediary!

For the rest of us, all was silence. The experience of a Lobby

67

friend, James Robertson, vividly illustrates Churchill's curious mixture of hostility and unease towards Press men. After being in the Gallery for many years Robertson was appointed political correspondent of the *Glasgow Herald* and therefore sought to establish contacts with Churchill and those members of the Government he had not known before. Seeing Churchill striding through the Lobby one afternoon after questions in the Commons, Robertson seized the opportunity of making himself known.

"Prime Minister, sir," Robertson opened. "May I introduce myself? I am James Robertson of the . . ."

"Do I know you?" growled Winston. "What right have you to . . ."

Robertson was overwhelmed by the forbidding response. "I am sorry, Prime Minister. If you object, forgive me, but as I'll be representing the *Glasgow Herald* I thought it right to introduce myself. . . . Scotland is interested in your leadership, and you have been very interested in Scotland in the past"—a sly dig at Churchill's alacrity in becoming M.P. for Dundee when he failed to find a seat in England.

Churchill stood scowling at Robertson, obviously fuming that someone should have the presumption to force himself upon his company. After a long pause, while other journalists and M.P.s witnessed the tense scene, the Prime Minister grunted something about "Out of my way . . ." and strode on in eloquent resentment.

His attitude to Fleet Street and particularly to the Lobby was best summed up by the first Earl of Swinton (with whom I collaborated on *Sixty Years of Power*). In 1953, when the Prime Minister was experiencing an exceptionally critical Press, a hostile opinion, and several by-election shocks he sent for Swinton, whose memories went back to Bonar Law and Balfour, and gave a long recital of complaints about the wicked and uninformed state of the British Press which misrepresented Government policies. He said that he had been advised by the Party's experts that all his disasters were due to his own failure as a communicator. What could be done, he asked, to rescue his Government, to get a better Press, and to communicate with the people? The conversation, Swinton told me, went along these lines:

Swinton: "You must stop living in your ivory tower, Winston; get into the market place, take the Press into your confidence, tell them what you're trying to do. They don't want to hear any of your grand orations written for history. Unbend. Confide in the journalists."

Churchill: "But I do, Philip, I do, all the time. I see Max [Beaverbrook] regularly. I have close relations with Bill [the first

68

Lord Camrose] and his brother, Gomer, too [the first Lord Kemsley]. And I've known Rothermere many years. I see them all from time to time, at dinner you know. And I talk freely to them."

Swinton: "Winston, you're wasting your bloody time. They're all proprietors. Not one of them writes a line, with the exception of Max, who stirs things up for the pure hell of it. Seeing you is just good for their self-esteem; not a line of what you tell them ever reaches the public. It just gives them a snobbish card to play over dinner, when they can tell their guests what you were saying to them; they like to create the impression that they're advising you. Wasting your time giving them dinner at all."

Churchill: "But, Philip, that's not all. I see some editors from time to time. . . . Haley of *The Times*, my old friend Colin Coote of the *Telegraph*—he was in the Commons with me just after the First World War, you know—and I see other editors at functions from time to time. I'm always open to see them at any time. I was very fond of Crozier of the *Manchester Guardian*."

Swinton: "But Winston you're wasting your time. The editors are mainly concerned with their leading articles, and nobody reads them nowadays except in times of national crisis. No, the fellows you've got to meet and explain what you're trying to do are the political correspondents in the Lobby; they're the chaps who are writing the stories every night which make the front pages of all the papers next morning. Have you ever met them? Do you know any of them, to ask along for an informal chat and a drink, off the record, background; that's how to get the real facts about the Government put across. . . ."

Churchill: "I'm too old, Philip, to learn these tricks [he was then seventy-nine]. I suppose it's the new American style of trying to persuade journalists they're important."

Swinton: "The Lobby system is unique to British politics, there's nothing like it anywhere else in the world. In America, where they've no daily contact with Parliament, Ministers exploit contacts with individual writers, because that's their only outlet. But in Britain the system is much more mature and subtle."

Churchill: "Philip, it's a new world to me. Will you handle all the contacts with the Press at all levels for me? I don't know these Lobby people."

So Swinton took charge of all information and public relations services on Churchill's behalf and was outstandingly successful.

The strange thing was that Churchill every day read all the newspapers in great detail. When he was not in power he would telephone my office at night seeking the latest news from Moscow or Washington. And when a newspaper strike closed Fleet Street

I had the job of collecting all the morning and evening papers in our regional group and delivering them twice a day to No. 10. Yet for all this intense interest in the Press, he never, to the end, understood the subtle balance in the power structure between Downing Street and Fleet Street.

On succeeding Chamberlain in 1940 Churchill rapidly revealed himself as the prime advocate of dictatorial controls on the Press, the sponsor of astonishing censorship. When faced with Press criticisms his anger in Cabinet became almost uncontrollable, his quest for vengeance endless. This is a little-known aspect of his character and confirms anew how absolute power, even in a democracy, begets dictatorial intolerance.

Yet in Churchill's case it should not occasion too much surprise. Even when he held office in the 1914–18 World War he was always the most enthusiastic advocate of the most total censorship and at one time vigorously (but unsuccessfully) pressed Asquith to take over *The Times* as a State organ. As First Lord of the Admiralty he forbade war correspondents to accompany the Royal Navy. During the General Strike in 1926, when he was editor of the Government's *British Gazette*, the only daily paper then published, he used his powers ruthlessly to suppress any reports which appeared to give a favourable view of the strikers; even the Archbishop of Canterbury's appeal for a negotiated settlement was spiked because it conflicted with the editor's determination to force unconditional surrender. His excuse for blacking out reports which might encourage peace initiatives was typically Churchillian: as between the fire brigade and the fire he could not be impartial!

His historic wartime orations in the Mother of Parliaments were always given great prominence and approval in all the papers; but this was not enough for Churchill. If the same papers also reported critical speeches by M.P.s he reacted bitterly. The situation became so tense that the censorship branch of the Ministry of Information started blacking out critical passages of Commons speeches on the grounds that if they were reproduced they would depress morale and hinder the war effort—notwithstanding that the speeches were reflecting the national mood of disquiet over the conduct of the war. I was a member of a small deputation of Westminster Lobbymen invited to lunch with Lord Beaverbrook at the Dorchester to discover a formula for reconciling the paramount freedom of Parliamentary democracy with the need to sustain a high morale when military disasters spread depression and gloom. Beaverbrook, who had a foot in both camps as a Minister in Churchill's Government and proprietor of the *Express* newspapers, came down strongly on our side: there could be no justification for censoring Parliament by censoring correspondents' reports of what was said and done at Westminster.

Nevertheless the struggle continued and a little later became a bizarre three-sided confrontation. Duff Cooper, Minister of Information, and Brendan Bracken formulated an inspired and realistic policy: always tell the British people the truth, however grim, and they will respond with courage. To prepare the civilian population for grim reality they briefed the political correspondents frankly on Hitler's plans for invasion, for assault by pilotless V-weapons and so on. Alas, the mandarins at Duff Cooper's own Ministry heavily blue-pencilled the harsh war tidings which he had shared with us. We protested vigorously and Duff Cooper, one of the few men to be able to stand up to Churchill, took our side against his own men. Never again was he censored, however indirectly or anonymously he was reported. It was not an insignificant victory.

Churchill's obsession with the Press is fully, and often frighteningly, depicted by the minutes of the War Cabinet meetings which confirm that discussions on complaints and inquiries about Press reports and articles were invariably raised on Churchill's personal initiative. Within a few weeks of his becoming Prime Minister comes evidence that he was determined to take an authoritarian line. At the Cabinet on 16 June 1940, he was telling his Ministers:

> It was unfortunate that there was a certain tendency by the Press to encourage inquests rather than to concentrate on the tasks ahead. It was essential that steps should be taken to make the Press realise that demands for inquests could only engender a spirit of doubt as to our strength and that such demands ought therefore to be sternly discouraged.

The next day, he was back on the same threatening tack, this time complaining that the Press

> could not refrain from indulging in one stunt after another. These stunts sometimes created a lack of confidence. Again, even the most reputable newspapers treated the guidance which they were given in a rather cavalier spirit. In the last resort, the only remedy in the hands of the Government was to order prosecutions, and it seemed undesirable to adopt this remedy at the present juncture.

These brief extracts, which show Churchill giving advance warning of the obedience and co-operation he expected from the newspapers, set the scene for much that was to follow during the next

71

five years. The record should be seen as part of the unending struggle over Press freedom on the one hand and, on the other, Prime Ministerial ambitions to subjugate newspapers.

The most serious and longest running crisis in Government–Press relations concerned Churchill's private war with the Mirror group under the editorial direction of Harry Bartholomew. We know from a variety of speeches, lectures and writings by Cecil King, later chairman of the *Mirror* empire; from Hugh Cudlipp (later Lord Cudlipp) his editorial director; and from Maurice Edelman's official history of the *Mirror* newspapers, how the war was seen and directed from the papers' side. It is important that gaps in knowledge should be filled in from the other side, from hitherto unplumbed official Cabinet minutes and papers. They show how extremely grave and explosive was the crisis as seen from inside No. 10 Downing Street and how frequently Churchill was warning his War Cabinet that the papers would have to be suppressed unless they ceased being critical of himself and his Government.

After much skirmishing, relations moved to a major crisis at the War Cabinet meeting on 7 October 1940, only a year after the out-break of war and within six months of Churchill's becoming Prime Minister. The Cabinet minute concerning the Press is extraordinarily long, running to about 1,100 words, with little attempt at summary. The issue was raised by Churchill himself, and the narrative style suggests that it was mainly a monologue by him. Here are the main points from the section, given by the Cabinet Secretariat the sinister heading: "The Press—Subversive Articles":

> The Prime Minister drew attention to an article in the *Sunday Pictorial* [now the *Sunday Mirror*] on the 29th September. This article, which had contained a lot of false information, had characterised the Dakar affair as "Another Blunder" and had used language of an insulting character to the Government. In the issue of the same journal of the previous day [i.e. 6 October, the day before the meeting] great prominence had been given to an article published by Mr H. G. Wells in an obscure pamphlet [the Bulletin of the Labour Book Service]. This article had contained a slashing attack on Field-Marshal Sir Edmund Ironside and General Viscount Gort. The general tenor of Mr H. G. Wells' article, reproduced in the *Sunday Pictorial* had been that, until the Army was better led, we stood no chance of beating the Germans.
>
> The same issue of the *Sunday Pictorial* had contained a leading article by the Editor, containing a scurrilous attack on several members of the Government, and obviously seeking to

72

undermine confidence in the Government. Much the same line had been taken in the leading article in that morning's *Daily Mirror*.

The immediate purpose of these articles seemed to be to affect the discipline of the Army, to attempt to shake the stability of the Government, and to make trouble between the Government and organised labour. In his considered judgment there was far more behind these articles than disgruntlement or frayed nerves. They stood for something most dangerous and sinister, namely, an attempt to bring about a situation in which the country would be ready for surrender peace.

It was not right that anyone bearing his heavy responsibilities should have to submit to attacks of this nature upon his Government. It was intolerable that any newspaper should indulge in criticism and abuse, far beyond what was tolerated in times of acute Party strife, in a time of great national peril.

After a lengthy debate in the Cabinet, in which Ministers are quoted as discussing the real ownership of the *Mirror* papers, ways in which the papers could be suppressed by the executive action of the Government and not by the courts, and how the articles represented "some unscrupulous and dangerous purpose", the record closes like this:

The Prime Minister, summing up the discussion, said that the solution which he hoped to see adopted and which he thought was generally favoured, was that two members of the War Cabinet should see the Newspaper Proprietors' Association and explain the situation to them. The articles complained of should be shown to the Association, and it should be made clear that the Government was not prepared to allow continued publication of such articles. It should also be made clear that, if the Newspaper Proprietors' Association were not ready or able to take action to stop further publication of such articles, the Government would have to deal with the matter in some other way.

It was clear, however, that, before action could be taken on these lines, the War Cabinet must decide definitely that they were prepared to take action against these newspapers if necessary. In view, however, of the fact that the Home Secretary had a quasi-judicial function to perform, it would clearly be right to defer a decision in order to give him time for further consideration.

These quotations recapture the high tensions and bitter hostility inside No. 10. Churchill was obviously determined to force a show-down with the Mirror group. Note how he built up his attack on "the most dangerous and sinister" meaning of the articles as "an attempt to bring about a situation in which the country would be ready for a surrender peace". In other words, Bartholemew, King, Cudlipp and Co were acting as defeatists, betraying their country as quislings and traitors.

Two days later the War Cabinet returned to the "Subversive articles" theme. Once again the record demonstrates Churchill's determination to demand and impose tough action, suppressing the *Mirror* papers if need be, while members of the War Cabinet such as Herbert Morrison, Home Secretary, and Lord Beaverbrook, Minister of Aircraft Production, fought shrewdly for more moderate action, hoping to avoid the head-on collision which the Prime Minister was patently anxious to bring about. The following extracts have an ominous tone:

> The War Cabinet resumed discussion of this question, and had before them a Memorandum by the Home Secretary (W.P. (40) 402) suggesting that while representations should be made to the Newspaper Proprietors' Association, this should be in the nature of a friendly appeal and not a threat of action under the Defence Regulations.
>
> The Prime Minister said that the articles in the *Sunday Pictorial* and *Daily Mirror* constituted, in his view, a serious danger to this country. First, these newspapers were trying to "rock the boat" and to shake the confidence of the country in Ministers. . . . He was determined to put a stop to these attacks and to obtain protection for the War Cabinet. It would be quite wrong that two members of the War Cabinet should be in the position of asking favours of the Newspaper Proprietors' Association.
>
> Discussion followed as to who exercised the controlling influence over these newspapers.
>
> The Lord Privy Seal [Clement Attlee] attached importance to finding out who had the controlling interest, in order to satisfy himself whether the underlying motive was definitely an attempt to exercise a disrupting influence and not merely irresponsible journalism. He regarded the matter very seriously and favoured strong action, but wanted to be sure that there was a cast-iron case. The Home Secretary was invited to take such steps as were in his power to find out the facts required, although the view was expressed that persons who went to the trouble to put their holdings in the name of bank nominees had

74

probably taken steps to make it very difficult to trace their connection with the paper. The Lord President of the Council [Sir John Anderson, later Lord Waverley] pointed out that, irrespective of the question of motive, the fact remained that grave harm undoubtedly followed from the fact that these malicious articles were published; he wished to stop mischievous articles in the Press, if powerful newspapers were allowed to publish articles of this kind. General agreement was expressed by the War Cabinet with the view that . . . a continuance of such articles could not be tolerated.

In further discussion it was suggested that the Minister of Aircraft Production and the Lord Privy Seal should summon representatives of the Newspaper Proprietors' Association to see them, and should explain to them that the War Cabinet were considering this whole matter and were gravely perturbed at the position. The Minister of Aircraft Production said that he had felt quite sure that the newspaper proprietors as a whole would wish to see action taken to restrain the *Daily Mirror* and the *Sunday Pictorial*. These two newspapers were conducted in a manner which was damaging to the repute of newspapers generally. The Newspaper Proprietors' Association had it in their power to exercise disciplinary action, by taking steps which would add substantially to the cost of running the papers; e.g., by refusing to allow these papers to be put on the newspaper trains.

The Prime Minister said that he was prepared to agree to the Minister of Aircraft Production and the Lord Privy Seal sending for representatives of the Newspaper Proprietors' Association and speaking to them on the lines suggested. But he wished it to be clear that, for his part, he receded in no way from the view he had taken, that the Government must be prepared to take firm action to deal with this menace. The Home Secretary (was invited) to take such steps as were in his power to ascertain who exercised the controlling influence over the *Sunday Pictorial* and the *Daily Mirror*."

A few days later the results of the "friendly talks" were duly reported to the Cabinet:

The Lord Privy Seal said that . . . he and the Minister of Aircraft Production had seen representatives of the Newspaper Proprietors' Association. They had explained that the Government took a serious view of the position. The impression left on his mind had been that these representatives recognised that the articles in the *Sunday Pictorial* and the *Daily Mirror* were mischievous, and that they would do what they could to remedy matters. Later, Mr Esmond Harmsworth [one of the representatives of the Newspaper Proprietors' Association at the interview] had rung up and asked whether he (the Lord Privy Seal) would see a representative of the *Sunday Pictorial* and the *Daily Mirror*. On the advice of Lord Beaverbrook he had agreed to do so. Two representatives had come to the meeting, Mr Bartholemew and Mr C. H. King. Mr Bartholemew had been the more reasonable of the two. Mr King had at first tried to adopt the attitude that he did not see what harm these articles were doing. The Lord Privy Seal said that he had made it clear that many people thought these articles were a deliberate Fifth Column activity. The representatives of the two newspapers had suggested than an approach might have been of the interview, however, they had both appeared somewhat chastened, and had undertaken to exercise care in the future.

The Minister of Aircraft Production said that he thought that these two newspapers would amend their behaviour, at any rate for the time being.

The Home Secretary said that he had ordered investigations to be made as to who exercised the controlling influence over these two newspapers, notwithstanding that there was some risk of its becoming known that these investigations were being made.

The War Cabinet took note of the above statements.

The serial continued. In the early days of 1941, Churchill wrote to Cecil King protesting at the "malevolence" shown by Cassandra (Bill, later Sir William, Connor). King replied in an amiable letter intended to pacify the great man. But Churchill was in no mood to be friendly. On 25 January 1941, he returned an astonishing letter accusing King and the *Mirror* writers of being defeatists, preparing to form a Fifth Column to undermine the war effort. In an explosive attack and insinuation about the papers' treachery he said:

Much the most effective way in which to conduct a Fifth Column movement would be the method followed by the *Daily Mirror* and the *Sunday Pictorial*. Lip service would no doubt be paid to the Prime Minister whose position at the moment may be difficult to undermine. A perfervid zeal for the intensification of the war effort would be used as a cloak behind which to insult and discredit one Minister after another. Every grievance would be exploited to the full, especially those grievances which lead to class dissension.

76

By this technique, Churchill added, readers could be brought into a state of despondency which after disaster or prolonged tribulation could suddenly be switched into naked defeatism and a demand for negotiated peace. "I am sure this is not your intention, nor the intention of the able writers you employ. It is, none-the-less, in my judgment, the result."

Cecil King has recalled the next round: "I answered that we were dedicated to victory and sought an interview. When I went to No. 10 I was subjected to a reprimand lasting one hour and ten minutes. Churchill kept getting up and striding up and down, relighting his cigar. The word he most used was 'malignancy'. He said that some of his colleagues felt that there were sinister figures among the owners of the paper. I told him that this was false and that the other four executive directors left politics to me. 'Well,' he said, looking me up and down, 'you look innocent enough'."

After the visit King wrote to Churchill saying: "You are wartime England," and explaining why the paper advocated a statement of war aims. Churchill's response was pointed: "All this fine thought about the rising generation ought not to lead you to try to discredit the Government in a period of extreme danger and difficulty. . . ."

It seems astonishing that even in the darkest hours of the war when "we stood alone", in Winston's famous phrase, and invasion, occupation and defeat seemed inevitable, the great man allowed himself to become so upset by Press criticisms. Invariably he overreacted, pressing his Cabinet to take extreme and direct action to compel proprietors, editors and journalists to co-operate with his judgment about their duties and responsibilities. At a War Cabinet meeting on 9 October 1941, concerned with the effects of Press criticisms on Britain's relations with foreign countries, especially neutrals (in this case Franco's Spain), it was on his insistence that a high-powered committee was set up to see what further action should be taken.

His three senior colleagues—Anthony Eden, Foreign Secretary; Herbert Morrison, Home Secretary; and Brendan Bracken, Information Minister—showed delicacy and discretion when they reported. They studied the problems and dangers of moving from voluntary to compulsory censorship, and of extending the powers from the greater demands of defence and security to reports and opinions on foreign affairs. Then followed their summing up in the eighth and ninth paragraphs:

8. Another possible course would be for a Government spokesman (and we doubt whether anyone less than the Prime

Minister would be effective) to make a statement in Parliament pointing out that a specified newspaper was not acting in the national interest, calling attention to the mischievous effect on foreign relations and commenting on any other misdemeanours of the paper in question, such as irresponsible and ill-informed excursions into the field of strategy and unfounded or exaggerated criticisms of the administration made for the purpose of attracting readers by sensational statements. Such a statement would in a proper case be very damaging to a newspaper so stigmatised; it would not be likely to provoke united opposition from other papers and could not be represented as an attempt to silence expressions of opinions inconvenient to the Government.

9. During the war numerous articles have appeared in the Press which at the time seemed likely to impair the war effort either by injuring foreign relations or by shaking confidence in the national Government or disrupting the national unity, but in retrospect it is seen that the effect of such articles has been comparatively insignificant.

While we fully realise that the freedom allowed to the Press presents special dangers in time of war and that a vigilant watch must be kept lest such freedom should endanger the successful prosecution of the war, we do not feel able to recommend—in present circumstances at any rate—the introduction of new methods of coercion, but we think the possibility of taking such action as is outlined in paragraph 8 above should be kept in mind.

The War Cabinet later "took note of this memorandum and agreed it was unnecessary to take any action in regard to this matter at the present time".

But nothing really changed. On 17 October, following *Sunday Pictorial* attacks on M.P.s, the War Cabinet agreed that "the Home Secretary should make inquiries whether the article constituted a breach of privilege of the House of Commons" and that he should report "whether the article offended against the Defence Regulations and in consultation with the Lord President (Sir John Anderson) and the Minister of Information (Duff Cooper) consider whether it would be desirable to obtain further powers to deal with articles of this description".

On 8 November, in the course of a long memorandum to Churchill, Morrison reported:

On the question of prosecution I have consulted the Director of Public Prosecutions who says that in his opinion the article does not offend against the existing Defence Regulations. He also thinks that it does not offend against the common law relating to sedition because "although the writer impliedly advocates a change in the present Government, he does not recommend unlawful or violent means for the purpose of effecting any such change". The Director adds that he cannot find in the article any material on which proceedings for criminal libel could be founded.

On the question of further powers I have, after consultation with the Lord President of the Council and the Minister of Information, come to the conclusion that no Defence Regulation could be devised which would cover the article in question without at the same time covering numerous other criticisms of the administration and raising the controversial issue whether the Government is to be clothed with extensive powers for the control of expressions of opinion. However limited may be the use which the Government would make of such powers in practice, any Regulations which would be effective for dealing with such an article as that in the *Sunday Pictorial* would have to be so framed as to cover a wide field and would be open to attack on the ground that it would empower a Government to exercise a much more extensive control over expressions of opinion that the present Government would in fact exercise or would think it right to exercise.

A week later, on 12 November 1941, Morrison submitted yet another wordy paper on the *Mirror–Pictorial* attacks. This brief extract captures the flavour:

The despicable character of the *Daily Mirror* and the *Sunday Pictorial* is unquestionable. The tone and policy of these newspapers reach as low a level of journalism as has been known in this country. The object of the papers in adopting these methods is to make money. There are no grounds for thinking that there are any subversive influences behind the papers. The financial interests are widely spread, and it appears that the shareholders and directors leave the widest liberty to the editorial staff to pursue any methods which will increase the circulation of the papers and augment the dividends. Since the outbreak of war the circulation of the *Daily Mirror* has, the Minister of Information informs me, greatly increased, and the paper has a wide circulation amongst the troops, but it is a matter of some doubt as to how far its leaders or political articles are much read, or have much influence. So far as is known, the Left-wing attitude of this paper is adopted because this attitude helps to sell the paper, and perhaps because in the view of the influential members of the editorial staff, such an attitude might conceivably be advantageous to them in the future.

Was this an astonishing case of foresight stretching into the Wilson era, when six life peerages were given to *Mirror* executives?

It was on 6 March 1942, that the issue came to a head. On that date, the day after Government approval of a petrol price increase of one penny a gallon, the *Mirror*'s cartoonist, Philip Zec, produced a powerful drawing showing a torpedoed sailor clinging to a raft in an empty sea. The caption read: "The price of petrol has been raised by a penny (official)". Churchill exploded. He demanded that the War Cabinet should take even stronger action against the *Mirror* because, he argued, the cartoon implied that the Government was allowing sailors to drown in order to increase petrol prices and profits. Zec's family background and past political views were probed at the request of Downing Street to discover whether he was of alien stock or a Nazi sympathiser.

On 9 March the Cabinet set up a committee under Anderson to investigate the effect of the Press on public morale. The minutes record:

> The view was strongly expressed that the attitude of certain organs of the Press was gravely prejudicial to the national morale. In particular certain sections of the Press, by persistent attacks on officers holding high ranking appointments, were undermining the morale of the army.
>
> It was also pointed out that messages frequently sent overseas by Press correspondents in this country were calculated to arouse ill-feeling between this country and certain of our Dominions or allies.
>
> Criticism was also made of the fact that it was not possible under existing regulations to stop publication here of the messages containing matter which had already been published overseas. The time had come when Parliament should be asked for the necessary powers in order to deal with the situation.
>
> The War Cabinet i) Agreed in principle that effective control should be established to prevent the publication in this country of articles, or the sending out of this country of messages, calculated to undermine public morale at home or to create ill-feeling between the united nations. ii) Appointed a Committee comprising the Lord President [Anderson]; Dominions Affairs Secretary [Attlee]; Lord Privy Seal [Cripps]; Foreign Secretary [Eden]; Minister for Labour & National Service

[Bevin]; Home Secretary and Minister for Home Security [Morrison]; Minister of Information [Bracken] to examine the methods of giving effect to this decision and to report in a week's time.

The committee duly reported on 17 March. The news for the Mirror group was not good:

In our view it is necessary in the first instance that the Government should make it clear that the continued publication of this kind of unwarranted and malignant criticism of those in authority may do the State a mortal injury by sapping public confidence and breaking down the spirit of unity in prosecuting the war. If a general statement on these lines were made, by the highest authority, all members of the Government should follow it up by countering this type of criticism, whenever it occurs, by vigorous correction and counter-statement. Above all, it would be helpful if an example could be made of one of the newspapers which has been a flagrant offender in this respect.

In view of these opinions, we have no doubt that there has been in the *Daily Mirror* systematic publication of material which would render it liable to suppression under ... Regulation (2D).

At the same time, we doubt whether it is realised by Parliament, Press or public that material of this kind comes within Regulation 2D—which was designed, and is at present regarded as an instrument for use rather against positive propaganda in opposition to the war or in favour of a negotiated peace.

If only for this reason, we do not think it would be expedient to take immediate action to suppress the *Daily Mirror* under Regulation 2D without previous warning. It should first be made clear that, in the view of the Government, the systematic publication of irresponsible and malignant criticism of this kind makes a newspaper liable to be suppressed under this Regulation. This would serve as a warning, not only to the *Daily Mirror* but to such other newspaper as may stand in need of it.

We therefore recommend that the Home Secretary should make a considered statement, in answer to a Parliamentary Question, explaining the Government's view of the publication of such material and making it clear that it is their intention to act under this Regulation against any newspaper which offends in the future.

We also recommend that the Home Secretary should at the

same time send for the editor of the *Daily Mirror* and warn him that the paper will be suppressed if the offence is repeated.

These tactics were agreed and on 19 March there was a full-scale Parliamentary debate on the *Mirror*'s record, during which public warning was given that the Government would be ready to suppress the *Mirror* papers unless they mended their ways. The method by which Herbert Morrison, acting under Churchill's angry insistence, built up his indictment of the *Mirror* provides a most alarming example of the way in which an authoritarian Government can silence all criticisms and tame editors and directors.

First there came an attack on the Zec cartoon involving "the paper's appetite for sensation, reckless indifference to the national interest, scurrilous distortions, insidious attacks, the need for Press freedom to be exercised with a proper sense of responsibility". Then he emphasised the dangers of depressing public morale "by poisoning the springs of National loyalty and by creating a spirit of despair and defeatism". Morrison ended with the ultimatum: "I have seen those responsible for the *Daily Mirror* and I have made clear to them the considerations which I have outlined to the House. A watch will be kept on this paper and the course which the Government may ultimately decide to take will depend on whether those concerned recognise their public responsibility and take care to refrain from further publication of matter calculated to foment opposition to the successful prosecution of the war."

Just how close the *Mirror* had come to being suppressed was revealed years later by W. P. Crozier, editor of the *Manchester Guardian*, who kept a detailed record, published after his death, of private interviews with Churchill and other prominent figures*. At a meeting on 28 May Morrison revealed to Crozier the flavour of the Cabinet debate on the Anderson report and the passionate nature of Churchill's concern over the *Mirror*:

> He and some others besides, whom you might not have expected—wanted to suppress the *Mirror* at once, without a word of warning. I wouldn't do that. Bevin was hot and strong about it—highly emotional. Well, you can't conduct your policy on the basis of emotion. You must base it on reason and then stick to your decision whatever happens . . . when it came before the Cabinet again I opposed the suppression bluntly. I said I couldn't agree but that I would cheerfully see the D.M. people and tell them what the position was and warn them, and if they did not amend I would certainly suppress them. And

* *Off the Record, Political Interviews 1933–45*, W. P. Crozier. Edited, with an Introduction, by A. J. P. Taylor, Hutchinson.

that was how it was settled, but Churchill didn't at all like it at the time.

Crozier is even more revealing than the Cabinet minutes on the strength of Churchill's disenchantment with the Press. After one meeting he records that of the *Manchester Guardian* the Prime Minister commented: "I always read it", and of the *Yorkshire Post*: "a good paper". Then he added: "But most of the papers infuriate me. They exasperate. The *News Chronicle*: All over the place. Geese! Geese! But the paper I can't stand, the worst of all, is the *Daily Mirror*. Yes, the *Daily Mirror*. It makes me spit."

And of a lunchtime meeting with Churchill at No. 10 on 20 March Crozier writes:

> He turned to the *Daily Mirror* question and was very hot and strong about it. He said it was dangerous to have a constant stream of stuff which was calculated to undermine the morale of the soldier; very serious issues were involved. He resented the "carping, niggling criticisms" that he and the Government received day by day from certain quarters and certain newspapers—from the *Daily Herald* "which represents the second largest Party in the Government", and from the *News Chronicle*—"the most stupid of all the papers."
>
> He was vehement about this, and I said: "You don't mind if I speak quite frankly about that?" and he replied "No, that's what I want you to do". I said: "Well, it puzzles me that you bother, or worry, about these papers so much. No doubt they irritate you but do they matter all that much? You have your great majority in the House and you know that you have the country behind you firmly. Why should you let one or two papers who nag day by day disturb you so much?" He said he didn't think he got reasonable treatment from such people, they were injuring the prestige of the Government which was very important etc. But what he obviously felt most was that the disaster in Malaya etc. hurt him bitterly—"anguish and self-reproach"—and that he did not get a fair deal from the daily critics. (Both A. Eden and B. Bracken told me how much he was hurt by these constant newspaper attacks.) He insisted that, though times were bad, he could and would pull the country through to victory, but "Give us a chance!" he said.

From Downing Street Crozier went to see Sir Archibald Sinclair, the Liberal leader, at the Air Ministry and wrote:

> I began by asking him what he thought about the *Daily Mirror* business. He said that speaking for himself he never saw the

Daily Mirror and therefore could only judge in the light of the passages which had been collected and put before him as a Minister; he was bound to say that they were pretty serious.

He would put it this way—that if the objectionable passages had been collected together by anyone in a leaflet and circulated to the troops in a camp, the printer and the author or authors would have been liable to be prosecuted for sedition, and he understood there would have been every reason to expect a conviction. It was not in his view a matter of freedom of criticism at all; it was a constant drip, drip, of an attack on the officer class in the army and it was likely to do serious harm.

These crises between the Churchill Government and Fleet Street continued over most of the war years, covering many papers—none so explosively as the Mirror group but nevertheless dangerously with frequent threats of suppression, libel and criminal law actions, and discipline under defence regulations. It was a miracle, particularly since newsprint rationing kept papers down to four or six pages, that journalism survived the experience.

In fact the *Mirror*–Churchill feud continued until 1955 when the papers finally latched on to the fact that there was something gravely wrong with Churchill's health. The *Mirror* demanded: "Is there any reason why the British people should not be told the facts about the health of their Prime Minister? Let us know whether Sir Winston is fit enough to lead us." Until that time Churchill's series of strokes and seizures had been a rigorously kept Downing Street secret and the massive tome by his medical adviser, Lord Moran, later revealed the fury inside No. 10 when the truth began to seep out. Churchill and his staff reacted as though the Official Secrets Act had been breached—for the answer to the *Mirror*'s question was that Sir Winston was in no position to lead anybody. For long periods he had been seriously incapacitated and should have retired gracefully in 1945. After one particularly bad stroke, which left his face and one side of his body paralysed, his family had been warned that he would not see out the weekend. Yet Government and Whitehall contrived to impose a complete blackout on news of the utmost national importance. If only No. 10 had been a little more forthcoming the hurt subsequently caused by such headings as "Twilight of a Giant" and "Giant in Decay" might have been avoided.

However one of the most bizarre aspects of this serious stroke was the emergency plan of succession devised by the inner, or

84

magic, circle following a suggestion by Sir John Colville, Churchill's personal aide and private secretary. Under this scheme Lord Salisbury would act as Prime Minister for six months until the designated successor, Sir Anthony Eden, was able to return from a serious operation in America. The odd feature about this scheme was that the Chancellor, R. A. Butler, had already been nominated as chairman of Cabinet and acting Prime Minister in the simultaneous absence of Churchill and Eden. So why bring in Salisbury when Butler was already running the show successfully?

The fear clearly was that if Butler actually became Prime Minister for six months the Tory Party might be so impressed by his performance and leadership that they would prefer him to remain in occupation, and not to vacate the seat of power for Eden. Another contingency to be guarded against was that Butler might himself organise a major campaign to cling to the Premiership. In short, he might resist the pressures to edge him back · into the shadows. This was the first of three occasions when the dice were loaded against him in the leadership race. Twice he was the front-runner, but finished weakly; against Harold Macmillan in the succession to Eden, and against Sir Alec Douglas-Home in the succession to Macmillan.

In the event, Moran's forecast about Churchill's survival prospects was confounded, so it remains a constitutional might-have-been as to whether Parliament and the country would have accepted a Prime Minister in the House of Lords even for a limited period; and much more profoundly, how far the weighting of the Queen's prerogative in order to resolve the Tories' domestic dilemma would have proved acceptable.

The final irony is that although the Salisbury masterplan was shared by only a handful of people close to Churchill, two of them were Press lords, Beaverbrook and Camrose. Yet not a word leaked out. Not a single whisper appeared even in a gossip column. Britain was only a heart-beat away from an astonishing constitutional dilemma—and Fleet Street teamed up with Downing Street to preserve an official secret. As ever, Butler loyally went along with the extraordinary formula for a PM *pro tem* without violent defence of his own interests. Why? Years afterwards I asked him. Only "Rab" could have given such a reply. "Well I knew the doctors were wrong in forecasting Winston's imminent death. His mouth and side were paralysed, his speech was slurred but he was holding in his good hand a big brandy with great determination. I knew a man with such spirit would not die that weekend, despite Lord Moran's prophecy. So why should I kick up hell on a situation which I knew would never arise?"

6

CLEMENT ATTLEE

July 1945–April 1955

"My cricket machine outside the Cabinet door is ticking out the decisions and subjects discussed at the Cabinet meeting this morning. How can it do that? What's going on around here?"
CLEMENT ATTLEE

Clement Attlee has had the last laugh. During six years in Downing Street he experienced a calamitous Press and was undoubtedly the most derided and under-rated of all my Prime Ministers. He was also the most unprepossessing: no personality or presence, un-inspiring, devoid of glamour, the despair of the advertising men and the addicts of Maddison Avenue packaging. Charisma? He did not recognise the word except as a clue in his beloved *Times* crossword. So Fleet Street made him into a figure of fun.

When he became Premier in 1945 his first job was to attend the Peace Conference of the victorious Allies, previously dominated by Churchill, Roosevelt and Stalin. The Big Three, we called them. When Attlee displaced Winston editorials and cartoons gave them a new title: The Big $2\frac{1}{2}$. Churchill, too, joined in: "An empty taxi pulled up at No. 10 and Attlee got out," he quipped. Modest? "He has so much to be modest about."

If this makes relations between Downing Street and Fleet Street appear waspishly humorous let me hasten to correct that impression. Relations were never so poisonous, bad-tempered and embittered as during the years of the Attlee Government. To be frank, I have never known the Press so consistently and irresponsibly political, slanted and prejudiced. One can only sympathise with Aneurin Bevan's protest about "the most prostituted Press in the world". But if Harold Wilson later over-rated the influence of the Press Attlee under-rated it in silence. He never once replied in kind. Yet this colourless little man whom the communications world so com-pletely misjudged and reviled is now being identified as one of the most substantial of Britain's Prime Ministers, while others who were seen as immeasurably more glamorous and dynamic when arriving at No. 10 are receding into the shadows of the half-forgotten. Attlee presided over the biggest social, political and economic revolutions of the century. He never lost a single by-election and after five years of ceaseless Press harassment he polled the highest popular vote at any election before or since—notwithstanding today's substantially increased electorate following the lowering of the voting age. As for the Press, they emerged from this shameful period to face a Royal Commission and the subsequent formation of a Press Council to monitor their performance and to impose standards. There can be no doubt as to which side fared the better.

Asquith, no mean judge, summed up Attlee's situation half a century in advance when speaking of Campbell-Bannerman: "There have been men who, in the cruel phrase of the ancient historian, were universally judged to be fit for the highest place until they attained and held it. Our late Prime Minister belonged to that rarer class whose fitness for such a place, until they attain and hold it, is never adequately understood."

This is all very well; but how exactly did Attlee do it? He underplayed every big occasion. He had no sense of showmanship, no love of the spotlight, no feel for the grand presentation, the dramatic peroration and exit, and he slurred his words and paid no attention to verbs. In short, he confounded all the popular and academic theories about power, personality and the Press. As my colleague Frederick Newman wrote in the *Daily Sketch*: "He was a man who tucked his personality behind a pipe and left colleagues and public to make what they could of all the smoke signals." Fleet Street became very angry with him precisely because he ignored what they were thundering about him. He just concentrated on doing what he felt was right, keeping his eyes focused on the future and not on instant history. This was not a pose. He simply did not care about being popular and grabbing favourable headlines. When told by a member of his personal staff that a particular paper that morning had attacked him violently, he would retort in his terse and elliptical style: "That so? Suppose they've to say something. Circulation slipping, you think?" But he would never dream of asking for a marked copy to be put in his tray so that he might read it for himself. Later Prime Ministers regarded the cuttings files as the first priority for the baggage train. But Attlee was still a Victorian, the last of the series, and he judged that as long as he had the support of the country and of Parliament, moving peacefully from its Imperial glory to its home-based role, he did not have to spare a thought for Fleet Street.

Among the Prime Ministers Balfour came closest to this attitude of mind, suffering the "Balfour Must Go" campaign with indifference. When advised by Lord Rosebery to ignore what the papers were saying he was dumbfounded; he never read them in the first place. When Churchill suggested that Press cuttings and comments might provide useful ammunition for speeches Balfour was astonished at what he regarded as trivial advice from an important man. He replied: "I have never put myself to the trouble of rummaging through an immense rubbish-heap on the problematical chance of discovering a cigar-end."

Attlee's personal newspaper reading habits were simple and reflected his devotion to the old standards of public and private life. He took *The Times* every morning, but he was not interested in news of events at home and abroad; for these he depended on official minutes, compiled by his staff, which had to be free of comment and wordiness. Instead, he concentrated on the births, marriages and deaths, appointments and promotions, and completed the crossword without fail. He used the paper to maintain contact with his private world of school, university, army and family. If an old friend or remote relation was mentioned he would at once scribble a note of congratulation or sympathy, address the envelope himself and put it with the family mail so that it would not be officially franked. When he saw a notice of a memorial service he would note date and place in his private diary and faithfully turn up (unless major Government business intervened, in which case he was always represented). Indeed, he was the only former Premier to attend regularly the annual Armistice Day service at the Cenotaph.

As for his other contacts with the Press, he would occasionally glance at the Labour *Daily Herald*: "to see what the chaps are doing, ye' know" and "to keep in touch with the Party's grass roots". The *Daily Mirror*? "To tell you the truth, I seldom see it." Proprietors and editors? "I see the editor of the *Herald* [Francis Williams] from time to time. I keep him in touch. He keeps me in touch. Good arrangement. It works. Nobody else, except when I bump into them at set dos."

In my own dealings with Attlee during his twenty years as Labour leader and Prime Minister I always found him friendly, courteous, understanding and patient. But his replies were confined to single sentences: "Nope, nothing in that"; "Can't say"; "Somebody been kidding you again"; "You've not done your homework" and "You shouldn't listen to gossip, it's all poppycock". If he used two sentences he was in danger of becoming long-winded. This was not personal to me; it was his invariable style with his staff, his colleagues and with other journalists either individually or *en masse*. He held surprisingly few formal Press meetings and conferences but before the war he and his deputy leader, Arthur Greenwood, did have weekly meetings with the Lobby correspondents and I recall that the leader discouraged any attempt to stray outside the confines of Parliamentary business. Queries about sensitive areas, such as Labour Party rows, were knocked for six, as he would have said. "That's a Party matter," he would snap, "and I'm sure you wouldn't like me to prattle on about Party politics to people like you who pride yourselves about being above squalid Party affairs. Poor show if I were to involve you in that. The Tories might suspect I was pulling you into the muddy waters. Must keep you clean, you know." That was Attlee caught in a verbose reply. If anyone tried to probe deeper he would retort: "I've just told you the answer at some length. Next question?"

The finest example of an Attlee Press performance was one of his rare big-time and no-holds-barred meetings with the Lobby. This was a special occasion arranged well in advance, with no limits set, a go-as-you-please affair. Knowing the Prime Minister's penchant for the six-or ten-word reply, rather than the discursive thinking-aloud style, the chairman arranged that each of the fifty or sixty Lobbymen should be armed with two or three questions on current affairs, in the hope of encouraging Attlee to unbend.

Alas, when the questions started, he was true to form. Everything was played back with the straight bat, laconic replies coloured by schoolboy or army slang: "Nothing in that"; "You're off beam again"; "I've never heard that, have you"; "That idea seems bonkers to me—the Cabinet's never looked at it"; "You can't expect me to answer that one". Within ten minutes the conference, scheduled to last an hour, was sagging, despite the chairman's frantic efforts to pull in even more tempting questions.

Finally, Ernest Hunter, political correspondent of the *Daily Herald*, stepped in, dead-pan: "Prime Minister," he said, "we're all stumped. You must share your secrets with us—just this once. What's number twelve across, two words, seven and six letters?" He was quoting from the crossword in *The Times* that morning. Instantly the little man came to life; for the first time he removed the pipe from his mouth and put it on the table. For ten to twelve minutes—longer indeed than the question-and-answer session so far—he proceeded to give us a lively commentary on the higher intellectual meaning of crossword clues.

"Your parents wasted their money sending you to college, Hunter. You've forgotten anything you ever knew about the classics." And on he went, with enthusiasm. Didn't the Lobby know that the first oblique reference was to Homer, that the fellow who set the puzzle that day liked to pop in Latin and Greek hints to put you off the scent? Indeed, the chap had a perfect flair for Biblical affairs as well: where he slipped in the passing reference to something being well marked, it was a clear pointer to St Mark's guidance. And so he continued, elucidating the concealed meaning of twelve across, seven and six, with wit, humour and education knit together in animated enthusiasm. This was the real Attlee in action. These were his priorities. The questions by Lobby correspondents seeking fodder for tomorrow's newsprint were irrelevant. But twelve across, seven and six—now that had made the conference worth while!

Attlee showed rare wisdom in the history of Government–Press relations by putting Francis Williams (later Lord Francis-Williams) in charge of his Press and public relations at No. 10. It was an inspired appointment. Williams was not only a great journalist and editor but a fluent communicator on the platform, radio and TV. It was an ideal partnership. This was not a case of a Prime Minister informing his spokesman of what to say—what should be disclosed and what should be kept under wraps—for Attlee had no understanding of what was entailed or any knowledge of whom Williams saw or what he said. Williams was left alone, to do the job as he saw fit. Indeed, he told me that he had to do his own lobbying of other Ministers and departments, supplemented by research into Cabinet papers, to discover what was happening on current and controversial subjects.

Attlee's other-worldly approach to the Press, public relations and the need to keep the nation informed, is well illustrated by Williams's experience on first moving into No. 10. He found he was totally isolated from the world, unaware of what was taking place and when journalists phoned him about outside events he was deeply embarrassed at having to expose his ignorance. He therefore proposed that a news agency tape service should be installed. Senior officials were suspicious of any move to bring the ballyhoo of the ticker-tape world into the hallowed precincts and advised the Prime Minister of the dangers of such an innovation. Thus briefed, Attlee in turn confessed to Williams that he doubted the value of the expense involved; what good could the service possibly do? Williams knew his man. He pointed out that the Exchange Telegraph service tape would prove of great value to Attlee personally. "Prime Minister," he said "you'll be able to keep up to date on the lunch-time and close of play scores, especially of Middlesex (the county team Attlee supported). The service will keep you informed; I'll put the machine just outside the Cabinet room, so that you can pop

8. Anthony Eden during the Suez Crisis

9. Harold Macmillan with Denis Hamilton, editor of the *Sunday Times* 1961–67, now chairman and editor-in-chief Times Newspapers Ltd

10. Lord Denning Master of the Rolls, who headed the inquiry into the Profumo Affair

11. The late Lord Radcliffe who was chairman of the inquiries into the Vassall Case, and D Notices

12. Sir Alec Douglas-Home

13. Edward Heath

14. David Astor of the *Observer*, the last of the great editor-proprietors

15. William Clark, the Downing Stre spokesman during the Suez crisis

16. The two famous Canadians, Press Lords Beaverbrook (*below left*) and Thomson

out to see the latest batting in the Tests as well as county games."
Not a word was said about the national need for No. 10 to be kept
in touch with the world outside. Cricket was the ticket, and the
machine was duly installed.

The following week, however, Attlee went rushing into Williams's
room in great alarm. "Francis, Francis," he cried. "You know my
cricket machine at the Cabinet door? When I checked it just now
for the lunch-time score at Lord's it was ticking out the decisions
and subjects discussed at the Cabinet meeting this morning. How
can it do that? What's going on around here?" The Prime Minister
was totally unaware that part of Williams's routine was to meet the
evening papers' political correspondents and brief them in broad
terms about what was going on and about the decisions likely to be
announced by Ministers in Parliament later that day. Williams
explained the situation but it was a strange world which Attlee did
not understand, had no wish to understand, and had no desire to
enter. "OK, Francis," he said. "I'll leave the show to you. Good
work."

While Attlee remained aloof from the buffeting of the Press his
leading Ministers traded blow for blow, giving at least as good as
they got. What they got, as censorship ended and newsprint rationing eased, was a series of vicious personal attacks going far beyond
the usual tensions inherent in the system. The Press blatantly ignored
C. P. Scott's distinction between fact and comment as the news
pages were turned over to political opinion and propaganda. (Television, then only restarting tentatively, was unable, unlike today,
to correct Press excesses.) As early as 1946, Sir Hartley Shawcross,
Attorney-General, set a hot pace in the counter-attack. In a speech
in Battersea on Saturday, 30 July, he lambasted the "campaign of
calumny and misrepresentation which the Tory Party and the Tory
stooge Press" had been directing against the Labour Government.
He defended the freedom of the Press—"there would be nothing
more dangerous to democratic Government in this country than that
the Press should be gagged"—but "the truth is that there has never
been a time when certain sections of the Press have more seriously
abused the freedom which is accorded them under our constitution.
Freedom of the Press does not mean freedom to tell lies." Tough,
rumbustious stuff indeed; Tony Benn would be derided as a menace
to civilisation if he used such language today. Nye Bevan's attack
on "the most prostituted Press in the world" was milksop stuff
when set against Sir Hartley in top gear.

In his speech Shawcross argued that it did not matter how
malicious, biased or extreme were the views which newspaper

proprietors expressed—provided that they did not "cook the news to suit their own views". And there was much more on the same theme, developed later by Shawcross and other Attlee Ministers, about the menace "of a mere handful of men who represent nobody but themselves, who are unable or unwilling to express their views publicly and personally in the legislature"—a dig at the Press barons who kept away from the House of Lords, where they would have faced the unaccustomed ordeal of public debate—"but who use their newspapers as a vehicle of propaganda to foist their views upon the public".

The Shawcross attack served only to worsen relations between Westminster and Fleet Street; and the next day my paper, the *Sunday Times* was one of many to hit back, condemning Shawcross for his "wildly abusive" and "grossly offensive" speech, full of "disreputable stuff, seasoned with personal insult". The final lofty rebuke for the learned Attorney was to remind him that "there are standards of decency in public life which the Law Officer especially ought to maintain".

Shawcross refused to be intimidated, and in the following weeks returned to the attack by accusing "certain sections" of the Press "of misrepresentation and chicanery", adding that the power had never been more abused, than by a "notorious section of the Tory Press". All through the wrangle Shawcross insisted that the freedom of the Press must be preserved: "For my part I do not think any legal control is possible". Even so, he indulged in astonishing personal vituperation: "No one cares a straw what the opinions of the proprietors of the gutter Press, Beaverbrook, Kemsley and the owners of the *News of the World* are. . . . They are distorting news, suppressing the evidence and the facts." (Twenty-fours hours later he withdrew his charge against the *News of the World* explaining that the paper was not included in the draft of his speech and that he had been confused by an interruption.)

The time had passed when Kemsley could sit idly by. The attacks on the way he ran his newspaper had become so extreme that he announced his intention to issue a writ against Shawcross for libel and defamation. It was unheard of for a Press lord to be the pursuer rather than the defender in a libel action and even more remarkable that the Government's principal Law Officer should be at the receiving end. A handsome apology was offered by Shawcross:

Dear Lord Kemsley,
I learn with regret that certain words of mine in speeches which I made on the 19th and 30th July have given you the impression that I intended to impugn your business and pro-

fessional integrity in the conduct of your newspapers, and, in particular, to allege that you were conducting a "gutter Press" and intentionally distorting and suppressing facts.

I can assure you that I did not intend to make any of these imputations upon you, and, if any words of mine appeared to make them, I desire unreservedly to withdraw them and express my regret.

I have always been strongly opposed to the introduction of personalities into political controversies, and I should be sorry to think that I had myself introduced them.

This was a unique situation. Here was the Government's Attorney-General having to eat humble pie before a Press baron, having slipped up over libel. Kemsley saw to it that over twenty million readers were informed of the scale of the Shawcross apology: his letter was displayed prominently on the front page of every one of Kemsley's morning, evening, Sunday, weekly and monthly papers.

In the anti-Press campaign Shawcross was the administration's front runner but the back-room mastermind and chief instigator was undoubtedly Herbert Morrison, Home Secretary. He was hypersensitive to criticism, and suspected that he was the target of a constant attack which might imperil his status as Deputy Prime Minister and his prospects of ever becoming Premier. (He never did, but that was due entirely to Attlee's stamina in staying on beyond his time deliberately to frustrate his aspirations.) Though not a lawyer, Morrison had a sensitive feel for libel hazards. So instead of attacking the Press lords by name, he built up a major generalised campaign in a series of speeches in the Commons and the country against what he derided as the "gramophone Press". His favourite story concerned a whirlwind tour during which he visited Cardiff, Manchester, Blackburn, Sheffield, York, Middlesbrough, Newcastle, Glasgow and Aberdeen (all Kemsley centres). At each town and city he eagerly bought the evening and morning papers to discover what the local editors were thinking on the issues of the day and how the pulse of the nation was beating outside London. Alas, he confessed sadly and with mock irony, his research was all in vain. The papers carried identical leading articles written by one hand in the London office, and equally, the names on all the major political news reports and articles were the same (including nine evening papers carrying James Margach's prose— and later six regional morning papers as well!). This, then, was the "gramophone Press", with every editor repeating "His Master's Voice"—in this case, clearly, the views of Lord Kemsley. Other groups which operated similarly were not singled out; the venom was concentrated, albeit obliquely, on Kemsley. Quite why this should have been so is unclear but one theory of mine was that it was because Morrison's Party support was strong in London and woefully weak north of Luton; in any leadership struggle Morrison therefore feared that the Kemsley papers—being entrenched in the regions, Scotland and Wales—would swing their local M.P.s against him.

But this was all a war of words. Morrison also took action. He adroitly encouraged the Labour M.P.s who were also members of the National Union of Journalists—a group far more numerous then than now—to sustain a vociferous campaign for a Commission to inquire into the "monopolistic tendencies" of ownership. The attack was clearly directed not so much against the concentration of ownership as such but against the megalomania and dictatorship of the Press lords who, in truth, were severely eroding the standing of the Press by shrieking about the freedom of the Press while abusing it. A full-scale Parliamentary debate took place on 30 October 1946, and by 270 votes to 157 the Commons decided in favour of setting up a Royal Commission. On 27 March 1947, the inquiry was appointed under the chairmanship of Sir David Ross, with sixteen members, to investigate the "control, management, ownership" of the Press as well as the "monopolistic tendencies".

The Commission, reporting with exemplary speed in June, cleared the Press of the more excitable and extreme charges of distortion and suppression but recommended that a Press Council should be set up to deal with future developments, standards and ethics of newspapers, with a view to supervising conduct and dealing with complaints. There followed some years of wrangling and delay within the industry, special problems being raised over the Council's powers, whether it should include lay members with an independent chairman and whether it would interfere with an editor's independence and judgment. With scant progress being made, a Bill was introduced to set up a Press Council which would have legal powers after two years and this measure, though delayed, helped to speed up the protracted arguments within all sections of the industry. The threat of State intervention persuaded all sides to come together. Their final scheme proposed a Council carefully balanced between the various sections of the Press but without lay members. Herbert Morrison retorted that unless there were lay members to represent the public interest he would have to consider legislative powers after all and so a lay element was duly introduced. In 1953 the Press Council, under the chairmanship of the Hon. J. J. Astor (later Lord Astor of Hever) began work. For the first time newspapers had an official watch-dog. And they had no one but themselves to blame.

During the Attlee years two individual and explosive cases worsened the already poor relations between Downing Street, Westminster and Fleet Street. The first, known as the "Allighan affair", provided startling evidence about the way in which some newspapers were paying M.P.s for private reports about what went on at Parliamentary Labour Party meetings—a form of retainer which many M.P.s on both sides of the House saw as a refined system of bribery and corruption. The second concerned the resignation of Attlee's Chancellor of the Exchequer, Dr Hugh Dalton, for revealing Budget secrets to a distinguished political correspondent a matter of minutes before he was due to deliver his Budget speech in the Commons. Both tempestuous cases increased the conviction inside the Government and Party that, for Party political purposes, the Press would go to any length to discredit and if possible destroy them.

First the Allighan affair. Because of the feuds and splits inside the Government and the Labour Party—the permanent identifying feature of Labour for the whole of this century—weekly Party meeting became the circus act at Westminster. There were invariably rows, explosive debates and acrimonious speeches and, like everybody else in the Lobby, I did my best to acquire information from M.P. friends on which to base my next instalments of the thriller. But one paper excelled: the London *Evening Standard*. Week after week it did more than describe the angry scenes—it actually provided long verbatim reports of key speeches. This not only mystified the Labour Party, it mystified the rest of the Lobby whose own resources could not produce the rival of such reports. Obviously the *Standard's* information was coming from someone inside, someone actually attending the meetings. But how was it being done? The speeches were reported in such detail that only one or two theories seemed tenable: the source was an expert shorthand writer or he was using a tape-recorder.

Soon we were all writing the mystery behind the mystery. Ministers and Whips had their own lists of suspects and week after week they arranged to sit on each side of those under suspicion, to observe whether they ever took notes or were switching on and off anything in their pockets. Never a clue was discovered. No suspect made so much as an occasional note or carried in his pockets anything more menacing than a pipe and a tobacco pouch.

To this day the riddle might have remained unsolved, but for one slip by the central character: the temptation to be a bit too clever, to show off his professional know-how, proved too much. Instead of keeping mum, Garry Allighan, Labour M.P. for Gravesend, tried to confuse the scent by airing his theories about how the *Standard*'s astonishingly accurate and lengthy reports were being compiled. In an article for the *World's Press News*, Fleet Street's trade paper at the time, he claimed that there was no real mystery at all: M.P.s were paid in money and in kind, and political correspondents were able to get first-hand reports of Party meetings by filling Members tight with liquor in "Annie's Bar" and other bars at Westminster. When the drink's in the wits are out, ran Allighan's scenario. Under the influence M.P.s talk their heads off. They spill the beans. Easy, my dear Watson! To spread confusion even wider he claimed in the article that every newspaper had "anything up to half-a-dozen M.P.s on its contact list".

At this juncture a full-scale inquiry was launched by the Committee of Privileges. It is important to note one point: it was not the leaking of reports from the private Labour Party meetings which triggered the investigation. Instead, it was the actual article which was raised as an issue of privilege by Quintin Hogg (later Lord Hailsham) on the grounds that it implied bribery and corruption by M.P.s as well as dishonourable conduct and drunkenness unbecoming to the dignity and honour of "this honourable House".

At first Allighan did not admit that he was the author of the *Standard* reports. It was left to the editor, Herbert Gunn, to tell the Committee that he paid a small Press agency £120 a month for them. The agency was owned and controlled by none other than Garry Allighan, but it was only under merciless questioning by Sir Hartley Shawcross that he finally confessed. The case inevitably widened. The editor of the London *Evening News*, Guy Schofield, and his political correspondent, Stanley Dobson, admitted in evidence that they paid an M.P. £5 a week for help and guidance in political reporting. But they refused to identify their informant. The Privileges Committee adjourned for twenty-four hours to consider the tense situation in which journalists were openly defying the all-powerful Committee. I remember how we all speculated on the probable upshot. One report, widely circulated, suggested that if anyone was sentenced to the Tower for defying the High Court of Parliament's demand for a source of information, it should not be Schofield and Dobson, but the proprietor, Lord Rothermere—after all, he was responsible for his papers and the actions of his staff. To complicate matters, however, Evelyn Walkden, Labour M.P. for Doncaster, then made a statement in the House admitting that he was the Member concerned and dire consequences for journalists and owner were avoided, the Committee deciding instead to report Schofield and Dobson to the House for refusing to name their informant. All honour to them for standing by Press freedom and the protection of sources.

Allighan himself was found guilty of "an aggravated contempt of the House" through spreading suspicions on others by persistently misleading the Committee when he knew he was the guilty Member —and of a "gross breach of privilege" and of corruptly accepting payments for disclosing information when under the obligation of secrecy. On 30 October 1947 he was expelled from Parliament—the first expulsion since that of Horatio Bottomley twenty-five years before. Curiously, however, Allighan was expelled only after an all-party revolt by M.P.s against the Government. Herbert Morrison, on behalf of the Cabinet, moved that Allighan should only be reprimanded by Mr Speaker and suspended for six months without salary. It was Winston Churchill and Quintin Hogg who moved an amendment to expel him and on a free vote the amendment was carried by 187 votes to 75 (the majority of M.P.s did not vote and most of the votes for expulsion came from the Labour side). It was an agonising experience to see Allighan, an able journalist and a man of great personal charm, being conducted from the precincts by a police inspector, never to cross the Parliamentary threshold again.

At the same sitting, and immediately after Allighan's expulsion, Evelyn Walkden was reprimanded for "dishonourable conduct" while Arthur Heighway, editor of *World's Press News*, was called to the Bar of the House and reprimanded by the Speaker for "publishing news containing unfounded implications against M.P.s— a gross offence against the House". Altogether, it was a squalid affair, leaving the impression that the worst features of cheque-book journalism were rampant at Westminster, as though jobbery, bribery and corruption had become the stock-in-trade of political corres-pondents, a gross libel on honourable men.

But all was not yet over. At the fag-end of a day which left us all exhausted by the emotion of the personal tragedies being played out, Morrison tried to slip in a motion as a consequential and minor issue. With Fleet Street clearly in his sights, he proposed that in any future case in which a Member was found guilty of accepting payment for the disclosure of information about matters "to be proceeded with in Parliament", then the paper concerned and any representative responsible for offering payments, should be excluded from Westminster. It was an obvious threat to gag and expel correspondents and papers on a permanent basis. Thanks to the objections instantly raised by M.P. journalists and editors of the standing of Vernon Bartlett, Wilson Harris, J. P. L. Mallalieu and

Haydn Davies, Morrison agreed to drop the motion. By way of explanation, he said: "We've all had a heavy day and I'm anxious that this should not be settled in the middle of the night or early morning." But his action carried a clear warning for the future conduct of the Press. It was a threat which was never implemented, but I am in no doubt that in the unending love-hate serial, Governments are just as ready to pounce when they feel themselves under attack.

The Dalton case, which also involved the sensitive area of contacts between M.P.s and the Lobby, convinced the more suspicious M.P.s that too-close relations should be avoided like the plague, for they could bring only disaster to politicians; it was the inevitable price to be paid for supping with the devil. Yet the case started innocently enough. On 11 November 1947, as Dalton was walking through the Lobby to the Commons chamber to present an interim Budget, he bumped into John Carvel, political correspondent of the London *Evening Star* (now alas defunct, for it was a lively paper). Carvel, a very experienced journalist and a dear friend of mine, as is his son Robert today, good-naturedly remarked to the Chancellor that everybody was braced for shocks. They were friends of many years standing, accustomed to sharing confidences as between trusted intimates, so Dalton proceeded to tell Carvel the three or four main tax changes which, a few minutes later, he would be announcing.

Carvel got on to his editor right away and reported what the major changes would be. A report was rushed in to an edition then running, for seldom could a forecast have been published with greater confidence. The report had only a trivial circulation at the back end of a main edition; it was simply a stop-gap report until Dalton started the Budget speech proper. But the crucial factor, although neither Carvel nor his editor knew it at the time, was this: Dalton, in only a few seconds with Carvel, had confided *all* his Budget proposals.

The matter became an issue because of a rival editor's peevish reaction to the *Star*'s hundred per cent Budget forecast: he tipped off an Opposition M.P., with dark hints about official secrets and sinister leaks. Within twenty-four hours the report was raised in the Commons as a grave breach of privilege and security; and in the instant chain-reaction the Lobby Committee, of which I was a member, became heavily involved in what was trumpeted as a major sensation—as though newspapers are not in business to breach security and then to publish and be damned.

Dalton apologised in the House and Churchill, then leading the

Opposition, refused to make a song and dance about the leak, expressing sympathy with Dalton in his experience and embarrassment. There the issue might well have rested and been forgotten but for some of the more belligerent spirits in his Shadow Cabinet and on his back-benches. The hunt was on. They wanted to hound Dalton for his indiscretion. They were not to be deprived of their fox and the final kill. So, under pressure, Churchill changed tack. Six hours after his sympathetic response to Dalton's apology he became master of the hunt. He wrote to Dalton that he wanted a Select Committee to investigate the whole incident, because he had received further details "about the very precise and comprehensive" form of the *Star*'s report.

This created an entirely new situation for Attlee and his Chancellor, so Dalton submitted his resignation the same night. Attlee accepted it. Any inclination to refuse to allow Dalton to go, and to face the music as a team, was over-powered by Stafford Cripps, who, as always, made much mileage out of his high principles and strongly advised the Prime Minister that only resignation could satisfy the constitutional issues at stake. The all-party Select Committee was at once set up. Its report accepted Dalton's admission of a "grave indiscretion" on his part; John Carvel's action was seen as an "error of judgment in good faith". In due course Dalton returned to the Attlee Cabinet and Carvel continued for many years as one of the most distinguished and respected newspapermen at Westminster. But the damage to Lobby relations was done.

One final comment is appropriate. Budget leaks terrify Chancellors, Cabinets and Whitehall because of the danger of someone making a fortune in a quick City killing. But in the Dalton–Carvel affair, nothing remotely like this happened. The chairman of the Stock Exchange Council gave evidence that "there were no movements of prices or sales which could in any way be attributed to the leakage of news which occurred". So why all the fuss, apart from its being a classic symptom of explosive Parliament–Press tensions? Certainly, Attlee himself was unconcerned by the hullabaloo. Indeed, in a typical gesture, he demonstrated his sympathy with an old friend. At the height of the storm he invited Mr and Mrs Carvel for a weekend at Chequers.

The ultimate irony is that nobody would ever have been aware of the Budget leak but for the action of the other editor. It was an unhappy reminder that it is not only Parliament, Downing Street and the mandarins of Whitehall who constantly threaten the freedom of the Press and the initiative of individual journalists, but that the highly developed streak of cannibalism in Fleet Street itself also exacts penalties in mutual self-destruction. Dog really does eat dog.

7

ANTHONY EDEN

April 1955–January 1957

"The power of the Government to deceive is so immense that fooling all of the people some of the time can successfully and easily lead to fooling them all of the time." WILLIAM CLARK*

By every conceivable test of history, politics and popularity Anthony Eden should have been one of Britain's truly great Prime Ministers. For almost thirty years he was trained for the most glittering prize of all. For twenty years he waited for the succession, first as Heir Apparent and then as the established Crown Prince. It is difficult to explain to a new generation the way in which Eden was the embodiment of hope and idealism in the grim 'twenties and 'thirties. For three decades he was the most glamorous and popular British figure on the world stage; the youngest Foreign Secretary since Lord Greville in 1791, a figure of international stature before he was forty. Yet when he finally reached the top his was a brief and disastrous Premiership which collapsed in personal tragedy.

He was the victim of his own past. He was created and shaped by the tumultuous crises created by Hitler, Mussolini and Franco. When he became Prime Minister, facing his first major international crises posed by President Nasser's nationalisation of the Suez Canal, he believed he was back in the 'thirties, re-living the dictators' crisis. Lord Blake explained the Eden failure in a single sentence of his obituary assessment in the *Sunday Times*: "He was the last Prime Minister to believe Britain was a great power and the first to confront a crisis which proved she was not."

Nevertheless, it remains extraordinary that one who had served such a long apprenticeship in power should ultimately prove so inept. He lost control over Parliament, which he had dominated with easy confidence for twenty years; and although he was a superb

* Spokesman at No. 10 Downing Street for Sir Anthony Eden; now vice-president, World Bank.

diplomat as Foreign Secretary when dealing with world leaders he lost all his skill and finesse as Prime Minister when dealing with editors and correspondents. The final eclipse was certain when, as a result of his isolation, he was defeated at every turn in his power battle with the Press and the BBC.

Apart from the ever-present shadows of the dictators I think that Eden lacked the three basic qualities or advantages of all successful Premiers: luck—Eden's ran out from the moment he became Prime Minister; health—he had the most appalling health record of all; and patience—on which he was seriously overdrawn, having been compelled to wait too long by obstinate old men. As Eden himself wrote in retrospect:

> The vows they make earlier that they would give way to a younger man when the years begin to blunt their faculties, when illness begins to twist their judgement, these they choose to ignore. Power has become a habit they cannot bear to cast off. . . . What neither he (Churchill) nor I could have foreseen was that when at last I stepped into his place I should have so short a run. Thirty years of political work at high tension and feckless disregard for my own health were to claim their forfeit."*

But one's doubts persist as to whether he genuinely possessed the armour for supreme power. Of course, by the time he succeeded Churchill in 1955 Eden was patently a sick man. But much earlier, in his prime, he still failed to demonstrate the consuming thrust of ambition, the killer instinct. When, as Foreign Secretary, he resigned from the Chamberlain Government in February 1938 in protest against appeasement he was identified by most of us in the Westminster Press corps, as well as in Parliament and by public opinion, as the next Prime Minister. He was then in a much more powerful position than Churchill and could have set himself at the head of all the anti-appeasement forces in the three parties. But he ducked the opportunity and the challenge when he could have changed the course of history. Instead, a year later, he returned to the Government as Dominions Secretary. As Eden wrote in his diary: "Max [Beaverbrook] girded at me for not understanding my strength when I resigned and for coming back as Dominions Secretary. He said had I played my hand strongly I must have succeeded Neville." His problem was that he had never been in conflict with his Party, and when he resigned he was therefore afraid of causing dissension and isolating himself from the Conservative Central Office machine.

* *The Eden Memoirs, The Reckoning*, Cassell.

He was totally unlike other rebels of the period such as Duff Cooper, Salisbury and, of course, Churchill himself. Having made his gesture of resignation he lacked the courage to continue the fight. He was a rebel with velvet gloves.

The "Eden Group", which attracted many prominent Tories including Harold Macmillan and Duff Cooper, was organised as a party within a party. It was the most potent anti-leadership group which I have ever known in the Tory Party—far more powerful than the Imperial India and pro-Suez groups or, for that matter, the Labour Party Bevanites. Its members were dedicated and highly organised meeting every week—to escape the Whips' espionage network—in the palatial Queen Anne's Gate home of the rich young Conservative Ronald Tree, which was equipped with division bells to enable the rebels to return to the nearby House of Commons in time to vote.

When I refer to an "espionage network" I do not exaggerate. What is not known is that these meetings came close to providing Britain with an early version of the Watergate scandal: Tree's telephone was being tapped by Chamberlain's very own department of dirty tricks. Tree, at the time, was actually tipped off about the tap but he regarded the notion as fantastic and took no evasive action beyond making more use of Members' phone boxes at the Commons. There were no Communists, Fascists or enemy sympathisers in the group so why should his line be under surveillance? He should have known better for his warning came from reliable sources—Helen Kirkpatrick of the Chicago *Daily News*, the first of the new generation of American women journalists breaking into a big-time man's world, and Victor Gordon-Lennox, diplomatic correspondent of the *Daily Telegraph*. At the time these two were co-operating in writing and editing a weekly broadsheet devoted to attacking Chamberlain's appeasement policies. Gordon-Lennox, who was a great help on foreign affairs in my younger days, had exceptionally close contacts inside the Foreign Office and embassies, while Miss Kirkpatrick had elevated sources in the Roosevelt White House and State Department.

To produce their broadsheet they hired rooms in a block which happened to be directly opposite Tree's house. Both from observation and private information they discovered that phone calls to and from the nerve-centre of the Eden group were being monitored in considerable detail and they exhorted Tree not to reveal his sources and contacts over the phone when speaking to third parties. Tree was always hearing odd clickings every time he picked up the phone in his house—bugging being relatively unsophisticated then —but was unable to solve the mystery: Who? Why?

The explanation was not furnished until two years later when Tree, then acting as Parliamentary Private Secretary to Duff Cooper at the Ministry of Information, met Sir Joseph Ball who had been head of the Conservative Party research department and was then chairman of the Security Service at the Ministry dealing with counter-espionage. Ball, a curiously shadowy figure who features in many biographies, histories and memoirs of the period, was a tough, ruthless operator, one of Chamberlain's hatchet-men and an intimate from the days when Chamberlain was chairman of the Party. He was forever on shady missions to Italian and other embassies— often with secret messages for Mussolini, thus by-passing the Foreign Office and allowing Chamberlain to deny all knowledge of rumoured accommodations with the Duce. Ball frequently briefed hand-picked Lobbymen and would sit in when Chamberlain and a few of us had lunch at the St Stephen's Club. Describing the revelatory meeting with Ball*, Tree says that he was "a dislikeable man with an unenviable reputation for doing some of Chamberlain's behind-the-scenes' work. We got into conversation and he had the gall to tell me that he had been responsible for having my telephone tapped."

That, then, was the Who? The Why? is not difficult to comprehend. Eden and his group were alarmingly well briefed on everything that was taking place on the international network and the wire-taps were intended to discover the sources of suspected leaks within the Foreign Office, the Defence Ministry and the Intelligence Service. Chamberlain was ruthless in dismissing officials whose loyalty to himself was suspect or whose contacts with Eden or Churchill were thought to be too close. The bitterness inside the Party had reached such an unimaginable pitch that anything was possible. Tree even found that his application to join the Royal Yacht Squadron had been blackballed by the Whips because he was known to be providing hospitality for the Tory derided Eden "Glamour Set".

In fact the top-level source of the leaks is now common knowledge. Sir Robert Vansittart (later Lord Vansittart), head of the Foreign Office and later Diplomatic Adviser, recorded in his memoirs that it was he who kept Eden, Churchill, Duff Cooper and others fully informed of developments. He had considered it his duty to do so. Moreover, the most recent Churchill biography*

* *When the Moon was High*, Macmillan.
* *Winston Churchill*, Vol. V, Martin Gilbert, Heinemann.

reveals that other senior officials, as well as service and intelligence officers, placed their careers in jeopardy by keeping Winston fully in the picture from top secret documents. The most sinister aspect of the eavesdropping on Eden and Co—as it was with Watergate—was that it was inspired and executed by Party functionaries in order to inform their political masters of the private moves of their political rivals and, in the case of Eden, to root out anti-appeasement men and women in the public service. It was certainly not inspired by any altruistic desire to preserve the security of the State against enemy agents and sympathisers.

If Ball and his merry men considered it worth while to tap the Eden group's phones, it is a reasonable inference that Churchill's lines, too, were bugged, especially since Martin Gilbert reveals that the Cabinet Secretary, Lord Hankey, wrote a lengthy letter of protest to Churchill about his access to official Cabinet papers. And even to my own knowledge the old-style clicking on certain numbers indicated that the Tree experience was not an isolated one. I also know that during the same period one or two Press Gallery correspondents suffered similarly. They were men who used to boost their income by providing daily reports to the Communist *Daily Worker* (now the *Morning Star*) in the days before the paper was allowed staffmen at Westminster. One of them—a senior member of *The Times* team—told me that for two years he sent the *Worker* news summaries from the Press Gallery and that every time he phoned the paper there was a sequence of clickings before the connection was established. Often the third party listening in could be heard breathing heavily. In no time at all it became an "in" joke. My friend would say: "When the three of us are sitting comfortably, with pencils sharpened, I'll start dictating", and the third man could be heard having a private chuckle.

Having failed to fight for Chamberlain's leadership Eden was in two ways lucky to be allowed to succeed Churchill. First, if the great man had clung to the Premiership for much longer Eden's own failing health might have denied him office. It was touch and go; the process of persuading Churchill that enough was enough was a long and delicate one. In the end it was subtle power-play by Lord Kemsley and Lord Woolton, the redoubtable Party chairman, which did the trick. Kemsley had already tried to point the way during the closing stages of the Attlee administration when his newspapers, including the *Sunday Times*, pointed out that the Tory leader was applying most of his energies to the production of memoirs and histories. Churchill was furious and summoned Kemsley to his presence. The proprietor, confronted by a combination of hectoring threats and impish banter, rapidly realised that Churchill had no intention of being persuaded to retire gracefully. But in the early 'fifties, when it became obvious that Churchill, then Prime Minister, had suffered strokes and was in decline, H. V. Hodson, editor of the *Sunday Times*, wrote a very firm leader which paid compliment to Winston's great age, his unique record of service to the country, and then stressed the need for the Prime Minister seriously to consider the country's future and the interests of the Conservative Party in stepping down in favour of a new leader before an election came too close. When Kemsley discovered what his editor was publishing he alerted Woolton, his close friend, and his cue was sufficient for the final act to unfold. Woolton at once went to Churchill and stressed the significance of the leading article. If the *Sunday Times* says that, he warned, other papers will take up the hint, but more stridently. Great harm would thus be done to the Party. He hated to say it, of course, to his dear old friend but the picture of the Party being led by an obstinate and ailing old man would cause great injury. Churchill was moved by the sincerity of the message from Woolton—and agreed to plan the timing of his retirement with care. The influence of Kemsley and Woolton was never identified at the time. It was a unique example of the interplay of Press and Party forces gently but firmly pushing a Prime Minister into retirement.

The second potential barrier to Eden's succession was Churchill's own grave second-thoughts as to his capacity to govern. As Sir John Colville, Principal Private Secretary at No. 10, confirmed to me later, Churchill had become significantly impressed by "Rab" Butler's record and was coming round to the view that he might prove the better bet for Government and country. Echoing this statement, the first Lord Swinton, talking to me for the record, put the Prime Minister's feelings somewhat more graphically:

A few weeks before Winston resigned we were lunching together—we did this about twice a week. He said to me: "I wonder if I've done right, not morally, but politically." I replied: "Well, your home affairs have been eighteenth century, and in Imperial affairs you've been in the nineteenth century. But in the things that matter, foreign affairs, defence and the war, you've been a hundred per cent right."

Winston said: "Oh no, you damn fool, I don't mean that. I'm talking about my successor. Do you not think that Rab would be better?" I said: "Well, frankly, Winston, anybody would be better than Anthony. I think Anthony would be the worst Prime Minister since Lord North. But you can't think like that now—it's too late. You announced him as your successor more than ten years ago."

Winston replied: "I think it was a great mistake." He was right, Anthony was the worst—he proved a prima donna, not a Prime Minister.

In his first-class history of the decline and fall of Lloyd George* Beaverbrook wrote that "in the moment of supreme triumph decline begins to do its work, undermining, weakening and finally destroying not only the reputations but also the power and the authority of our heroes". This was even truer of Anthony Eden. Scarcely had he succeeded Churchill and with astonishing flair won the 1955 general election than decay set in. Of all Prime Ministers' honeymoons his was the briefest.

It is a complete misreading of history to regard him as a one-issue man, for long before Nasser even thought of nationalising the Suez Canal in July 1956 Eden was fighting desperately for survival. Suez provided the final push for a man already losing his balance on the edge of the precipice. In January 1956, six months after his convincing election victory, an "Eden Must Go" campaign was sweeping through the Tory Party. What is more, it was led by the ultra-loyalist Conservative *Daily Telegraph*, displaying uncharacteristic zest for scalp-hunting. The deputy editor, Donald McLachlan, wrote an article pointing out how indecisive and weak the Prime Minister and his Government appeared to be; they were constantly changing, delaying and confusing policy decisions. The situation, said McLachlan, demanded the smack of firm Government. The phrase was not accidental; he was referring to a characteristic mannerism of Eden when emphasising a point during a speech. He would hold up both hands like a boxer and then bring the right fist down into the open left palm—but instead of the expected resounding smack no sound resulted.

After this early trial salvo, Eden rapidly demonstrated that he was a shell-shocked case, his physical and nervous system shot to pieces before he ever joined battle. Within days, an official Downing Street statement was denying reports that he was on the point of resigning. It was a clear indication that he did not have the stamina to stay the course. It proved in advance that in the conflict for power between Downing Street and Fleet Street Anthony Eden was the natural loser—the easiest and quickest Fleet Street victim on record.

The *Telegraph* people were so embarrassed by the reactions to

* *Decline and Fall of Lloyd George*, Collins.

their comments—which were interpreted at home and overseas as an attack inspired by powerful Conservatives anxious to ditch Eden —that another article was written to explain that, of course, there was nothing personal in the earlier criticisms. But, at the same time, the anti-Tory papers, headed by the *Daily Mirror*, were in full cry: "Eden is a Flop", "Eden Must Go". The Press campaign went on for months, eroding Eden's vulnerable political position and sapping his over-strained physical resources. No commercial is intended or necessary, but the political correspondent of the *Sunday Times* was writing on 11 March 1956—with the firm smack of authority of course: "The Prime Minister is showing signs of nervous tension. This is not surprising, for the Government is passing through a testing time in foreign and economic affairs. When the head of the Government shows obvious signs of the intense and inescapable strain of his office, a sort of psychological inquest must follow. Is he the man for the job? Can he stand it? What's wrong with the Government?" And so on. I quote from the record simply to emphasise that long before Suez Eden's morale was cracking, his defences crumbling.

But when the heat was on and he was fighting for survival it was his appallingly patchy Press relations which hastened his downfall. He was lonely and isolated just at the moment when he should have been accessible to all in order to communicate his feelings with Parliament and people. It is an odd feature of his record at Westminster that despite his thirty-odd years as an M.P. and his long career as a senior Minister and front-bencher, he had so few contacts with the corps of political correspondents and so few close friends in Fleet Street. Even after his resignation in 1938 he remained aloof from the Press and news of the activities of the "Eden Group" had to be gleaned through Ronald Tree and his Parliamentary Private Secretary, J. P. L. Thomas. Eden's closest friend was Iverach McDonald, deputy editor of *The Times* (the editor, Sir William Haley, also met him privately from time to time). But his main contact with the Press world—since for thirty years he had been exclusively bound up with foreign affairs—was through the diplomatic correspondents, among whom were an inner circle of special confidants, identified as an arm of the Foreign Office, who adored him with total loyalty. He had a flair for warm friendship, but it was not enough. Many of these old friends disagreed with his Suez policy. And then he was on his own.

Not quite on his own, perhaps. For shortly after becoming Prime Minister he made an excellent appointment as his Press and Broadcasting Adviser to No. 10: William Clark, a senior *Observer* man with excellent contacts and wide knowledge of home and international affairs, and a regular current affairs performer on radio and television. He was thus a highly skilled and articulate professional, a man destined to be a significant influence on the Eden Government. But then came Suez. The partnership had not time to bloom.

Instead, a situation unique in my experience was created at the centre of power. For Clark profoundly disagreed with his Prime Minister's plan. He was convinced that by trying to overthrow Nasser and seize the Canal by armed invasion Eden was making a calamitous misjudgment. Clark's advice to his chief was that by equating Nasser with Hitler, by seeing 1956 through the eyes of 1936, and by ignoring the realities of power in the post-war world he was heading for certain disaster.

Clearly, enormous strains were placed on both the Prime Minister and the official spokesman who had to interpret his politics to the British and world media. Yet all through the long explosive Suez crisis Clark acted honourably and loyally. I saw him regularly and privately in Downing Street and elsewhere, as a professional seeker after truth and a friend, and while it was obvious to me that he was suffering great anguish of heart he always explained and interpreted the policies of his Prime Minister and Government with total loyalty. Never once did he attempt to thrust his privately critical views into our countless conversations. Indeed, during the military build-up of August and September he was so successful in convincing communicators that Eden meant business that Crossman denounced "Clark's sabre-rattling" and dubbed him as a sort of "Nasser's Burgess and Maclean".

He stayed on, in personal agony, purely to avoid the public embarrassment to Eden which would have resulted if he had resigned at once. He promised that he would remain at No. 10 until the official cease-fire was established, and then resign.

This was precisely what happened. Of course, Clark was widely courted by editors and publishers who pressed handsome cheques on him in return for the real inside story of Suez. But Clark turned down the tempting offers and at once went to India on a year-long assignment for the *Observer*, in order to avoid involvement in the inevitable post-Suez inquests and controversies. His personal papers and records of the period are now in the banker's safe and will not be made public until the end of the century.

However, years later he did in a general sense analyse in a book* what went wrong over Suez. His experience reveals in sharp focus

* *Secrecy*, O.U.P., New York.

the issues with which this book is concerned: secrecy, disclosures, access to information and decision-making, open government, communications, and trust between Government and Press. He wrote that in the Government's strategy the element of surprise was essential—not against the enemy but against public opinion at home and abroad. He said:

What was worse, Parliament, the public and the bureaucracy were not only unconsulted, not only surprised, they were deceived. . . . Public opinion at home and particularly abroad was sufficiently potent that it could not be ignored, it had to be fooled. News management became news invention. (He added:) This is not just moral judgment about deception; it is based on the knowledge that the power of Government to deceive is so immense that fooling all of the people some of the time can successfully and easily lead to fooling them all of the time. That is why a Press Officer who is being used for fooling the Press should break the rules of the Civil Service and resign.

It was on this very point, of course, that Clark himself reached breaking point. It is possible to tell the truth and nothing but the truth while stopping well short of the whole truth—and in between are an infinite number of gradations. Clark, knowing much, if not all, of the details of the French and Israeli "collusion" over the invasion, could not reconcile himself to delivering a string of half-truths. Thus he practised what he preached and resolved to resign. An eloquent example for today's massed bands of Government Press and Information Officers.

Until the cease-fire, however, the faithful Clark continued in his pivotal role of attempting to reconcile his Prime Minister to the existence of a free Press and BBC, the latter at one stage coming under unbelievable pressure from No. 10. Even the highest echelons of Fleet Street were far from immune from the direct intervention of Eden. In his despair he felt compelled to forge some contact with the newspapers but since his grass-roots Press contacts were so few he began to summon editors, in groups of six or eight, to Downing Street. Had he then proceeded to discuss policy with them some good might have come from these gatherings. As it was, however, the editors found a Prime Minister close to the point of physical and nervous collapse, lecturing them on their duty to inform readers of the need to rally round the armed forces in action. Some editors did not take kindly to this approach and began to peel off, sending subordinates instead. As Michael Curtis editor of the *News*

Chronicle, told me: "I can't keep coming round to No. 10 to be harangued by the P.M. on what I should be thinking and saying in the national interest." He obviously agreed with Hazlitt that editors should stay in their garrets.

Perhaps Eden's paranoia about the Press had some justification since the chief Eden-baiter over Suez was Randolph Churchill— as he had been ever since Eden succeeded his father and despite Eden's loyalty to Winston well beyond the calls of duty. Through his links with the proprietors and their families Randolph tried hard to orchestrate Fleet Street's attacks while himself writing hostile articles in Beaverbrook's London *Evening Standard*. But worse than this, he was frequently on the phone to his cousin Clarissa, Lady Eden, making it clear, in his hectoring style, just how disastrous a Premier he considered her husband to be. These personalised battering-ram onslaughts—and Randolph had a cruel and wicked tongue when he was trying to destroy anyone, which was often— added enormously to the anguish of Lady Eden, already at the point of exhaustion by worry over her husband's health. By carrying his attacks from the printed page into the private apartments of Downing Street he added tragically to the unhappiness of the Eden family. But then, Randolph Churchill believed that battles at the top should be fought with jungle-like ferocity.

When Eden's *soirees* with the editors proved pointless he turned to the telephone instead. It became like a drug. After the morning papers reached No. 10 at 6 a.m. he at once phoned proprietors, editors and writers to complain about items which he read as hostile to his Suez policy. His most regular dawn contact was Esmond Harmsworth, chief proprietor of the *Daily Mail*. The calls succeeded in adding greatly to the pressures on the *Mail*'s famous leader writer, George Murray, but he continued to be consistently fair in trying to interpret Eden's policies while at the same time setting out the way in which they injured Britain's reputation in the world. Lord Kemsley, too, was constantly at the receiving end of urgent phone conversations at all hours, reflecting the grotesquely excitable state of the incumbent of No. 10. If Kemsley himself was not available, then his eldest son Lionel Berry, his personal assistant (Denis Hamilton) or H. V. Hodson, editor of the *Sunday Times*, would have to take the calls. Yet Eden was protesting not about the attitude of the *Sunday Times* (always loyal to Eden during Suez) or the Kemsley papers but about the national dailies. Indeed, so faithful was the *Sunday Times* that Eden was at pains to ensure that I, as its political correspondent, fully understood the detailed and secret version of his policies. And because Clark was known to disapprove of the Suez adventure the Prime Minister arranged that I should be briefed twice, as a cross-check. He need not have worried for, as a first-class professional, Clark did his job with great skill and fidelity. However, every Saturday, before going to press, I also talked privately to Bobby Allan (later Lord Allan of Kilmahew), Eden's Parliamentary Private Secretary and personal aide. He was briefed personally by the Prime Minister to guide me on the facts and the Government's plans just in case Clark had softened one aspect or hardened another to influence the overall picture. In practice my questions always elicited the same information from both, but the story illustrates the care with which even a Prime Minister on the point of breakdown made certain that he was fully insured against third-party risks in the control of news and information.

Clark, of course, was the one man who was consistently rung when the papers hit Downing Street, with Eden demanding instant reaction to leading articles and even news reports and headlines. Overwrought, Eden did not realise that an incident such as the Russian threat to bomb if British troops were not withdrawn was news of national importance, that events at the Security Council or in Washington merited prominent reports. However, Clark, then living in Albany, always said he would go round to No. 10 at once to discuss the problems with his master. But, ten minutes later, just as he was on the point of leaving his flat, there would come a follow-up call from the Prime Minister: "Don't worry, dear William," would be the burden of the message. "You must go back to bed, you need all the rest you can get; you've a busy day ahead of you. Have a little more sleep, don't worry about me. We must take care of you."

It was Eden's phone calls which convinced Cabinet Ministers, top permanent secretaries, Fleet Street, and most writers, that he had not the stamina for the supreme challenge. He was always flapping. It was for this reason that when Lord Hailsham first described Harold Macmillan as "unflappable", it became an instant catchword, distancing the incoming Prime Minister from his predecessor. Clark did his best. With the approval of Eden's personal staff and of Sir Norman Brook (later Lord Normanbrook), Secretary of the Cabinet, he regularly advised the Prime Minister to stop ringing editors and proprietors. The calls only made matters worse, he argued, because writers did not like him going behind their backs. Instead, Eden was repeatedly advised by Clark that he should start regular meetings with the political and defence correspondents. But he never did.

In the long build-up towards the landings of British and French paratroops at Port Said on 5 November 1956, Eden became increasingly short-tempered over what he regarded as the openly hostile criticisms of his policy broadcast by the BBC. The point to note is that there was no editorialising in these broadcasts; they roused his anger because they included straight reports of critical speeches made in Parliament by Hugh Gaitskell, leader of the Labour Opposition, and of critical editorials in the *Guardian*, *Observer* and other papers. Eden believed that once British forces were committed they were fighting the Queen's enemies: and in such a situation any criticism should be treated as subversion. In short, Eden saw himself as a war leader against Nasser just as Churchill was war leader against Hitler and Mussolini. His answer, like Churchill's, was censorship.

William Clark was responsible in great measure for heading off this potentially grave interference with the freedom of communication and in his memoirs* Harman Grisewood, former chief personal assistant to Director-General Sir Ian Jacobs, pays tribute to his "delicacy and discernment, tact and initiative, in restraining Eden and calming the BBC". Events, Grisewood recalls, followed a familiar pattern. The first indication that Eden was determined, if possible, to coerce the BBC into co-operation came when Grisewood discovered that he had gone over the heads of BBC executives straight to the Corporation Chairman, Sir Alexander Cadogan, a former head of the Foreign Office who had been close to Eden for many years. This was followed, in the last weeks of October, by an invitation to Grisewood, in the Director-General's absence overseas, to visit the Ministry of Defence where he was told that as military operations were about to start there would be a reintroduction of the war-time powers requiring the BBC to be subject to censorship. The modern analogy might be that because British forces were involved in Northern Ireland there should be censorship of any criticism of relevant British policy.

As the main channel of communication between Downing Street and Broadcasting House, Clark's powers of diplomacy were taxed to the full, and the pressure on him was increased when Eden ordered his Lord Chancellor, Lord Kilmuir, to prepare emergency powers under which all criticism of the Suez operation would be silenced in broadcasts to Egypt and the Middle East. Clark's fears were scarcely alleviated when the Prime Minister, refusing to countenance any half-measures, returned Kilmuir's first draft, demanding tougher legislation. But Clark warned the BBC to what was being prepared at the Premier's request and when confronted

* *One thing at a time*, Hutchinson.

by the combined opposition of the Board of Governors and top executives Eden was compelled to retreat from his hostile stance. To what extent this was purely a bargaining position is open to question for, as a skilled diplomat, he might well have pitched his demands higher than his target. Indeed, he may well have succeeded in his gagging move for even after his so-called "defeat" it was agreed that a Foreign Office official should sit in at Bush House, headquarters of the BBC's overseas broadcasts, to keep an eye on propaganda and to attempt to monitor anything he considered slanted against the Government. Much worse, the Foreign Office sent a senior expert to Cyprus to broadcast "black" propaganda to Egypt and the Middle East on an old BBC wavelength.

But whoever might be judged the victor, this BBC crisis served to reinforce something which Sir John Reith, the first Director-General, had established in the 'thirties: that the freedom of the spoken word must be fought for just as vigorously as the freedom of the written word. For both are pillars of the same arch.

When all the secret files are open, Eden's brief and unlucky Premiership may get a squarer deal than from the instant histories of the period. He was obviously a victim of history, caught between the old Imperial might of the Empire and its total eclipse as a world power. However, some of the top insiders at the time have assured me that in their judgment Eden's prime intention was—by demands, propaganda and threats of force—to keep up the pressure on Egypt in the hope of toppling President Nasser. It was part of the bluff and counter-bluff on the edge of the precipice. Unfortunately, according to these sources, he was overwhelmed by demands for military action from the hawks in his Cabinet, the most powerful of whom was Harold Macmillan. Yet he it was who first sounded the retreat, compelling Eden to cave in; the message on the inner Whitehall circuit was clear—Macmillan was first in and first out.

One of the morals of my studies of twelve Prime Ministers is that the one who loses control over his Cabinet loses himself. So it was with Anthony Eden.

The full story of the heartbreaking denouement has still to be told. Lord Butler has come closest to it in his memoirs* where he refers to the Cabinet's decisions not to proceed further with armed landings. Butler says that the debate "seemed to nonplus the Prime Minister. He said he must go upstairs to consider his position." In fact, the scene was much more moving. Eden was emotionally overcome. He broke down in tears and cried: "You are all deserting me, deserting me". He was in total collapse, weeping unashamedly.

* *The Art of the Possible*, Hamilton.

Then he went upstairs to compose himself. For such is the agony of power when it denies you.

Suez destroyed not only Eden, but left all parties suffering from shell-shock, the more nervous having breakdowns in public. Inevitably the Press was engulfed in the emotional backlash, and John Junor, editor of the *Sunday Express*, was grabbed as the first victim. He was in danger of being sentenced to the Tower, to be incarcerated in a lonely cell, all because he affronted the *amour propre* of M.P.s, releasing the basic anti-Press prejudice which exists just below the Westminster surface.

His crime was that, coinciding with the final agonies of Suez and Eden's Premiership, he wrote a barbed leader in the *Sunday Express* about politicians exempting themselves from the full rigours of petrol rationing (introduced as a price for Suez). He drew attention to the "prodigious allowances" earmarked for politicians and demanded to know what the M.P.s were doing about the blatant injustice. From the far Right came an immediate complaint about a breach of privilege; the full panoply of the Committee of Privileges was invoked to deal with Junor's irreverence. Hauled before the Committee he stood his ground; he regretted the leading article had been misunderstood . . . "its purpose was to comment on a system whereby, while ordinary members of the public are subject to the most stringent rationing petrol for motoring, up to 3,700 miles a month is to be allowed for political party use".

This was not good enough. The Committee on 9 January 1957 (the day Eden resigned) duly reported that they found John Junor guilty of "serious contempt", recommended a "severe reprimand", for an offence "aggravated by his demeanour before the Committee." Next day he was arraigned at the bar of the Commons. Had he anything to say before sentence was passed? In my time I have heard many maiden speeches, but Junor's, in a taut situation, excelled them all for brevity, dignity and courage. He dutifully expressed his regrets for any imputations on M.P.s. He never meant any discourtesy to Parliament. He added:

"My one aim was to focus attention on what I considered to be an injustice . . . in my judgment these allowances were a proper—and indeed inescapable—subject of comment in a free Press. That was the view which I held then and hold now, Sir."

When is an apology not an apology? The House concurred that no further action was necessary, though few M.P.s noticed that in saluting the dignity of Parliament he had asserted the freedom of the Press without retreating an inch. It was a worthy battle fought and won in a hostile anti-Press atmosphere.

8

HAROLD MACMILLAN

January 1957—October 1963

"If it hadn't been for the war Macmillan would have joined the Labour Party. Approaches and talks were going on. . . . I approved. If that had happened d'ye know the state of play? Macmillan would have been Labour's Prime Minister—and not me." CLEMENT ATTLEE

Harold Macmillan was the first person to recognise that in the modern world of constant media exposure a Prime Minister has to be something of a showman, equally at home in the theatre spotlight or the sawdust of the circus ring. He was the man to match the mood of the times—a brilliant communicator, a sophisticated performer, an actor-manager with an instinct for productions with appeal for all.

Like all good actors he made everything seem so easy, an amiable stroll through the corridors of power. But his real work was all behind the scenes where he was a shrewd, tough and cunning manipulator of Government, Party, Parliament and Press. It was not for nothing that he had the longest uninterrupted tenancy of No. 10 on record—even though, in accord with immutable law, it ended in panic and squalor.

I have no hesitation in placing him second only to Baldwin as the country's most successful and impressive peace-time Prime Minister. He pulled off an astonishing nap hand of major achievements. He rescued the Conservative Party and Government from the complete disintegration which seemed certain after the humiliation and splits of Suez in 1957 and followed up, two years later, with a general election majority of one hundred. He presided over the birth of Britain's new affluent society—"You've never had it so good" later became a mockery, but at the time he used the phrase as a warning. He restored Britain's world status by re-establishing the Anglo-American partnership so gravely ruptured by Suez. Despite the sharp opposition of America and West Germany he thawed the cold war by creating a new *détente* with Russia—the last occasion we are likely to see a Prime Minister undertake an independent British initiative on the old world scale. Agreement of the Nuclear Test Ban Treaty was exclusively due to Macmillan's personal drive, as President Kennedy publicly affirmed. Although he had known the Empire at its peak, he directed Britain's "Last Post" retreat from Imperial power, especially showing courage over the "wind of change" in Africa. And he set the stage for Britain's new destiny in Europe.

All these achievements, except the first, represented major policy changes which the traditional Conservative Party would not have approved in advance—if only they had known where Macmillan was leading them. His skill lay in the fact that he appeared to be charting to the Right whilst in reality he was steering hard to the Left. The truth of the matter is—and to appreciate the Macmillan Age it is essential to recognise the fact—that he was the most un-conservative Conservative of all time. As M.P. for Stockton in the 'thirties he had, after all, resigned the Tory Whip in protest at the Party's reactionary policies. Yet after the Suez debacle the Conservatives chose him in preference to "Rab" Butler in the belief that they were getting a tough-muscled Right-winger. The Party might have had second thoughts, thus substantially altering post-war political history, had they known how close he had once been to becoming a Labour Prime Minister.

I am not letting my imagination run away with me. My evidence is a conversation between Prime Minister Attlee and Sir David Llewellyn, Tory M.P. for Cardiff, on a train journey from Cardiff to Paddington in 1951. It is deeply revealing of the inter-war Macmillan, the more so since Attlee is here to be found still talking about him—and at considerable length—over a decade later:

> Llewellyn: "Is Aneurin Bevan the greatest Left-winger you've known?"
>
> Attlee (sharply): "Good gracious no. Far from it."
>
> Llewellyn: "Who then?"
>
> Attlee: "By far the most radical man I've known in politics wasn't on the Labour side at all—Harold Macmillan."
>
> Llewellyn: "The Middle Way, his Stockton conscience, and all that?"
>
> Attlee: "Far beyond that. If it hadn't been for the war he'd have joined the Labour Party. Approaches and talks were going on. I was in at some. I knew what was going on. I approved. If that had happened, d'ye know the state of play? Macmillan would have been Labour's Prime Minister—and not me."

Llewellyn: "But that would have been a startling change, from Tory to Labour. Far more fundamental than Churchill, Gladstone and Joe Chamberlain crossing the floor."

Attlee: "Take it from me, but for the war, Macmillan would have made it, a natural progression in his case. He was a real Left-wing radical in his social, human and economic thinking."

Llewellyn: "Was he so disillusioned then with the Tories, and couldn't take them any longer?"

Attlee: "No doubt at all. His experiences of the depression, the hunger, the poverty, fathers on the dole, kids not getting food, changed Macmillan completely. That's why he was moving strongly towards joining us. Macmillan was the most radical fellow I've known. A great future still awaits him."

Before including that conversation in this volume I met Mr Macmillan at the Carlton Club to tell him what Attlee had said about his coming so close to being a Labour Prime Minister. After I had read over the exchanges he sat back, pondered for a few moments, and remarked: "That's very interesting, you know, very interesting indeed. It's a revealing flash-back to much that was happening in those terrible years." Yes, but was it an accurate reconstruction of what was happening, or on the point of happening? "Oh well, you know what it is for a man of eighty-two . . . one's memory is not so good when so much was going on in the world then." He then set off on one of those classic elliptical chats which tell more than they say; his sentences or thoughts broken off in mid-air with perfect timing once their meaning is clear: Ah, Attlee now, under-rated at the time, but coming into his own in history . . . a substantial Prime Minister. A man of honesty and character. He had always a warm regard for him. And Sir David Llewellyn? But of course, he remembered him well, a very impressive and successful Tory M.P. Very good indeed. Wasn't he a journalist and writer as well? But of course! And didn't he write a very good vignette of Aneurin Bevan? Yes, memory is still good, you see. What was it called again? *The Real Nye*. That's it, a good title, that*. Titles are always so important. Who published it again? The *Western Mail* was it? Mmphm. He thought for a moment it might have been on the Macmillan list. And so on.

Behind the studied tribute to Attlee and Llewellyn, each delivered with equal sincerity, the message was clear. How could two such eminent men talking about him as the centre of a conversation in a train travelling from Cardiff to Paddington all those years ago have got things wrong? He did not say so in as many words, but the

* Actually the title was *Nye: The Beloved Patrician*.

moral was crystal clear: Attlee was no romancer when it came to facts, Llewellyn was a man of great character, an experienced writer and journalist. There was no reason for Attlee to dream up such a picture of Macmillan; there was no reason why Llewellyn should put words into Attlee's mouth! Thus he browsed on in his easy chair, savouring the subtleties and political shadings of the Attlee story. Report the conversation in your book? Of course, who was he to question the testimony of Clem Attlee and the accuracy of David Llewellyn? As ever, the delivery was perfect. And he doubtless savoured the irony of my reading Attlee's view of his socialistic radicalism in the Carlton, the mandarins of which seriously debated in the 'thirties expelling him as an undesirable.

Macmillan's public panache—the more remarkable since he was shy to the point of sickness before big occasions—is testimony to the value of highly professional public relations behind the scenes. In this crucial sector of power Macmillan avoided the errors committed by so many other Prime Ministers. He did not ask for any of the very able Information and Press Officers who had served him at his major Ministries: Treasury, Foreign Officers, Defence, Housing and Local Government. To do so would identify a career civil servant too closely with a particular Minister. He did not ask the Tory Central Office to provide him with a Press Secretary from the Party. He did not seek to bring in a friend from publishing, advertising or the media. Instead, he asked the Head of the Civil Service to find him the best man in the public service. At the same time Dr Charles Hill (later Lord Hill), Cabinet Minister co-ordinating information services, conducted his own survey of Westminster and Fleet Street opinion. They recommended Harold Evans (later Sir Harold Evans, Bart.), then in the Colonial Office, and he proved the most outstanding No. 10 spokesman in my long experience. He understood better than most what power at the top is all about: he never attempted hard or soft sells and always avoided becoming involved even remotely with Party politics. The subtle lesson of the Evans success is that you do not create the newspaper myths—in his case Supermac, MacWonder, etc.—you create the situations which inspire Fleet Street to invent them themselves!

One innovation of the Macmillan–Evans era was the on-the-record interviews, now commonplace but then unheard-of. I can claim a modest place in this development in open government for it was I who first submitted the idea of a personal interview. The Prime Minister, on Evans's recommendation, agreed to the innovation and it proved highly important and successful for all concerned. Macmillan told me, for the record, that the future of the world depended on breaking down the barriers between East and West.

The *Sunday Times* published his words and within forty-eight hours of the interview came a response from the Kremlin: an invitation to visit Moscow. The result was *détente*, an easing of the Cold War tensions for the first time since the war.

What is even more illuminating, however, is the typical top-level Civil Service resistance to the motion that Prime Ministers and other leaders should share their thoughts and forward thinking with the Media. When the details for my interview were being arranged Sir Norman Brook, Secretary of the Cabinet, minuted serious misgivings. He was worried about the constitutional proprieties. What would be the status of the interview? To what extent could it commit the Government on policy? A speech outside the House of Commons by the Prime Minister had its due place in the order of things, copies if necessary could be placed in the Commons library. But an interview! This was a novel device in Government and Whitehall for which no precedent could be discovered. There would be no draft, nothing on the official record, nothing to be circulated to other Departments for information and guidance. James Margach might not report accurately, or fully; there might be vital omissions unknown to the Prime Minister. The rumpus was so great that the interview was delayed for a few days until the machine could catch up. But Macmillan was not to be discouraged—and the interview went ahead as envisaged. (Might I say here that I am sorry that any wanton initiative of mine should have involuntarily led to a problem for editors and political correspondents—the problem of knowing how to decline with thanks countless pressing Whitehall suggestions that the Prime Minister of the day would consider granting a special interview! The courting of television, particularly, appears to increase in ratio to the decline of the popularity graphs.)

Macmillan's style in handling interviews was unique. Other Premiers and leaders usually sat immobile in their chairs in the Cabinet room or in their studies, in the set formula of question-and-answer sessions. But Supermac found he could think aloud for the record only if he kept moving. On the first occasion he began by sitting beside me, then suddenly he got up and walked around the Cabinet room, drawing a curtain here, moving a chair there, bending down to turn on a little electric fire, re-arranging a pile of notepaper at the far end of the Cabinet table, putting a quill pen back on its proper desk. And as he walked he kept his conversation going without a pause or diversion; perfect continuity. Not a word or a shade of meaning had to be changed even in the minutest detail.

His fluency and fast footwork were of enormous help at moments of crisis. The Macmillan touch is perfectly illustrated by a hitherto untold story of the 1962 Commonwealth conference in London which gave its blessing, albeit without too much enthusiasm, to his application to join Europe. John Diefenbaker, Canada's Prime Minister, arrived making fiery noises about the great Imperial mission being betrayed. Halfway through the conference the papers carried detailed reports that the Commonwealth was on the point of backing Britain's EEC application, despite the "negative attitude" of the Canadian leader. Diefenbaker exploded over breakfast and demanded an interview with the Prime Minister and protested against the unauthorised leaks and guidance which so patently had been given by Whitehall. This evoked vintage Macmillan. Leaks? In the papers? Incredible! Actually, he added soothingly to Diefenbaker, he never looked at the papers—and advised Diefenbaker to do the same. Then, as a languid afterthought, he confessed that this was not quite true—he did look at one paper, the *Daily Mail*, to see what Flook was up to. "Flook?" said Diefenbaker, "Flook; never heard of him. Is he their political writer, commentator?" No, No, nothing like that. Flook was a strip cartoon character. Never missed him. Actually it wasn't only for pleasure. Business came into it too, he might just as well confess, because his family publishing firm issued the book of the Flook strips. But Flook, apart, he paid no attention to the papers. It saved a great deal of unnecessary worry. Diefenbaker should do the same!

That gives the true flavour of Macmillan's instinctive ability to defuse a highly tense situation; any other approach could only have provoked yet more tension and recrimination. Macmillan, of course, knew full well that the accurate briefings had been given, as always, by Evans. But behind his play-acting, as I can testify at first hand, Macmillan was more genuinely worried and nervous over the need to carry the "old Empire" with him in his advance into Europe than about anything else.

Peel and Baldwin both judged that five years as a Prime Minister was about the maximum for effective leadership and Government. The Macmillan era supports this thesis to the full. He had a remarkably long honeymoon with the country, the Party and the Press but after rather more than five years of sweeping successes the rot set in. After the glory came the sadness; after the bouquets, the brickbats.

Over the final couple of years Macmillan was overwhelmed by political and economic crises which led to his panic sacking of seven members of his own Cabinet in 1962. The purge really marked the start of his final decline, because it was followed by the Vassall and Profumo scandals which gravely injured the character, standing and credibility of his Government. The Tories' hopes of new continental frontiers for post-Imperial Britain were also destroyed when General de Gaulle vetoed Britain's entry in January 1963. Suddenly, the Supermac image lay in pieces. In all my experience I have never seen a really great Prime Minister plummet from the exhilarating peaks to the depressing valleys with such speed. And, as always, the power battle between Downing Street and Fleet Street became squalid and intemperate on both sides.

The first setback came on the economic front. When, inevitably, the "You've never had it so good" prosperity was overtaken by price and wage inflation, leading to unemployment, tough deflation and hardship, Macmillan was the target of an intolerant campaign. Harold Wilson accused him of presiding over a "candy-floss society". He was blamed for a dissipated free-spending society. The evidence was lovingly recited: premium bonds; betting shops and bingo halls in every town and village; enormous hire-purchase debts as the people went on a never-never spree (stimulated, of course, by the advertising wizards who certainly had never had it so good) with as much prosperity; the spread of pornography under the more liberal obscenity laws; the lifting of film and theatre censorship.

Macmillan paid a heavy price for "setting the people free". Yet he had no regrets, I remember him, in defiance, saying to me: "I'm *not* ashamed of 'having it so good'. The temptations of comfort and affluence are not an argument in favour of poverty. Our purpose should be to keep it good and make it better. The people who object most violently to the new affluence being shared by the mass of working people are those who are doing exceptionally well out of the new capitalism through fat expense accounts, expensive meals and other perks on the company's account". I always found him very angry with the "superior" people who accused him of spreading the joys of affluence too widely. He was determined not to be stampeded to a return to the mass unemployment and hard times which he had known at Stockton. "The expansionist is the optimist" was his theme whenever I saw him "because he believes in the future. The deflationist is the pessimist because he fears the future."

But the skids were under him. In July 1962 after a run of disastrous by-elections, the unflappable Supreme lost his cool. On Friday the thirteenth he sacked seven Cabinet Ministers, many of them his oldest friends, in the "night of the long knives". Things were never the same again for Macmillan. I have never seen a Party so pole-axed by shock as when the massacre was announced. The reaction was captured in the sardonic wit of arch-critic Nigel Birch (late Lord Rhyl) when he congratulated the Prime Minister on keeping his head when all about him were losing theirs! Even so,

Macmillan might have recovered from the effects of the butchery had he not been overtaken by the Vassall (later in 1962) and Profumo (in May 1963) scandals. It was a disreputable period from which both the Press and the Prime Minister emerged with their reputations disfigured.

Vassall was an Admiralty clerk sentenced to prison for acting as a spy for Russia. His trial was followed by sensational newspaper allegations that other top people were involved, principal among them being Lord Carrington, Defence Secretary, and Tom Galbraith, Under-Secretary at the Admiralty. They were pursued in some papers by a campaign full of innuendo and smear, made worse when private letters between Galbraith and Vassall (who had been his private secretary) were given a sinister meaning when published. As the campaign reached fever pitch Galbraith felt compelled to offer his resignation, and this Macmillan accepted. It was his biggest mistake for it made a public exhibition of his loss of nerve and lack of loyalty (and as Viscount Kilmuir, later axed as Lord Chancellor by Macmillan, always claimed: loyalty was the Tories' secret weapon.) It seemed to the Tories as though Galbraith was being offered as a blood sacrifice to assuage the gods of Fleet Street. But the gods were not appeased. Having hounded Galbraith without mercy or responsibility, the papers then switched their attacks to Carrington, as though the big fish had escaped while the small fry had been hooked.

Exceptional anger prevailed on both sides. I remember one incident in particular at a meeting between the Prime Minister and a group of political correspondents. Macmillan, sitting at the top table beside the Lobby chairman, waiting for late arrivals, suddenly identified a correspondent from a Sunday paper. Instantly he exploded: "What do you mean," he demanded, "by writing such nonsense last weekend? You ought to be ashamed of yourself. You are a disgrace to the profession . . . lies, lies, falsehoods." The outburst continued for several minutes, stunning the meeting. The journalist concerned reacted quietly and with impressive dignity, refusing to be provoked into a public brawl with the Prime Minister and the experienced chairman rescued the situation by calmly intervening at a pause in Macmillan's tirade: "May we now proceed to ask some questions of the Prime Minister? First . . ." Thanks to the calming influence of Sir Harold Evans and Spencer Shew, representing the Press, nothing further was heard of this highly temperamental fracas, and good relations were resumed at once. But it shows how the best nerves can snap.

Finally, in November 1962, Macmillan felt compelled to set up an inquiry into the Vassall affair under the chairmanship of Lord

Radcliffe. Their report, published the following April, completely exonerated Carrington and Galbraith, who was deservedly reinstated. But it was devastating for the Press. Radcliffe reported that he and his colleagues had examined in the greatest detail over 250 separate newspaper reports. The humiliating verdict was that not a single one of them could be justified, even after all editors, news executives and reporters had been given every opportunity and offered the protection of privilege to justify their allegations. Radcliffe offered wholesale and detailed condemnation of the stories: they were pure fiction. No wonder that the whole of Fleet Street was stunned, demoralised and exposed. When two reporters were sent to prison for refusing to tell the Tribunal the source of some reports about Galbraith, feeble protests about the "freedom of the Press" fell on extremely stony ground. Frankly, the Press had plumbed disgraceful depths of irresponsible character assassination in circulating the most sordid and totally false reports about Galbraith and others—made worse by snide but nameless smears about "big names" being involved in a huge cover-up.

After the Radcliffe exposure Parliament and public opinion treated the Press with contempt. The moral universally drawn was simple: editors and journalists who clamour most about the "freedom of the Press" are often the first to abuse it. Macmillan himself made no attempt to conceal his disgust about the newspapers' conduct and the way in which proprietors, editors and working journalists had demeaned themselves and an honourable profession. The experience led to a strengthening of the powers of the Press Council and a reform of its procedures and composition as well as changes in the seamy practice of cheque-book journalism.

But there was an ironic twist to the Vassall affair: it appeared to give the Prime Minister a false sense of security. When the much more compulsive Profumo scandal burst on the national scene, he believed that the newspapers were once more engaged merely on an irresponsible campaign to denigrate Ministers and other public figures—and at the same time to wipe off the old Radcliffe score. It was to prove a grievous miscalculation.

The crisis centred on John Profumo, War Secretary, around whom rumours were circulating that he had had an affair with Christine Keeler, a prostitute who simultaneously had a regular liaison with the naval attache at the Russian Embassy, thus clearly involving a security risk. At first Profumo denied the rumours in the House of Commons. But when the paper printed his love-letters to Keeler, with, in particular, a "Darling" letter signed by the Ministerial recipient of her favours, he was in a hopeless situation

—not because of his morals but because he had told a deliberate lie. He resigned. But events did not stop there. Various names prominent in the public eye were bandied about, and the Parliament–Press agitation reached such intensity, with widespread innuendo, that Macmillan set up yet another judicial inquiry into the whole affair, this time by Lord Denning, Master of the Rolls. His investigation proved disastrous for Macmillan and his Government, who were condemned for mishandling the case: "It was the responsibility of the Prime Minister and his colleagues, and of them only, to deal with this situation: and they did not succeed in doing so."

I cannot recall such a period of intensive breast-beating over morality in public and private life as that which followed the Vassall and Profumo controversies. A spasm of conscience rapidly engulfed politics and, indeed, all forms of national life. Most people joined enthusiastically in a campaign denigrating Britain as a sick society. Inevitably this soul-searching and the epidemic of high morality cut the ground even further from underneath Macmillan's expansionist economic policies. He was held responsible for creating the avaricious, acquisitive, bingo-and-betting society. Against such an unexpected upsurge of self-righteousness he could not win and the Tories clamoured to sacrifice him in time for the next general election, due not later than the autumn of 1964. But they could not agree on any successor. Macmillan's own design was to announce, at the October 1963 Tory Party conference in Blackpool, that he would lead the Party into the 1964 election and then retire within eighteen months once a new leader had been chosen. However, this plan was destroyed by his sudden prostate operation. He decided to resign and there ensued rancorous public brawling over the successor. Lord Poole, Party Chairman, confided in me: "If only Harold had held on, given himself time to recover from the operation and returned to even partial fitness, I'm certain he would have won the 1964 election—and even if I had had to arrange a limited touring campaign for him on a pair of crutches!"

He went out, as he came in, amidst blazing controversies about the leadership—but this time he was unable to prevent his Party from tearing itself to pieces. As he surveyed the wreckage of Blackpool he doubtless echoed his own words: "Power? It's like a dead sea fruit. When you achieve it, there's nothing there!" But in the struggle between Downing Street and Fleet Street which clouded his final couple of years, he probably derived wry satisfaction from the fact that even if the scandals over Vassall and

Profumo hastened his own departure, he had succeeded in compelling the Press to clean up its own stables.

At least the Vassall and Profumo affairs were power battles which took place in the open, others did not. And probably the most sinister of these, because it struck at the very heart of the freedom of the Press, was a political hatchet job which challenged the professional integrity of one of Westminster's outstanding journalists. The details demand to go on record as a permanent warning to Prime Ministers, Governments and political parties on the one hand, and proprietors, editors and working journalists on the other, about the dangers which develop when politicians expect, and then demand, that journalists should become their allies.

When the days of Macmillan's Premiership were clearly numbered there was widespread speculation as to how long he could survive at No. 10, whether he would go voluntarily or be overtaken in a Party putsch. Inside the Conservative Party at Westminster, the tide against Macmillan ran with menacing force, the more ominous because it was manipulated in secret. However, David Wood, then political correspondent of *The Times*, proved exceptionally well-informed about every move inside the Parliamentary Party. In particular, he regularly reported in great detail all that was being said, demanded and plotted, not merely by talkative Tories in the lobbies—they seldom count for much—and at official group meetings of the 1922 Committee, which comprises all Tory M.P.s, but, most important of all, he discussed every refinement and shading of opinion inside the 1922 Executive itself. The eighteen or so elected members of the Executive are the true centre of the Party at Westminster, assembling before the full 1922 meetings to decide business, attitudes and the running order. It is through these Cardinals that real power is exercised. They determine what the Party in the mass will decide, what the next moves will be, and how each card will be played. When the Executive sneezes, the Party leader catches pneumonia. Wood was thus able to trace the sensitive clinical graph of Macmillan's high temperature.

The Executive decided they could stand Wood's detailed and only-too-accurate relevations no longer. There was a traitor in their midst, but his identity could not be established and as each and every one came under suspicion, mutual trust broke down. To re-establish unity and authority the inner guard decided that *The Times* must be told that its political correspondent was no gentleman, indeed a bounder, sir, who was doing great disservice to the Party. He was, too, inflicting a grave injury on the national interest by such splendid journalistic enterprise which, alas, they regarded as disloyalty. In effect, they wanted Wood cashiered, reduced to the ranks, expelled from the regiment in dishonour. In short, withdrawn from the Lobby and a successor appointed, who would prove more acceptable to the Party's establishment and more understanding of the Party's anxieties over the leadership.

In the best military tradition, they decided that before any frontal assault could be undertaken it was desirable to conduct a reconnaissance and this was entrusted to Colonel John Morrison (later Lord Margadale), the 1922 Committee chairman. Altogether he held three meetings with Wood. The first was all very friendly; Morrison said he did not mind leaks from the full meetings of the 1922 Committee so much as from the Executive. Wood advised him to speak, if he desired, to Sir William Haley, editor of *The Times*, and if he agreed with him—highly unlikely indeed!—then *The Times* would not print the reports. Morrison nodded, but indicated that he was no great admirer of the editor and could not bring himself to speak to him. The second meeting was tougher. The third was acerbic to the point of confrontation. Morrison threatened Wood that he would get him on breach of privilege, apparently having in mind the Gerry Allighan case (which is fully covered in Chapter 6). Wood replied that Morrison was mistaken if he imagined that the political correspondent of *The Times* would ever dream of bribing M.P.s for information.

Having failed to make any dent in Wood's defences, the Executive decided to go to the very top and sought a meeting with Gavin Astor, then the chief proprietor of *The Times*. The party was headed by Morrison and principally included knights and baronets from the rolling shires, men admired by Wood himself for their gallantry, integrity and devotion to standards in public life. Their message to Astor was clear and emphatic. David Wood was *persona non grata*. They had lost confidence in him. Far from showing in his reports sympathy and understanding of the difficulties confronting Party, Prime Minister and Government, he was actually breaching and publishing the Party's most sacred secrets. It was most unfriendly of him. The ambassador had been discovered spying on the country to which he was accredited and the preservation of good relations required him to be recalled.

Astor was placed in a position of great embarrassment. Brought up in the great tradition of *The Times* he had other opinions about the issues raised. However, he explained courteously that these were, of course, a matter for the editor and that he would report to him. In due course Sir William Haley reacted in a manner worthy of his model and Victorian predecessor Delane. This was, he said, an attack not on the paper's political correspondent but on himself as editor. He was constitutionally and editorially responsible for everything that appeared in *The Times*; everything that Wood had written for the paper had his wholehearted authority and approval, and would not have appeared otherwise. Wood enjoyed his complete and unqualified confidence. There was only one way in which honour and editorial integrity could be satisfied: *he* demanded an apology for this grave affront. Sir William received an apology.

By this time the Conservatives at Westminster were in a highly-strung state, many of them displaying signs of nervous breakdown and exhaustion. It was not only Wood who was seen as unfriendly. Derek Marks, then political correspondent of the *Daily Express* and one of Westminster's really great journalists—he became editor before his early death—was also exceptionally well informed about the plots and counter-plots in the 1922 Committee. His reports proved to be so textually accurate, quoting in first person what various M.P.s had said, that a few Tories formed themselves into a counter-espionage group to discover his sources and name the guilty Members as quislings. The group was initially convinced that Marks must be aided by concealed microphones and so one of the M.P.s, who was connected with one of the large technological groups, brought in a top professional to test the Commons Committee room for bugging devices. He drew a blank. One imaginative and over-excited M.P. even suggested that a check should be made in the private wards of St Thomas's Hospital across the Thames in order to see whether any window was available from which an experienced lip-reader, with racing glasses, might observe the conclave! This, too, was to no avail. The final zero followed a check on suspect M.P.s, who might have been using miniature recorders or even transmitters.

Leaks from Labour Party meetings added, of course, to the gaiety of nations. Leaks from the Conservative Party meant betrayal and espionage by alien forces hostile to the national interest. But the sources of David Wood, Derek Marks and other newspapermen remained secret. They made their contribution to the worthy ideal of open government, robust debate within the parties and a well-informed public opinion. As the incomparable Delane said: "Newspapers live by disclosure".

9

SIR ALEC DOUGLAS-HOME

October 1963—October 1964

"They must find someone else.... Even if they can't agree on Rab or Quintin there must be someone else. But please, please not me!" SIR ALEC DOUGLAS-HOME

Sir Alec Douglas-Home was the Prime Minister who was never given a chance. He had the shortest run this century as Premier and Party leader yet in only a year at No. 10 he was responsible for two major achievements. First, in a few short months, he transformed the Tories from a feuding, demoralised and disintegrating party facing electoral massacre, into a party with restored morale—so much so that instead of being engulfed by a Labour landslide they were only just pipped at the post. His second achievement was to restore dignity and honesty to public life after a series of sleazy scandals. At a time when so few public figures enjoyed respect or trust he stood out as a leader of probity. In the standards of conduct which he set for himself and others I have no hesitation in saying that he excelled all the Prime Ministers I have known. Yet his Tory critics never gave him due credit for his double rescue operation and, when the moon was high, he was offered up as a political sacrifice from motives compounded of fear, cynicism and self-interest.

Douglas-Home was unique. He will be seen by history as the last of the lost generation of gentlemen amateurs in an age dedicated to the worship of professional players. He never sought power, pursued power or had ambitions for power.

I recall going to see him privately during the frenzied Party conference at Blackpool after Macmillan had announced his resignation. I told him that I had done my home-work on form and that, in the racing terms which he savoured, the pace-setters were collapsing through lack of stamina; that Rab Butler could never make it because there were too many against him in the Parliamentary Party, the constituencies, the organisation and the regions; and that Lord Hailsham had blown all the fuses through overloading his campaign with histrionics. All my information and researchers confirmed that there would be a mass popular draft for him. In all my life, dealing with many ambitious politicians, I have never seen anyone so aghast at the prospect of power. Where all other heirs, some more presumptive than apparent, had been anxious to discover how their bandwagons were rolling, he thought the prospect personally appalling. "Oh, they must find someone else, once they get away from this Blackpool hot-house. Even if they can't agree on Rab or Quintin there must be someone else. But please, please not me!" I like to think that I can identify sincerity, and I remain completely convinced that Home's reluctance was sincere, not a cover for cunning ambition.

But it was no good. The Foreign Secretary and fourteenth Earl of Home had the Premiership thrust upon him. He cantered home in the most elegant style imaginable by never trying. He renounced his peerage, fought a by-election to become an M.P. and took office.

"If I have one regret", he said to me once, "it is that I never took any steps to prepare myself for the Premiership. I never dreamed it could happen to me." He reached the top of the greasy pole never having studied the techniques of government, Press and public relations, how to get on with the media. As for courting proprietors, editors, opinion-formers, political writers, he was simply not interested and left that side of the business to those professional politicians who were obsessed with power and the need to kow-tow to or exploit the media to advance their ambitions. Charisma, the image, the profile, packaging and selling personality for the headlines or the small screen, were simply the vogue words of the hucksters. "I prefer," he said, "my politicians in the flesh to their bloodless image."

He was the despair of the Downing Street and Central Office experts who suddenly became responsible for projecting him on the national scene. He was totally unconcerned about how he appeared or what he said, so long as he remained himself. But ill-considered words are dangerous. Most Prime Ministers have slipped up in their time and a casual phrase has dogged them for years if not for ever. Asquith's was "Wait and see", Lloyd George's "A land fit for heroes", Baldwin's "Safety first", Chamberlain's "Hitler has missed the bus", Churchill's was his "Gestapo" smear, Macmillan's, of course, "You've never had it so good". With Douglas-Home it was "Matchsticks". When asked in an *Observer* interview with Kenneth Harris whether he could ever become Prime Minister he replied that it was unlikely because the only way he could get his sums right was by using matchsticks. When he actually became Premier his political and Press critics capitalised on this mercilessly, portraying him as a blue-blooded economic simpleton—far removed, by implication, from the white-hot technology of the celebrated Wilson slide rule.

But he did learn a few tricks—and quickly. My first on-the-record interview with him was on the plane from Heathrow to Edinburgh for the start of his by-election campaign in Perth and Kinross. He proved so natural in his reactions that he would comment: "That's a nasty one"; "Oh, what's the answer to your query? There must be one, I'm sure"; "That's a teasing one which I know I should hit for six", and so on, oblivious of the fact that every word was going on tape. A couple of months later I had another interview with him in London, again on tape. This time instead of commenting on how difficult or deceptive any question might be, he would lean over and stop the recorder for a few seconds until he had considered the most telling reply. Then, with a smile, he would switch on the tape once more and start his answer.

He would have made life easier for the projectors of personality if only he had allowed them to bring his family and grandchildren before the cameras. His flat on the twelfth floor of a modern block off Victoria was the perfect setting for putting across the picture of the Prime Minister at home. I have seen play-pens and toys scattered across the room with the grandchildren crawling noisily around under the eye of Lady Douglas-Home, while grandfather got on with his job of reading and marking official documents.

He was equally unconventional when it came to speeches. Harold Wilson used to boast that he did not require speech writers to help him communicate with mass meetings (though after his peak he required considerable assistance in drafting entire speeches), the inference being that his adversary was but the dummy in a ventriloquist act. Certainly, Douglas-Home was assisted by two experienced journalists and politicians, Nigel Lawson and Eldon Griffiths, but this did not mean that they wrote his speeches for him. The fact was that he read fewer speeches than did Wilson—the latter, without a detailed script, was not good at impromptu performances, becoming wordy and repetitive. Churchill had established a pattern, followed by Eden and Macmillan, in which prepared briefs were set out in what the old Downing Street hands identified as the psalm-style—with lines slanted to make it easier for the eyes to pick up the crucial sentences. But largely because he was a bad reader, Douglas-Home always tried to avoid being so tethered, preferring his naturally relaxed free-ranging style. So when presented with the final speech, including the main lines on which he had thought aloud to his aides over the previous days, he would scribble the principal points, cablese-style, on two or three sheets of notepaper with key sentences underlined and with facts, figures and linking passages noted. The resulting spontaneity enabled him to develop a more intimate rapport with his audience, allowing his integrity and honesty to come through.

"Honest to the point of simplicity," jeered the cynics of Bonar Law fifty years earlier when comparing him with the clever manoeuvrers of the day. "By God, that's the type of man we've been looking for," responded the country to the appeal of simple, straight honesty, and rallied to Law as Prime Minister and party leader. It was very nearly the same for Douglas-Home but he ran out of two indispensable commodities: loyalty and time.

If only he had had two or three extra weeks I remain convinced that he would have snatched victory at the 1964 general election, instead of losing by four seats. As the results came in it was clear that Sir Alec had led the Tories from a hopeless position to a photo-finish and on the Friday morning, as the later results were being announced, even the super-optimist Harold Wilson was on the brink of conceding defeat. He confided: "It's no good, we shan't make it. I've checked with the slide-rule. We've lost the election to Alec by one seat." Perhaps he should have tried matchsticks!

As for loyalty, the Tories' secret weapon, it was in short supply. The decision by Ian Macleod and Enoch Powell not to serve in the Douglas-Home Government poses one of the great political "Ifs" of the 'sixties and 'seventies. Their decision spread confusion, disunity and depression among the mass of Tory supporters, hardly the recipe for inspiring the troops for an uphill election battle only months later. Reconciliation was not made easier when Iain Macleod, then editor of the *Spectator* weekly, wrote an article protesting violently against the machinations of the "magic circle" in deciding for Home rather than Butler. For good measure he stirred the pot with the view that Macmillan had deliberately stayed on longer than necessary in order to destroy Butler's prospects. Curiously, despite the fact that Macleod was joint Party chairman he felt very much an outsider looking in. He was so much out of touch that on the very night when the Home succession was certain he was still advising the correspondents of *The Times* and *Daily Telegraph* that Butler was the favourite—a misreading which forced the two papers to make embarrassing somersaults at midnight when it was clear that Home was romping home. For Powell this was the second in what was to become a series of occasions on which he showed fastidiousness in choosing the leader he was prepared to serve; he resigned from the Macmillan Government, refused to serve in Douglas-Home's, denounced Edward Heath's, provided an election bonus to Harold Wilson in urging the country to vote Labour and came full circle by deriding Margaret Thatcher. Sir Alec's final burden was Fleet Street. The papers enthusiastically joined the Macleod–Powell school of dissension and indulged in a running attack on the grouse-moor image, the faceless peer, the anachronistic aristocrat out of touch with the thrusting brave new world.

In the teeth of such Press and Party opposition, and with desperately little time, it was a magnificent election performance by Sir Alec. But what finally tipped the delicately poised scales against him was Edward Heath's Bill to abolish Retail Price Maintenance. Heath insisted that it should be pushed through in order to make firms and industries more competitive even though its threat to small traders was having a disruptive effect on both the Party and its M.P.s. It is worth recalling that fifty-six Tories voted against the Government—an extraordinary grass-roots rebellion at a time when Douglas-Home was preparing to press the election button—and many more M.P.s were protesting to the Whips. But the Bill became law and at the polls bitter resentment provoked a Poujadist-style revolt among the nation of shopkeepers, traditionally Conservative supporters. It cost the Party several marginal seats by a handful of votes.

But there is more to this than arithmetic. RPM was specifically significant for the Party's future leadership pattern. Inside the Cabinet there was strong opposition to Heath's Bill and in favour of alternative remedies. But Heath would not allow any tinkering with his masterpiece. Despite the obvious split his scheme was causing Heath remained adamant: it had to be his Bill, his whole Bill, and nothing but his Bill. Since it could only lose votes it was to widespread surprise that Douglas-Home sided with Heath to push the Bill through Cabinet and Parliament. The reason for his apparently suicidal action—and it has since remained a tightly guarded secret within the "magic circle"—is that he had no option; Heath had put a pistol to his head. He threatened that if he did not get his Bill through intact he would resign from the Government. Douglas-Home was in a vulnerable position. Macleod and Powell had already refused to join his Cabinet; if Heath walked out, too, only a few months before an election, the Tories would be more demoralised than ever and the Prime Minister even more on the defensive. He could do no other, he confided to me years later, but go along with Heath's diktat and influence several doubting Ministers to accept the controversial Bill.

This disclosure actually tells more about Heath than about Douglas-Home. Despite solemn warning that the RPM measure would cost the Government a number of vital seats, he was not prepared to compromise. For Ministers round the Cabinet table it was their first indication that he was so authoritarian, a man determined to get his own way irrespective of warnings about the injury being done to Party and Government interests. This insensitivity to the subtler shading of pre-election politics was evidenced once again a decade later when he landed himself with a miners' dispute as the issue for another election. The RPM Bill was really his first taste of power in a showdown with his Prime Minister and Cabinet colleagues—and in the process it set the scene for Douglas-Home's surrender of leadership the following year.

Sir Alec announced his resignation on 22 July 1965. The carefully nurtured Party myth suggests that he sacrificed himself voluntarily, greatly to the dismay of the high priests and elders who claimed that they were dedicated and tireless in their zeal to avoid the sickening sight of immolation on the high altar. But the myth conceals the true story. I am not in the slightest doubt that he was told he had to go, as befitted a man of honour and a gentleman, with a pat on the shoulder and a watery eye to soften the reality of the push; that the interests of the Party demanded that he should go quietly and with dignity, without any raucous squabbles about power. There is a clue hidden in his resignation statement: "I would never allow disunity in the Party, least of all over myself."

Politics at the top—especially at the top of the Tory Party—is a cruel, even merciless, business. The Party's doctrine that it is best to be off with the old and on with the new had paid handsome dividends: three general elections had been won by three new leaders. Douglas-Home failed to make it four in a row. He had to go. But why did he have to go so soon? There is no doubt in my mind that the Party panicked. The fact was self-evident that Harold Wilson, then at the peak of his tactical flair and struggling with knife-edge majorities varying between one and four, would seize the first opportunity to hold a quick election, pleading for a new mandate. Douglas-Home was prepared to soldier on, endure a second defeat at an early election and then bow out gracefully, having prepared a more democratic system for electing his successor. (And with hindsight it is obvious that the interests of that successor, Edward Heath, would have been better served if the Party had allowed Douglas-Home to be on the receiving end of Wilson's 1966 election victory. Heath could then have led the Party as a great white hope rather than as an instant loser.) But the Party was in no mood to tarry.

Apart from fear of Wilson's razor-sharp tactical brain two other factors encouraged haste over Douglas-Home's departure: a formidable combination of virulent Press criticism and poor opinion poll findings, each feeding on the other, and intrigues by the abrasive young men who supported Heath. (Heath was not himself an active campaigner but it was only he who could have called off the pack.) Douglas-Home was the first Prime Minister to be toppled as a result of the influence of opinion polls yet it is an aspect of his departure which has never to my knowledge been discussed. Sir Alec himself was always puzzled by the polls and by the attention paid to them by the Press, the public and the Party professionals. In addition to the voting intentions he was fascinated by the public's views of leading politicians built up into character profiles through subsidiary questions. How was it done? Did the figures and inferences justify the sanctity of holy writ? To enlighten him, Sir Neill Cooper-Key, Tory M.P. for Hastings, arranged for him to make a private and unreported visit to the offices of National Opinion Polls (controlled by Cooper-Key's father-in-law Lord Rothermere) at a time when several thousands cards were due to be processed, analysed and fed through the computers to produce the latest poll findings. The Conservative leader was duly impressed by the speed and complexity of the operation and the main discovery of the poll, that Labour's lead was trimmed from 5.3 per cent to 4.6 per cent, brought him encouragement. While Douglas-Home was studying the breakdown of the figures into regions, age groups, classes and so forth, a well-intentioned analyst approached the official party with a processed card and asked if Sir Alec would care to see the latest character profiles. Cooper-Key glanced quickly at the tables, realised the appalling effect the figures would have on his leader, and murmured: "No, no. Sir Alec hasn't the time to be troubled with details at the moment." "Oh yes he has," interjected Sir Alec. "Let me see them. What do they say?" The card set out, as follows, the ratings of Sir Alec and Harold Wilson based on percentage responses. The analysis was never published.

	Wilson	Douglas-Home
Tough	62	29
Sincere	74	67
Straight	75	57
Very intelligent	82	81
Sound judgment	59	52
In touch with people	67	28
Very capable	72	57
Pleasant	57	27

Sir Alec was incredulous. Wilson the more sincere, straight, intelligent and pleasant! His reaction was to smile, shake his head unbelievingly, and mutter something about "If people believe that they'll believe anything". But that night he travelled to his home in the Borders with his mind disposed, for the first time, to consider resignation.

On the Sunday the papers were once more demanding that the time had come for a change. Otherwise how could young executives, university teachers, the pace-setters, modernists and entrepreneurs, be advised to vote Tory? And on the same day, several hundred miles away in London there was a big turn-out of Fleet Street proprietors and editors for the service celebrating the centenary of Northcliff's birth. By a coincidence too persistent to be disregarded, many of the Fleet Street leaders approached Cooper-Key and warned him that the Conservative Party had no future under Douglas-Home, and that an early change must be made so that the Party could romp home under an abrasive modern leader and thus rescue the country from otherwise inevitable disaster under Wilson. Cooper-Key, a supporter of the leader, told me that he considered he had been deliberately selected by the Fleet Street "mafia" to collect their voices. He therefore felt it was his responsibility to convey the opinions of the Press to William Whitelaw, then Chief Whip, and to Edward du Cann, the Party chairman.

Whitelaw himself had been collecting views among the back-bench Tories and considered it his duty to inform Sir Alec that there was a substantial tide of opinion at Westminster in favour of his resignation. Edward du Cann reported in similar vein from the organisation, placing special emphasis on the fact that opinion among supporters in the country was becoming very confused because of constant Press speculation about Sir Alec's being forced out. While du Cann personally wanted the leader to continue he was afraid that, if he did, morale would be dangerously low by the time the election came.

Lord Home has since confided in me that the factor which finally decided him to resign was du Cann's report on the introspective state of grass-roots Tories. He told me:

> The persistent campaign by a group of young inexperienced critics in the House of Commons did not worry me. Willie Whitelaw would have been able to sort them out very quickly, by demanding they stand up and be counted, and identify themselves. Of course we knew who they were. I was activated by the interests of the Conservative Party away from Westminster; that was the consideration which finally decided me

to go. Anyway, I was never very impressed by the Tweedledum and Tweedledum form of politics in the Commons. It didn't make sense to me to go bashing ahead against a Government's policies, which perhaps had much to commend them, simply for the sake of keeping back-benchers happy. That makes Opposition fractious and silly. Just because the Labour Government had a majority of only four or so my people wanted a helluva row all the time. That to my simple way of thinking doesn't make for a responsible alternative Government.

Could Douglas-Home have survived the intrigues of the Party's young pretenders and the persistent Fleet Street campaign? Certainly he could have launched a major campaign against the papers following the successful Baldwin precedent; and a Party leader more interested than him in clinging to power could easily, as he said, have smoked out his detractors in the Parliamentary Party. Moreover, when Sir Alec announced his new formula for democratising the election of future Tory leaders—by all M.P.s and bearing in mind the views of the constituencies—he was advised by his friends to offer himself for re-election. I am assured that Macmillan, too, strongly advised him to fight. Nobody of importance would have opposed him. Thus by a vigorous campaign, carrying the fight into Fleet Street and demanding that the Party critics show courage in public instead of intriguing in secret, he could have consolidated his leadership beyond challenge.

But such counter-attacks would have struck him as squalid manoeuvres, alien to his standards of conduct and straight dealing. And so, on 22 July 1965—only nine days after his fateful visit to the Opinion poll offices—Sir Alec became the last Tory leader to be deposed by the machinations of the "magic circle". He resigned with honour, unlike his successor who was constitutionally deposed by the Party's majority and was dragged screeching from his perch despite the support of the very newspapers which had been heavily committed to the removal of Douglas-Home. Though Lord Home denied any such reaction when I put it to him, I am sure that even a fourteenth earl may be permitted a certain wry satisfaction when, ten years later, he saw that the first heads to roll under the axe of Margaret Thatcher were those of the very men who had worked so assiduously for his eclipse.

Douglas-Home was not long enough at No. 10 to enable an accurate historical judgment of his performance to be attempted. He succeeded Macmillan in an atmosphere highly charged with electioneering and for almost the next twelve months spent much time touring the country rallying the Party. But it is possible to make some assessment of the man. I was struck, for instance, by the fact that senior Downing Street and Whitehall officials privately expressed to me great praise for his innate flair for the top job. Although he said that he regretted having failed to study the overall organisation of government with a view to becoming Premier he had, of course, been at, or near, the centre of affairs since his period as Parliamentary Private Secretary to Neville Chamberlain. I was assured by those responsible for the administration of the Cabinet and Government that he learned more quickly than most incoming Premiers. His particular strengths were his ability to delegate to colleagues once central decisions had been made, and his briskness in disposing of business. He had an instinct for dealing with the major subjects and allowing the more routine papers to be dealt with by the machine.

Senior staff at the Conservative Central Office confirmed this judgment. Of all the post-war Party leaders, Sir Alec proved best able to preside over crucial meetings of the high command. He kept things going at a sharp pace, encouraging everyone to have his say but quick to move in when anyone started roaming round a subject or repeating an argument in various forms. (Heath, too, was highly efficient as leader at the Central Office but he was often in danger of being intolerant to views in conflict with his own.)

It was the same story at the Foreign Office where he had been placed by Macmillan. It was an inspired appointment yet even then his Press critics were in full cry: "The most reckless appointment since the Roman Emperor Caligula made his favourite horse a consul" and "This is carrying a joke too far". But he was capable of a light-hearted disregard of the most wounding attacks and proved to be among the most independently-minded of all Foreign Secretaries—"the best this century" in the opinion of Emmanuel Shinwell who, over seventy years, had known most of them. Douglas-Home shared with Bevin the rare quality of making the right decision without losing himself in mountains of paper. He appreciated that there was no point in spending hours reading countless files when he was mainly required to minute his approval or disapproval of the recommendation before him. I like the story of the occasion on which he received an extraordinarily long Ambassadorial telegram, with background and guidance papers attached, and the comment from the Private Secretary: "In view of the great importance of this subject I consider the Secretary of State may prefer to read all the relevant documents in full before reaching his decisions." Lord Home's reply was brief: "Oh no you don't," he minuted. "Submit your precis and appreciation in the usual way, on one sheet of paper, please."

His great achievement as Foreign Secretary was to ensure that Britain exerted the maximum influence in the world, that her voice was still strong and respected, even though British power had substantially declined. He saw his role as that of a British Ambassador resident in London, but on constant global tours; he logged over 300,000 miles by air, undertaking more journeys than any other Foreign Secretary before or since. At heart he was a great traditionalist in his global view of future British influence—as evidenced by his initiative towards China and his belief in a new role for Japan. But during his many years as Foreign Secretary and Commonwealth Secretary, and while shadowing these Departments from the Tory front bench, he principally established a reputation as a hard-liner on relations with Russia and other Communist powers. For such a gentle, mild-mannered man his speeches on the menace of Russian Communism were often exceptionally controversial and were given an even wider impact when he condemned Russia for encouraging the emerging Third World to abuse the United Nations by applying double standards.

On several occasions I raised with him this picture of outspoken criticism of Communist aspirations but he always rebutted the suggestion that he was out to obstruct successive Prime Ministers in their efforts to achieve East–West *détente* and ease the dangers of a Cold War. "Not at all," he would say, "I am the realist, I know that the Communists' objectives never vary, despite the smiling faces they display when we're at the Kremlin or they're in Downing Street. Their methods vary, never their ultimate ends."

He was probably the best-read Foreign Secretary on the writings of Marx, Lenin and the histories of Communism. When he was compelled to spend more than two painful years immobile on his back, suffering from spinal tuberculosis and encased from head to toe in plaster, he spent the time swotting up every last detail of the Communists' testament. The result was that at countless international conferences the Secretary of State earned the respect of the Russian leaders by his facility and accuracy in quoting, during the more relaxing off-duty dinner parties and receptions, the words of Marx and Lenin. When he ordered the expulsion of a hundred and five Russians from the Soviet Embassy in London, on the grounds that they were primarily concerned with spying and not diplomacy, he argued that Russia's Communist leaders respected tough talk and action and not soft words. Nor was it any secret at the time that Home was disenchanted with Macmillan's mission to Moscow and, for that matter, his "Wind of change" policies throughout

Africa. He firmly established his view that by speeding the rush for independence in Africa, Macmillan was encouraging the rapid spread of militant black nationalism. He was nobody's Yes-man.

I knew him for close on forty years at Westminster, ever since he became M.P. for Lanark with the courstesy title of Lord Dunglass. As Lobby and Gallery correspondent at the time for the Aberdeen and Glasgow papers I established close contact with him on Scottish affairs. He was no hard-line patrician. In fact he was always very much at home with the revolutionaries of the "Red Clydeside" of those days, being accepted by them as a liberal-minded aristocrat. A close friend of his was James Maxton, Clydeside's idol as leader of the Left-wing and anti-Communist Independent Labour Party. Maxton used to say: "Come the revolution, Alec, rather than string you up upon a lamp-post, I'll give you a cup of tea." But then it is a feature of our society that members of the old aristocracy and those of the traditional working class mix naturally: class prejudice in politics comes mainly from those people who belong to neither. Sir Alec was always puzzled by the English preoccupation with class: "The test for me," he said, "is character, not class."

Character is something that he himself had in abundance. It was a quality which the Tories desperately needed at a time when the Party was at a low ebb. And after he had re-formed their ranks with a chirpy assurance, it enabled him to move on without a word of reproach against those who did not stand by him. What Lloyd George said of the Tories' selection of Bonar Law in 1912 was worth repeating in 1963: "The fools have picked their best man by accident." The pity was that the fools never realised it!

10

HAROLD WILSON

October 1964–June 1970
March 1974–April 1976

"Oh my God, he's off again we would moan to each other, as Harold got on his high horse and ranted on endlessly about leaks." ANTHONY CROSLAND

Harold Wilson was Britain's most media-obsessed Prime Minister. It was not merely a case of being fascinated by the techniques of modern communication; for him it became a way of life. Government by public relations was the glittering prize after which he strove. He believed that political power and survival depended on his achieving ascendancy over the proprietors and editors of Fleet Street and their political writers at Westminster. He failed to achieve it—and, having failed, he started to live in his world of conspiracies, leaks and coups; the target of a nationwide revolution masterminded by an unlikely combination of editors and political correspondents.

It was the largely fantasy. What he preferred to forget was that after Hugh Gaitskell's sudden death, when he became leader in 1963 and indeed in the first eighteen months of his Premiership, he had the sunniest honeymoon, in my experience, of any national leader. He was a new, unknown Opposition leader and as a young (forty-eight) Prime Minister on a knife-edge majority of between one and four he revitalised politics after thirteen years of Tory government. He made news and made life exciting. He seemed to be a man in harmony with the mood of the country. Everything was going his way and he ought to have been thankful for such a send-off as Gaitskell's heir.

But when his policies started to collapse and he and his Ministers were seen to be failing disastrously—on Rhodesia, devaluation, the economy, and so on—he inevitably suffered a bad Press because the Government's performance was bad. But he did not see it that way and in 1966 started huffing about "traitorous Lobby correspondents". From that time on the conspiracy theory grew, and in order to have moved, sacked or superseded those journalists whom he feared or simply did not like, he resorted to the most astonishing accusations about their integrity, professional capacity and even their private morals. Suppression is an ugly word, but coming mighty close to it was the pressure exerted on proprietors and editors to remove uncongenial jounalists from Westminster. Wilson appeared to see that as a legitimate exercise of power. Never once did it strike him that his conduct was irresponsible and unforgiveable. I simply add that I derive no pleasure from setting out the sordid facts—but it is essential to get the record straight as a permanent warning about the possibilities of executive abuse in the relations between Downing Street and Fleet Street, Whitehall and the Press.

Yet if, instead of spending so much of his time and energies on the Press and Media Wilson had concentrated his very substantial abilities on his primary job of ruling the country I am certain that he would have broken through as one of Britain's great national leaders. More than most, he possessed the qualities. Among all the Premiers I have known he was the most professional in the techniques of running his Government and his Party. But he lost his way. From the moment he entered No. 10 in 1964 he became enraptured by the role of *being* Premier, captivated by the thrilling interplay of today's performance and tomorrow's headlines. He typecast himself for the role of instant government.

To understand this picture it is necessary to identify Wilson as the loneliest of all the Prime Ministers, a man bedevilled by a great sense of insecurity. He had no friends as the rest of us know personal and family friends and so, in his solitude, his political entourage assumed a greater importance in his life than would otherwise have been necessary. It was this over-dependence upon an odd assortment of acolytes—his "Kitchen Cabinet"—which prevented his becoming a Prime Minister of substance.

In particular, it is impossible to understand the real Wilson and ignore Mrs Marcia Williams, whom he later created Lady Falkender. For more than twenty years she remained the greatest political influence in his life. I knew her in the old days as private secretary to Wilson when he was a hard-working back-bencher out in the cold during the Gaitskell–Bevan era. Indeed, having frequently visited them both in his room in the House of Commons upper committee corridor I doubt very much whether Harold Wilson would ever have become Party leader and Prime Minister but for the ambitious thrust provided by Mrs Williams. Of one thing I am certain: she had much the better political flair. Her tragedy was that she was not prepared to conceal it.

As the central figure in his entourage observers found it increasingly difficult to distinguish between the roles of the secretary and the Prime Minister, and this does much to explain Wilson's apparent hyper-sensitivity when newspapers mentioned them both when writing about what struck them as her political and party influence at No. 10. It also casts considerable light on the tensions between Mrs Williams and top-flight civil servants which developed within months of Wilson's first becoming Premier. Lady Falkender has written one book on life at No. 10—perhaps another is on the way—but she has thus far overlooked a couple of incidents within my own first-hand knowledge which demonstrate the true flavour of the Wilson years in Downing Street and the interaction of personalities in the exercise of power.

The first was the bizarre affair of the gorgeous garden-room girls, which took place during Wilson's urgent visit to Salisbury in October 1965 in the hope of rescuing Rhodesia from Ian Smith's unilateral declaration of independence. Garden-room girls, in Downing Street parlance, are skilled shorthand typists working on top-secret documents in offices overlooking the gardens. As the official delegation was preparing to fly out to central Africa four of these girls were spotted by alert photographers leaving No. 10 and in response to the photographers' requests they waved and turned on happy smiles. The result was a perfect picture of beauty and gaiety; by far the happiest of the countless thousands of photographs taken on that familiar doorstep. Newspaper readers' reactions next morning were unanimous: what lovely ladies and, according to the various captions, what a lucky dog Wilson was to have them as his confidential or private or political secretaries.

Oh, innocent caption writers! When the papers reached Salisbury the reaction in the most exclusive sector of the Wilson entourage was far from rapturous. These were garden-room girls. Who were they to be taken for private, confidential and political secretaries?

At a time when I and other humble seekers after truth might reasonably have expected Wilson to be devoting all his energies and negotiating skills to averting UDI and establishing the abiding verities of the five principles which Smith must satisfy before Britain could agree to independence, he became involved in this ridiculous and small-time affair—one of the earliest instances of how he could allow trivia to escalate into matters of high principle. In his well-known desire for peace he decided that never again must cameramen have the joy of photographing lovely girls tripping in and out of No. 10 to the obvious dereliction of their duty to record the solemn entrances and exits of Prime Ministers. While still in Salisbury he instructed Derek Mitchell, his principal private secretary and thus in charge of all Prime Ministerial staff, to ensure that in future the four secretaries and their like should use the back entrance.

Mitchell's response should go on permanent record as one of the blandest but most barbed comments ever made to a Prime Minister by his principal private secretary: "Prime Minister," he said, "I'm not to be responsible for introducing apartheid into No. 10 Downing Street." Given that moment of history, its setting in Rhodesia, and all that has happened since in Southern Africa, I doubt whether anyone could rival such an inspired single-sentence comment. The girls, and other members of the No. 10 staff, continue to use the front door. The whole ridiculous affair was one of the earliest examples of the pattern of life ahead. Wilson remained the least self-important of men, forever modest and friendly; but the vignette over the garden-room girls reveals how he could not resist becoming involved in small-time incidents which he should never have been troubled with.

My second sample of the Downing Street atmosphere concerns the dual roles of Mrs Williams at No. 10 while officially still being on the Transport House list as a shorthand-typist and being paid the rate for the job. Since she always popped up at the right hand of Wilson in Salisbury, Moscow and other capitals of the world Fleet Street began to speculate on the reasons which made her presence so imperative on official Government visits. Questions were even asked in the House of Commons. Who was paying? Was the cost coming out of Wilson's pocket or from Government expenses? Were her journeys really necessary in the national interest? Wilson's reply was that her presence was essential to keep him in touch with politics back home, particularly with his constituents of Huyton.

For an impending trip to Washington, she was again on the list for the flight, presumably to ensure that Huyton would be kept in the forefront of the White House talks, and a number of solemn conferences were held by the "Kitchen Cabinet". How could poison pen paragraphs about her presence on a Government plane and in Government accommodation be avoided? Wilson turned to Derek Mitchell for suggestions to avoid embarrassment. (It could easily have been avoided by her *not* going on the trip, but that was another story.) Well, suggested the principal private secretary, "all questions, even Parliamentary questions, could be avoided if we put Marcia on the list of staff passengers as Mrs Wilson's lady's maid".

The topmost branches of Whitehall's most cultivated grapevine vastly enjoyed recounting this example of Mitchell's dead-pan, mordant sense of humour. The picture it conjures in the mind's eye of Marcia Williams making down Mrs Wilson's bed at night, placing the nightie on the pillow, ensuring that the sheets were properly aired, running the bath in the morning for her lady after serving the morning cup of tea, provides one of the gems of Whitehall folklore.

With Wilson himself Mitchell established a personal rapport—not, perhaps, surprisingly, since his private sympathies with many of the Labour Opposition's proposed social and administrative reforms had been one of the factors behind his appointment. Even while Sir Alec Douglas-Home was in office Sir Laurence Helsby, head of the Civil Service, Sir Norman Brook, Cabinet Secretary, and Sir William Armstrong, head of the Treasury, were making preparations for the change of Government which they felt was inevitable and imminent. They all agreed that one of the most brilliant young men in Whitehall must be groomed as principal private secretary under Sir Alec so as to enable him to ease in the untried Labour leader after the election. Mitchell was the high flyer selected for the job. It therefore provoked a few raised eyebrows when Mitchell was moved on earlier than usual to another department (he is now a director of the bankers Guiness Mahon). Into his shoes stepped Michael Halls, who died while at No. 10. He was specially asked for by Wilson because sixteen years earlier he had been his private secretary during Wilson's stint as President of the Board of Trade under Attlee.

In his first volume of diaries Cecil King, the deposed chairman of the *Mirror* group, wrote under the date 22 September 1967: "He (Wilson) sees James Margach every week, but all this has done is to weaken Margach's position in the *Sunday Times* office. He will be transferred elsewhere before long." An inaccurate prediction by King, who ought to have known better. I did see Wilson regularly (and other Prime Ministers just as often) but then senior correspondents, whether in London, Washington, Paris or Bonn, are only doing their jobs properly if they see a great deal of Premiers, Presidents and Chancellors. And one becomes accustomed to sentiments such as King's; over the years it was said that I saw too much of *all* Prime Ministers. But with Wilson there was a difference: he expected political correspondents to become his permanent allies.

The perennial Walter Mitty in the man wanted every defeat and retreat to be represented as a victory and an advance. When the Lobbymen failed to live up to his expectations he decided, in his insecurity, that they and their editors must be engaged in a vast conspiracy in cahoots with his enemies: the Tories, the Gaitskellites and Jenkinsites of the Labour right, the Bevanites and Tribunites of the Left. It was in his more panic-stricken moments, when overcome by the spectre of Lobby friends plotting to destroy him, that he made his extreme charges against journalists and his outrageous demands on proprietors and editors: if they wanted to retain his goodwill and friendship they should get rid of the offending journalists from the Lobby–Westminster–Whitehall circuit. Writers of thrillers set on the Downing Street and Fleet Street axis would be suspected of pushing credulity too far if they picture a Prime Ministers exploiting political muscle in order to threaten the careers of correspondents he did not like. In the cruder world of reality, Harold Wilson in effect several times demanded such sacrifices.

His first target was David Wood, political correspondent of *The Times*, and he first wielded his axe in my presence. It was an astonishing scene in which he simultaneously demonstrated for the first time his new-found hostility towards the Lobby in general. Considering that for nearly two years he had done more than any other Premier to manage the Lobby system it was a breath-taking U-turn.

I recall the occasion vividly. It was in the late autumn of 1966 and at the time the Monopolies Commission was considering the proposed take-over of *The Times* by the Thomson Organisation which already owned the *Sunday Times*. I was weekending at Chequers and on the Sunday evening the dinner guests were Roy Thomson—Lord Thomson of Fleet—Denis Hamilton, then editor of the *Sunday Times*, and the deputy editor, William Rees-Mogg. After dinner, over coffee, Roy, in that folksy but always penetrating style which proved so endearing and disarming, turned to Wilson and asked: "Tell me, Prime Minister, just assuming that I get *The Times*, what do *you* think I should do for its future?"

Wilson's answer was swift: "Well, you can start by giving a golden handshake to four people on your staff, starting with the political correspondent, David Wood. Get rid of him first, that's what I'd do if I were the new owner of *The Times*." He then regaled his guests with a bitter discourse on Wood's defects as seen by the Prime Minister, his bias against him, his planting of news and commentaries in favour of Wilson's critics such as Roy Jenkins.

But he was not content merely to attack the professional integrity of David Wood and Charles Douglas-Home, later joint deputy editor of *The Times*, who was then specialising in diplomatic, defence and Whitehall affairs. He embarked on a comprehensive count-down of Lobby ratings. One honoured senior correspondent was "over the hill, past it, tippling too much. His editor knows about it, I know for certain." Of another correspondent representing a major national daily, he opinioned: "He doesn't understand politics, he's just a shorthand writer. Anything anybody says to him is transcribed for straight reporting; he never goes behind the scene to see Ministers to discover what's going on. He's just a shorthand slave, not a political writer." And of an experienced Lobby correspondent he commented: "She missed the last Lobby briefing, I hear. Under the vet with hard pad I suppose." And: "If you gave her a monumental scoop at dictation speed she would still get it wrong."

I did my best to defend my colleagues individually and the Lobby in particular against such highly personalised attacks—a difficult exercise when one is a guest at Chequers and instinctive good manners require one not to become involved in argument with one's host. Next morning I had the satisfaction of a personal call from my editor, Denis Hamilton, complimenting me on my firm defiance while observing dignity and respect to my host.

Such outbursts became commonplace. He eagerly accepted Fleet Street invitations to lunch with proprietors and editors, then proceed to deliver peevish and embittered attacks on them, their papers, and especially their political writers. On four occasions over lunch at *The Times* he returned to his unhealthy fixation about David Wood. Hamilton, by then chairman and editor-in-chief of Times Newspapers, and Rees-Mogg, then *Times* editor, dismissed or ignored his attacks as so much petulance. They showed what they thought of the Prime Minister's criticisms by promoting David Wood to political editor in 1968, with added freedom of comment as a political columnist. Hamilton, who is always without rancour for anyone who tries to influence him in this way, was nevertheless able, while preserving his total independence, to keep a constant dialogue going with Wilson until the latter's resignation in 1976. Hamilton's life, incidently, is full of pressure of this sort from ambassadors and book publishers and business men.

Wilson was particularly ambitious to eliminate writers whom he regarded as close friends of Hugh Gaitskell. He even tried to achieve the transfer from politics of Harold Hutchinson, a father figure and veteran political correspondent of the *Daily Herald* (later the *Sun*). After a sharp and perceptive report on one of Wilson's Washington initiatives the Prime Minister complained to his editor: "I cannot understand why you employ that man; he does not like me and never gives me a fair deal in the paper. He is still one of the Gaitskellites. They all hate me."

Probably the most amazing, even melodramatic, attempt by Harold Wilson to get at a political correspondent was directed against Nora Beloff of the *Observer*, the most experienced doyenne of journalists, having been the *Observer*'s correspondent for many years in Paris, Moscow and Washington. She aroused Wilson's fury more than anyone else, which says a great deal. The reason is once again personal. To her credit, she was the first correspondent to latch on to the odd nature of the "Kitchen Cabinet" and the excessive impact of Marcia Williams on the Prime Minister, his policies and his appointments. According to the diaries of Ministers, Wilson often advised his Cabinet against seeing this "dangerous woman" whom he described as a committed enemy of the Government. He alleged, among other things, that she went straight to Ted Heath to inform him of what Ministers had said at Lobby meetings! I have in my possession a note from Richard Crossman (gratifyingly saying, as in his diaries, that he regarded me and David Watt of the *Financial Times* as the top two of the profession) in which he confirms the lengths to which the Prime Minister went at Cabinet meetings to isolate Miss Beloff from all Ministerial contacts. But the bans had little effect. Ministers continued to see all those correspondents they trusted without difficulty, no matter who might be on Wilson's blacklist.

Over Miss Beloff Wilson grew more than angry, he became a man possessed. In the spring of 1968 David Astor of the *Observer*, the last in the tradition of editor-proprietors, was informed by Lord Goodman that the Prime Minister seemed worried about things being written by Miss Beloff about him, his staff and his Government. Goodman kept a perfect balance in his dual role as chairman of the *Observer* Trust and legal adviser to Wilson in private matters; he reported the situation without bias or comment. In the light of Goodman's information Astor decided that he had better see the Prime Minister himself to discover what all the fuss was about. And at 6.30 p.m. on 2 April a meeting took place in the Premier's room at the House of Commons.

Instead of the relaxed, friendly and mature conversation between two men of the world—and Astor over his many years in Fleet Street had dealt personally with a great many Premiers—Wilson went as a man obsessed into his favourite subject. He went to a filing cabinet and produced bulky files of Nora Beloff's newspaper cuttings. He had obviously dwelt at length over them for he was almost word-perfect in his commentary. Pointing to sentences heavily underlined or encircled, or marked with marginal comments about suspected sources, he sustained a fast monologue: wrong, inaccurate, malicious, inspired by Gaitskellites, slanted, getting at Marcia. His rudeness about her was oblique and only came after he had warmed up. On and on he went in this fashion, thumbing through the mass of clippings and holding them out, and asking in a chatty but barbed fashion, "Read this, for example. And this one."

As there seemed to be a formidable number of files still in reserve and as Wilson was running out of epithets, beginning to parody himself in his phrases about lies, inaccuracies and slants, Astor interposed in low key on the lines of: "There is really no point in you going through those old cuttings. What you are really saying is that you don't like what she is writing, think it unfair, and so on. Well, I come from a family that has been much more unfairly treated by the Press than ever you have, and I really don't think you need feel so aggrieved. Put away the file, Prime Minister, and we'll talk about the general problems, your criticisms, the general principles at stake, the freedom of comment, the freedom of the Press."

Wilson appeared to accept the suggestion and returned the bulky files to the locked steel cabinet. But instead of thereafter cooling down for a relaxed talk about issues he renewed the personal onslaught: "That woman hates me, she hates me," he said. "She's always slanting things against me; she repeats in your paper all the gossip she picks up from my enemies. She's no good as a journalist; she peddles gossip only; she can't deal with serious politics and policies; everything she writes is riddled with lies and half-truths, lending herself as a gossip columnist."

To Astor's amazement, Wilson then revealed the febrile world in which he lived, a world of spies, conspiracies and intrigues. Supporting his allegations that Nora Beloff talked only to critics who wanted to destroy him, he played what he obviously regarded as his ace: "Of course, I know all the people she sees (mentioning several names). In fact, our people keep an eye on her to see just what she is up to." Offices and rooms were mentioned in detail. When the names were subsequently checked back against her own diary entries and notes they proved totally accurate.

Wilson seemed not to appreciate what this grotesque surveillance told about him, that keeping tabs on Miss Beloff smacked of KGB and CIA "observing" methods. Of course, nobody could suggest that Her Majesty's Secret Service agents were involved in the trailing. "Our people" suggested to David Astor as much more like one or two characters from the "Kitchen Cabinet" acting as amateur sleuths. Looking back at the incident years afterwards Astor commented: "It was just the fact that he was foolish enough to say that he had had her followed that astonished me, as it lent itself so easily to misinterpretation." Moreover, perhaps because Astor showed no sense of awe over his espionage techniques, the Prime

Minister rounded off with the smear that it might even appear that she could have been having an affair with one of her regular Ministerial contacts—a nasty innuendo that she was prepared to sleep with the Minister in return for tit-bits from the Cabinet table.

Astor never took a single word of the attack on his political correspondent seriously. "I tried to conduct the conversation by refusing to continue talking on his terms. Whenever it was that I went over to the counter-attack and told him that he had no experience of Press persecution comparable to my family's, this rather took the wind out of his sails and after that he quietened down." Later, when it was arranged that Nora Beloff was going to the United States to stand in for a few months until the new resident correspondent could take over, Astor wrote saying that he hoped, after Wilson's criticisms, that she would have the full facilities in Washington. The Prime Minister replied in a brief note saying that he had never criticised her!

One final detail captures the atmosphere. Astor was conducted to the Prime Minister's room at the Commons by a private entrance, apparently so as not to have to pass through the ante-room where Marcia sat. "I somehow gained the impression that this was done so as to indicate how painful Nora's reports (which were perfectly straightforward political commentary) were supposed to have been to the future Lady Falkender." He regarded the Premier's performance as characterised by nimbleness and obliquity, sometimes by sneering entertainment, rather than angry aggression.

But all was not yet over. Shortly after David Astor's defence of the professionalism of his political correspondent, Nora Beloff told me that she was in serious trouble with the Prime Minister and that she had been summoned to No. 10 to be rebuked. I advised her not to go since even Prime Ministers have no authority to hold trials in secret. But she told me it was too late, a meeting had already been fixed for later that afternoon. I then offered to accompany her to the inquisition on the grounds that even someone charged with mutiny is entitled to be defended by a friend. As I happened to be what is euphemistically described as the "father", or doyen, of the Lobby, I thought my presence might widen the issue to one covering the Lobby's integrity as a whole and encompassing the principles of Press freedom. But time was too brief to enable a switch from her established arrangement and so she was accompanied by the late Ivan Yates, the *Observer*'s chief leader writer and a man with a wonderful flair for gentle mockery.

They were received by Gerald Kaufman, a close "Kitchen Cabinet" colleague of Marcia Williams, in his role as Press adviser (he later became a Minister of State in the Wilson and Callaghan

Governments). As a former journalist and a close friend of his visitors for many years, Kaufman was obviously embarrassed by the whole exercise. He explained the problem. The P.M., he said, always went "through the roof" every time he saw Marcia's name in a newspaper report about him, and justified the invitation-cum-summons to visit No. 10 by the fact that Wilson was the victim of a widespread smear campaign, with poison pen letters sent to most M.P.s making objectionable accusations. It so happened, he added gently, that Nora Beloff, by writing about her political influence, mentioned Mrs Williams more frequently than others. Kaufman obviously felt so unhappy about the role allotted him that Nora Beloff and Ivan Yates were sorry for him. Indeed, so gentle was he that they did not feel required to make even a formal protest about being summoned to discuss Miss Beloff's writings.

The monitoring of the Press became a routine. Many nights until midnight and beyond the Prime Minister and his little coterie, headed by Kaufman and Marcia Williams, would pore over the first editions of Fleet Street papers, studying the variety of political stories, with the added spice of mystery in trying to guess the possible sources of leaks: which Cabinet Ministers had been talking to particular Lobbymen, and who had been at this or that Soho lunch spreading anti-Wilson propaganda. Any signs of co-operation between two or more political writers fired anew Wilson's suspicions that a colleague was plotting with the Press to overthrow him. For weeks James Callaghan would be seen as the great threat, then it would be Roy Jenkins, George Brown or Tony Crosland. Richard Crossman, in his diaries, records that he always had to be careful in his meetings with Jenkins in case "Harold suspected (us) of hatching a new conspiracy against him, and that would be bad for his morale". As for the Left-wing, Tony Benn was, of course, continuously marked down as a villain.

Their late-night seances often resulted in another member of the inner circle, George Wigg, the Paymaster General, ringing up an editor or a correspondent with the request from the top that something should be done to correct paragraphs which might be damaging. Over breakfast the final editions were again meticulously examined to see if any changes had been made in the early hours. This ritual dissection of the papers was carried out with such intensity that it was not unknown for Wilson to intervene personally as, for example, when the old *Sun* one day carried four reports referring to him in various contexts. Three were favourable; one struck a critical note. It was about the fourth that he telephoned the editor.

On one occasion, when commissioned to discover from which Ministers a number of leaks on Cabinet decisions had emanated, Wigg returned with a list of cuttings, the dates and information that Marcia Williams herself had been lunching or dining with the newspaperman concerned. Wigg also informed Wilson of Mrs Williams's relationship with a political correspondent and, with Harold Davies, Wilson's Parliamentary Private Secretary, pointed out the prima facie dangers of the association. For his pains Wigg in 1967 was encouraged to put politics behind him and move on to greater things, the chairmanship of the Horserace Betting Levy Board. When he had left it was clear that he had, after all, been a symptom rather than the cause of the ailment. For the anti-Press neurosis continued unabated—confirmation that he could not be accused of having fed his master's fears of newspapermen's conspiracies. Later the phobia over edition changes abated somewhat when it was shown that these were due to later news stories coming in overnight unconnected with No. 10.

Wilson found it difficult to come to terms with reality. Often he could not accept the fact that many of the newspaper stories to which he objected so violently were straightforward reports of the conduct of himself and his entourage, the legitimate subjects of national attention. This, for instance, was the situation over the celebrated slag-heap episode in which, after the election of February 1974, the *Daily Mail* reported that Marcia Williams and her brother, Anthony Field (who had been head of Wilson's private office) had been engaged on what the papers described as land speculation. Wilson, convinced that once again the Press was hounding him through the "Kitchen Cabinet" and embarrassed that the traditional Labour bogey of land speculation should appear on his own doorstep, became vigorously involved in their defence—striving all the time to make a distinction between land speculation and land reclamation for the benefit of the nation. A few weeks later, when the Press reported that in August 1968 and June 1969, while his principal aide at No. 10, Mrs Williams had given birth to two baby boys by her affair with a Lobby correspondent, Wilson's sense of persecution was fed to the point of uncontrollable fury. And when he heard that the actual birth certificates were circulating in Fleet Street (shades of Horatio Bottomley's assault on Ramsay MacDonald's birth) to appear with a story under the heading "The Babes of No 10" his lawyers moved in with threats of injunctions. In the event, the editor of the *Express*, Ian McColl, did not publish the certificates, although the lawyer failed to trace the proprietor, Sir Max Aitken.

It was after the storm over the land deals that Wilson decided to make Mrs Williams a Life Peer but not before he had strongly attacked another political journalist for anticipating her elevation too accurately. This time it was Noyes Thomas who confidently forecast her ennoblement in his paper, the *News of the World*. Wilson was so furious that he demanded that Joe Haines, who in June 1969 had succeeded Trevor Lloyd Hughes in the unenviable role of Press Secretary, should denounce the report as a pack of lies. Then, the following week, he instructed Haines not to give briefings to the Lobby if Thomas was present. The Lobby, when informed of this command from on high, repudiated the clear suggestion that at the direct behest of Downing Street it should connive in blacklisting a colleague, in effect barring him from continuing his job. His editor, Peter Stephens, also protested vigorously and No. 10 backed down —though without any semblance of an apology. (The truth is that Haines did not carry out his master's instruction to send Thomas to Coventry). In due course the forecast was vindicated when Mrs Williams took the ermine as Lady Falkender. Much later, in a television interview, Wilson confessed that he had conferred the honour in order to spite the Press—as good a reason as any, one imagines, if a Premier is hard-pressed to explain why a report denounced as a lie should miraculously be confirmed by events.

Wilson's tragedy was that he could not see reports such as Thomas's as transient, passing incidents to be savoured for a day in Fleet Street hostelries and then quickly forgotten. Perhaps the best illustration of his inability to keep cool over an issue of passing importance is what became known as the "D-Notice Affair", which centred on a startling story published on the front page of the *Daily Express* on 21 February 1967. Chapman Pincher, the defence correspondent, reported that "thousands of private cables and telegrams sent out of Britain . . . were regularly made available to the security authorities for scrutiny . . . were regularly vetted by security officials". Wilson saw the story as part of a "Big Brother is Watching You" campaign, yet another attempt to discredit his Government. He over-reacted. He should have poked fun at the revelation, pointing out that the system of security checks had operated smoothly for almost half a century, that in any case the security men could scarcely ignore this communication loophole. Instead, he gave the story an exaggerated importance, by claiming that it breached established "D-Notice" security arrangements under which Fleet Street editors co-operate with the security services on matters of importance to defence. He proceeded to set up a powerful Committee of Privy Councillors under Lord Radcliffe (who also chaired the Vassall Tribunal), but their report in June rejected the Prime Minister's accusations. By nature, Wilson found it a strain to admit he was ever wrong, and on this occasion he actually issued a White Paper rejecting the Radcliffe Committee's findings—which inevitably landed him in more trouble than ever, inflicting great injury on his reputation. If only he had employed the Baldwin touch, defusing a security challenge by complimenting the journalist on his initiative and playing the side-issues in a low key, the whole thing would have been forgotten in twenty-four hours.

Wilson's obsession with the Press menace, as I saw it from the ringside, is now being confirmed many times over from the Cabinet room itself. The diaries, memoirs and papers of a wide variety of Ministers in the Wilson Government—notably those of Richard Crossman and Barbara Castle, reinforced by the memories of others then on the inside—all pay eloquent testimony to the frequency with which he lectured them on the subject. Anthony Crosland once pictured the scene for me like this: "Oh my God, he's off again, we would moan to each other, as Harold got on his high horse and ranted on endlessly about leaks and demanded that we should stop speaking to Lobby people out of favour at the time—all to the neglect of much more important Cabinet business which had either to be rushed or delayed for another meeting."

The amount of time and energy expended on Cabinet leaks and Press relations must have been enormous. Wilson would lecture his entire Cabinet on their disloyalty: "I know who's been talking to the Lobby," he would say. "The fingerprints of two Ministers are all over the stories in the *Guardian*, *Times* and *Financial Times* this morning." And so on, endlessly. He suspected even his friend, Richard Crossman, of talking too freely to me. In attempts to scare Ministers from seeing political correspondents he would at one meeting of the Cabinet invoke the "leak security system", whereby civil servants would check out people's access to relevant information; at the next meeting he would authorise the issuing of a questionnaire to Ministers demanding to know who had been talking to whom. In a different situation the Lord Chancellor himself, Lord Gardiner, would be mobilised to conduct a quasi-legal probe into leaks and sources.

Of course, it all depended on who was doing the leaking. When Wilson discovered that Peter Jenkins of the *Guardian* was writing the inside story of the "In Place of Strife" proposals for a legal code on trade unions over which he and Employment Secretary Barbara Castle were humiliatingly defeated, he feared that Crosland, Callaghan and others were leaking anti-Wilson versions and that the book would therefore discredit him. "Leak like hell," he commanded Barbara. Yet, almost inevitably, no leaks were ever pinned down. And, indeed, the more he berated his Cabinet on the sin of communication in a modern society and the more he tried to bar the Lobby's access to Ministers, the more frequent the leaks became.

When Anthony Howard (later editor of the *New Statesman*) was appointed in 1965 Whitehall correspondent of the *Sunday Times*, Wilson issued a personal directive to Ministers and civil servants warning them that he was a dangerous man and must not be seen by any of them. For once diaries, memoirs and papers available to me, all agree with Crossman about what happened at the Cabinet on Tuesday 23 February 1965. Crossman wrote about: ". . . the first Whitehall correspondent in history, looking into the secrets of the Civil Service rather than leaking the secrets of the politicians. . . . The Prime Minister said that this was outrageous and he was going to accept the challenge of the *Sunday Times*. In order to kill Tony Howard's new job he forbade any of us (and the officials as well) to speak to him." Another Minister with a sharper memory and note recalls that Wilson said: "We can't understand any such Whitehall animal". Another snapshot of the same Cabinet shows Wilson in a state of fury saying: "This is a dangerous man doing a very dangerous job".

The new dimension of power which the *Sunday Times* sought to disclose in Whitehall was identical to the problem identified by the grand journalist, James Reston of the New York *Times*, as rampant in Washington. He said: "The power of the executive to decide things in secret is growing all the time; what reporters have to do is to move in much earlier in the development of policy—never before has there been such a need for aggressive reporting. . . ." The best journalists in London and Washington had their sights on the same bulls-eye. As William Rees-Mogg put it at the time: "The job of a newspaper is to bring into public information the acts and processes of power", and to this end a paper should be able to discuss "the attitudes of Civil Servants with the same freedom that it discusses the attitude of politicians".

The need for such ambitious journalism was never better demonstrated than by the way in which the Executive instantly closed ranks, Government and Civil Service coming together to beat off the intruder and preserve the mystique of secrecy. For ever after, Harold Wilson claimed that this was one of the most significant victories in the clash of power between the two empires: "I saw Tony Howard off with his tail between his legs".

Wilson even carried his obsession with the Press through his years in Opposition. It was in the election atmosphere of early 1974 that

17. The author with Harold Wilson

18. Marcia Williams (Lady Falkender) on the day her life peerage was announced

19. (*above left*) Nora Beloff, former|
political correspondent of the *Observe*

20. (*above right*) David Wood, Europea|
Political Editor of *The Times*

21. (*left*) Sir William Haley, editor *
The Times 1952–66

(*above left*) Lord Armstrong of
ﾑderstead who, as Sir William Arm-
ﾑong was Joint Permanent Secretary to
The Treasury 1962–68

(*above right*) Sir Derek Mitchell who
ﾑs Principal Private Secretary to the
Prime Minister 1964–66

(*right*) The author talking to Denis
Healey

25. James Callaghan

26. The author with Bernard
Donoughue, Senior Policy
Advisor to Harold Wilson and
James Callaghan

he made his most sweeping allegations against the Press as a whole when he claimed that "hordes" of newspapermen were scouring the country in search of damaging disclosures about him and his close friends. When pressed for the evidence, he excused himself by stating that the facts could not be disclosed because of legal action which he had initiated. When these were finally disposed of and he was pressured into submitting proof to the Royal Commission on the Press the "evidence" was such that the controversy spluttered out like the proverbial damp squib.

One last story illustrates how totally Wilson lost his sense of perspective. When in Opposition, in the spring and summer months of 1972, Fleet Street editors and American newsmen found how much his mind was preoccupied with his old Lobby worries. They were anxious to discover something of the Opposition leader's future plans if he became Prime Minister again. His visitors expected, in response to questions, some forty minutes of elevated thinking on future economic policies, what he was to do about sterling, overseas confidence, Britain's role in the world, the future of the Common Market, economic planning and growth; his new visions, his brave horizons. Wilson confounded all hopes. His plans? Well, he would start, he said, with the Lobby. The political correspondents were his enemies. He was determined to ignore them when he became Prime Minister again. Ignore them completely. The journalists could not believe their ears: Wilson's topmost priority on re-entering No. 10 was to ditch the Lobby! Indeed, he carried out his 1972 threat to put the Lobby in limbo four years later when, as Prime Minister, he ordered Joe Haines to break off all formal contacts, but this was effected in a petty punitive spirit and not as a reform to make the system more open and less rigid, controlled and centralised.

Instead, said Wilson, he would develop his contacts with the best performers on television and radio and communicate with the country through them. Yet it was not as though his relations with the BBC were any less tempestuous than with the Lobby, despite the fact that when Macmillan and Douglas-Home were in power the BBC was seen as a hot-bed of anti-Toryism, with Left-wing producers given full scope to satirise the nation's leaders through debunking shows like "That Was The Week That Was" and other lampoons. When his turn came Wilson became convinced that many regulars in television news and current affairs were anxious to damage his image and that performers and interviewers were far too hostile in their questions and comments. When personal appearances were discussed in advance, No. 10 tried to condition the atmosphere by suggesting that certain "personalities" were "unsympathetic" or too abrasive and that the Prime Minister would really be happier and more relaxed with X, Y or Z. Such was the atmosphere of tension although the only total ban imposed was on David Dimbleby, because he was responsible for a BBC programme "Yesterday's Men" which satirised Wilson and his Ministers.

The final paradox about Wilson is that the more embittered his relations with the media became the more compulsively he sought to mix personally with the communicators, despite the fact that the social contacts often terminated amidst displays of bad temper and recrimination, with Wilson particularly accusing the media of devoting too much time to Marcia Williams. If he had opted instead for total withdrawal from the communications field the atmosphere would have proved healthier for Wilson, the media, the Government and the country. He was encouraged to cool it, and detach himself from the constant crises with the media, by Joe Haines, his Press secretary. Haines was appointed to No. 10 in late 1969, after Wilson had been Prime Minister for five years, so it proved difficult for the master to change his style and habits. Haines had been an experienced Lobby correspondent himself, so knew the system well from both sides of the blanket. But his was an impossible mission, as his book* on life inside Downing Street and the high tensions he experienced with Lady Falkender makes only too clear. As it was in the field of Press relations the Wilson years were disfigured by an endless series of tempestuous battles and slanging matches with the media, on which he wasted so much of his time, energy and passion, and misdirected so much of his very considerable abilities and potential as a great national leader.

* *The Politics of Power*, Jonathan Cape.

II

EDWARD HEATH

June 1970–March 1974

"It is only when the opaque windows on to Whitehall and around our working lives are opened that we shall find ourselves braced to make the immense efforts which are required in Britain today." EDWARD HEATH

Edward Heath was once news editor of the *Church Times*. It was a part of his career that he kept in the background. As Prime Minister he disliked journalists and distrusted newspapers. Political correspondents he felt had been willing parties in their seduction by the arch-villain Harold Wilson. And he had an open contempt for the way in which Fleet Street harried public figures; in his mind the issue of Press freedom was inextricably linked to the need for Press responsibility in the delicate area between public interest and the privacy of the individual. His feelings crossed party lines; he resented alike the pursuit of Labour and Tory Ministers. Fleet Street, in his view, had debased standards in the Vassall, Profumo, Lambton and Jellicoe scandals—particularly since the so-called responsible papers had felt compelled by the bad example of others to join the hunt. He never expected a good Press and was always wary of journalists.

Though this attitude burgeoned on his becoming Premier the seeds were sown during his days as Opposition leader. "Oh, he's a Wilson tool, just a Wilson toady", he would say of one distinguished Lobby correspondent. "He's a Maoist, that's why his leaders are so bloody awful, he's ruining what used to be a great newspaper, always nit-picking and nagging." When in due course a courteous protest was made to his staff about the reflections on a journalist's integrity, the reply was that of course Mr Heath never intended such a smear, only to say the writer was predisposed to being small-minded, self-centred and self-righteous! When Wilson tried to steal the limelight from the Conservative Party conference at Blackpool 1968 by attempting a peace parley with Ian Smith at Gibralter, Heath was furious that so many correspondents deserted the resort in favour of Wilson's Mediterranean initiative. Even those who remained at the conference were given no thanks; rather, they earned his angry sarcasm: "I suppose you're frustrated having to stay and listen to me at Blackpool instead of kneeling at the feet of Wilson at Gib."

The point was well made by William Davis, later editor of *Punch*, that if only Heath had "lost his temper in public in the way he does in private" he' would have become a more commanding and successful national leader. Davis had front-line experience to back his judgment about the potency of the Conservative leader's fury. In the days when Davis was financial editor of the *Guardian* and Heath Leader of the Opposition, he had lunch at Heath's flat in Albany, while preparing a profile article, and for two hours took voluminous notes. Finally he asked Heath to outline the main features he would include in a Tory Budget and Heath promised to prepare an outline in a few days. But despite reminders to the Party officials then servicing the leader, the "Shadow Budget" failed to appear and so Davis wrote an article for the *Guardian* under the headline: "Where is Your Budget, Mr Heath?", recalling the promise over lunch. Heath was incensed. A couple of days later, in a TV studio, he accused Davis of "the most disgraceful conduct I've ever experienced in my political career". He became even more livid when Davis wrote a second piece under the title "Barking from the Doghouse" about his tense relations with the Conservative leader, who ignored invitations to write his own reply. Yet a careful reading and re-reading of the offending article failed to discover any cause for the leader's anger. It was only much later that the reason emerged: his outbursts were concerned with the one brief sentence in which Davis mentioned that he had had lunch as Heath's guest in exclusive Albany; that was the "disgraceful misconduct". It had nothing to do with any errors or misrepresentations about economic and financial policies.

The story illustrates, firstly, Heath's inability to get on with journalists in the Media Age, and secondly the way in which he could allow an initially trivial incident to fester into a major issue of high principle and honour—for, in this case, the wound was still deep nine months later. At a Stock Exchange lunch he saw Davis among those gathered and shocked the City establishment by objecting to the presence of a distinguished journalist performing his professional duties: "Either he goes", exploded Heath, "or I go".

A relaxed Prime Minister would have given the impression that he was too busy and too thick-skinned to pay attention to the scribes and pharisees. But Heath was not relaxed and between the lines of any editorially critical comment he espied a malicious personal attack on himself. A classic instance of his inability to rise above such matters concerns a lunch which he was due to have at the *Financial Times* on 16 May 1973, with the then chairman, Lord Drogheda, and senior editorial staff. On the previous day, however, the *Financial Times* carried an article by Joe Rogaly, a specialist commentator of substantial reputation in Fleet Street, entitled "A Government of Little Stature". It was displayed across the main feature page and was highly critical of Heath and his Ministers: "The Government is not blessed with men of stature. This is hardly surprising in a declining country whose elite is demonstrably mediocre ... our politicians drawn from the more unprepossessing of that rump ... we have certainly not had a Prime Minister of quality since Mr Harold Macmillan ... not blessed with men of stature." There was much besides on these lines, ending with the body blow: "There will be no true solutions while we continue to be governed by pygmies".

Heath was furious when he read the article. He considered it outrageous conduct by a paper due to do him honour in the directors' dining room within twenty-four hours of publication. He therefore ordered his staff to cancel his appointment to lunch and to tell his hosts that he considered their action despicable. He suspected that publication had been deliberately timed to insult him but in fact the writer and the executive responsible for the display were unaware of the Premier's impending visit. It was one of those hapless coincidences which can occur in the best organised enterprise.

Again, the wound was slow to heal. Shortly afterwards Heath was at the opera when, during the interval, he bumped into one of the *Financial Times*'s most powerful executives. "I must say," hissed Heath, "there's a limit to what a prospective guest should be expected to take from his prospective hosts."

During his Premiership Heath's distrust of all journalists developed to such an extent that he often did not extend the normal courtesies of personal relations. When a meeting was arranged at No. 10 in June 1972, specially to enable him to meet a new editor of the *Daily Mirror*, there was not a word of greeting or a couple of friendly sentences to enable the two men, who had never met previously, to get over the preliminaries. "Well, what's to be your first question then?" Heath snapped. The ending was handled with equal abruptness. This was not an isolated example and the politics of the paper or the political reporting of the journalists concerned had nothing to do with the type of treatment handed out; Heath became frigid and brusque with most of them, including those who had known him well over many years. It was as though he believed that the machinations of journalists were responsible for the failure of his policies. Even that redoubtable Conservative commentator Peregrine Worsthorne, deputy editor of the *Sunday Telegraph*, was given astonishingly cold treatment during an hour's on-the-record interview in the Cabinet room. The scene was so bizarre that he felt impelled to publish barbed comments about the Prime Minister's behaviour: "the atmosphere of impatient formality . . . no warming up or exchange of civilities or small talk . . . I was hustled out . . . no jokes or private confidences, not a trace of the charm or bonhomie with which these rather gaunt occasions are usually enlivened". That was Premier Heath at close quarters with the Press—cold, formal, abrupt, hostile.

Yet it was not always so and it is regrettable that this is the way in which historians will see him. Before he became leader I knew him for twenty years, often on a day-to-day basis, and even when under considerable pressure as a Cabinet Minister he was in the main friendly, outgoing and understanding of the problems of newspapermen. More importantly, during his days in Opposition a pledge of an open administration and frank Press relations lay at the heart of his proposed "New Style of Government": everyone would share in the decision-making through constant disclosure of what was going on inside Whitehall. Was it not Heath who said in 1966: "It is only when the opaque windows of Whitehall and around our working lives are opened that we shall find ourselves braced to make the immense efforts which are required in Britain today." After the tantrums, bitter arguments and high tensions of Wilson's Mark-1 government there was therefore a sense of optimism as Heath moved in to No. 10. Perhaps at long last, the great ideal would be realised: access to Whitehall secrets, a genuine share in the great national debate; the door of Downing Street flung open wide, a welcome on the mat, come on in, so pleased to see you.

Alas, power, which has the ability to mellow some of those who achieve it, adding greatness where none was suspected, in Heath's case changed his personality almost overnight. When Prime Minister he became authoritarian and intolerant. The opaque windows and the front door were not open for long. The shutters were fastened and the door opened only to a select few by a Government which was the most secrecy-conscious since the war. Downing Street became the most closed society in all my experience.

Heath had the shortest honeymoon of all with the political correspondents. Within months he dismissed them as an unfriendly lot, not simply because he identified them as dupes of Harold Wilson. Within three months of his becoming P.M. he decided to banish them to outer darkness. In the autumn of 1970 he released Leila Khaled, a Palestinian Arab terrorist, who had attempted to hijack an El Al Boeing plane flying to London. As a guerrilla he ordered her release in exchange for the terrorists' freeing hostages in other hijacked planes. The Lobbymen duly reported that many leading Conservatives, notably Enoch Powell and Duncan Sandys, regarded his action as surrender to terrorism, and showing lack of courage on his part. From that moment onwards he more or less broke off relations with the political corps for their lack of co-operation and understanding. Things were never the same again. He and his P.R.O., Sir Donald Maitland, opted instead to operate through the diplomatic corps. In the end this encompassed his downfall. By the time of his defeat in 1974 he had cut himself off from political reality, and his base of political power, without the crucial daily contacts with the world outside, by his misguided decision to ostracise the media at Westminster.

Heath made no attempt to model himself on any of the Prime Ministers with whom he had worked closely. Instead he modelled his administration on the autocratic presidential style of de Gaulle, even adopting the Gaullist fashion of holding Press conferences which really became TV spectaculars—with Press men used as extras—during which the leader could expatiate on national and world affairs without the necessity of answering tiresome questions. Heath was so encouraged by his own Lancaster House experiments along these lines that he urged his advisers to plan a series of fire-side chat shows to be broadcast simultaneously on both TV channels —thus enabling him to reach the carpet-slippered nation while by-passing Parliament, Fleet Street and the Lobby. "Sunday Night at No. 10" was seen as a rival to "Sunday Night at the Palladium". Obviously the initial idea had come from officials who had spent too much time in Paris and Washington where Presidents do not customarily go through the Parliamentary-question hoop twice a week at the hands of people somewhat more motivated than television cameras. But as a new channel of power and communication it clearly carried attractive opportunities for news management, since the format, the issues, and even the choice of question, would be firmly in the hands of No. 10. The formula would have brought to Britain a new kind of political broadcast masquerading as an exercise in Prime Ministerial briefings to the public on the making of Government policies. In the event, however, the idea foundered when it was pointed out that it would be exceedingly difficult to differentiate between Ministerial and Party broadcasts and that the Opposition would inevitably demand equal air-time in which to reply.

Another aspect of his presidential approach to power was his domination of the Cabinet. In my experience no Prime Minister rivalled his control. It was a one-man Government. Even those Ministers who were naturally good communicators, with a sympathy for more open government, became afraid to talk even privately about their departmental policies. Even in Opposition when he objected in 1968 to the tone of Enoch Powell's first speech on race, colour and immigration he was quite ruthless in sacking him from the Shadow Cabinet. When in power all his Ministers seemed apprehensive about his reactions and always appeared overawed in his presence. As part of a serious study of power not one of them has to this day written any book—or even a series of articles—about the Heath Government from the inside. As a result, less is known about the workings of the 1970-74 Government than of any other government this century. Heath was against any form of instant history. If he had suspected any Cabinet colleague of keeping notes on paper or tape he would have dismissed him at once.

Heath was the first lower middle-class grammar schoolboy to become leader. If, in the end, he was thwarted in his passion to modernise the Conservative Party as well as the country at least he compelled it to face the realities of economics and social change. But his misfortune was that he became leader too soon—not before *he* was ready but before the Party was ready for him. At no time did he become a hero symbol; he was never accepted with the unqualified affection near to idolatory which it traditionally accords its leaders. This, I believe, had nothing to do with class snobbery— the boy from the modest home in Broadstairs without the broad acres of the landed gentry or the patina of big-business success— it was that he never adjusted himself in style, conviction and person to being Party leader. He commanded the troops from on high with an authoritative smack to which they were not accustomed. He was never a comfortable, chummy leader. He found it almost impossible to unbend.

It is a point well illustrated from an interview I once had with Heath when in Opposition. With me was the *Sunday Times* photographer, Steve Brodie, now picture editor, and for twenty minutes, as Heath and I talked informally, he took pictures of the Tory leader from a variety of angles. Then he withdrew to let us get on with our talk for the record. After he had done so Heath said: "A very good photographer that, and a very friendly man." I was somewhat surprised. "Oh, you know him, then?" I said. "But of course. He came with me on a couple of overseas trips by plane. His name is Brodie, isn't it? He's a great friend of mine. He's been very good to me. First class. I like him." Despite the fact that he obviously knew my colleague well, he had not been able to "give" in friendship and recognise him from their former tours together. Harold Wilson, who knew him similarly from political tours, always made a point of hailing him by his Christian name. Heath had no less warm regard for him than Wilson, but he found it difficult to break his natural reserve.

This aspect of his character was well summed up in army terms by a former prominent Conservative M.P., Colonel Sir "Toby" Lancaster, one of the knights and baronets of the old Tory brigade. He told me:

> The difficulty with Ted is that you never know him. You can spend hours and hours with him and you never know him any better at the end of it. You get the feeling that you've had the most interesting conversation with him, but you leave him with the impression that he has never been interested in you as a person. A man with wonderful drive and energy, but totally lacking the personal warmth of personality. In the army as C.O. you had to develop a relationship with your troops, and when a man came back from illness or family troubles at home you remembered to ask him how he was and how his family were getting on; or if a corporal came back from a course you had to remember to ask him if he enjoyed it and that you liked the report he earned. They feel you are interested in them, in their problems or achievements, and thus you develop a mutual sympathy, understanding and contact. That's a very good test for a Party leader, in fact; but with Heath you always get the impression that he is unbelievably impersonal in human relationships.

So it was that when Heath had lost his third out of four elections the implacable Party formbook decreed that he was a no-hoper, and he was overthrown in a palace revolution led by Margaret Thatcher. But whereas the mass of Tories were heartbroken and conscience-stricken when Douglas-Home was forced into resignation by the "magic circle", this time there were no tears, no regrets.

The Party had cast Heath in the role of a David who would cut

Goliath Wilson down to size; indeed they hoped he would prove to be a Tory version of Wilson himself, a tough and abrasive product of the new generation. As Quintin Hogg said to me: "They wanted a popular leader who would impress as a grammar schoolboy. They also wanted an able public relations man who would look more democratic than Alec. They abandoned King Log and did not realise they had bought King Stork!"

In the early days Heath tried very hard to get across to the public. Sometimes he would be touching in his boyish anxiety, as for instance when he would write me: "Dear James: Thank you so much for your kind references on Sunday. As ever. Ted." But as an essential shy man, full of humanity—before being transformed by power—he began to suffer great internal agonies at his lack of success in leadership. He became increasingly sensitive when reports began to appear suggesting that the Tories were beginning to doubt whether they had made the right decision in 1965 in "getting rid of Alec for Ted". In particular, he allowed Wilson's rampant Parliamentary ascendancy to shatter his morale and self-confidence. I recall one night when I had arranged to have a taped interview with him in Albany on the future of development of Party policy. He came rushing in, markedly late due to some delay, to his obvious annoyance, in getting decisions through his Shadow Cabinet. After a brief chat, he asked if I could wait a little longer before starting the interview so that he could go next door to change from his formal lounge suit into more relaxing slacks and open-neck sports shirt. Then he showed me the beautiful grand piano which he had recently bought with the proceeds of the Charlemagne Prize for his historic work for Europe. He was justly proud of the magnificent grand, even prouder of the reasons for the prize—but through it all I detected from his manner that he was still seething over something that had been said or done at the earlier meeting. Abruptly he said: "James, do you mind if I play a little. I'm sorry, but it means so much to me." He sat down and played for at least half an hour. I am no music buff, and I could easily be mistaken, but I fancy that he began with a Chopin prelude before sweeping on to something dramatic by Lizst into which he threw his whole personality. He was uplifted to another world. When it was over he exclaimed with relief: "Now I feel I'll do a job worthy of your interview on which I know you've done your homework."

I was fascinated, not so much by the actual performance on the piano, but by the man, totally changed in temperament and appearance. Gone were the tell-tale signs of tension. I asked: "Do you play every night when you come home, even late from the House of Commons?"

"Yes," he replied. "Not every night, but very often. I've got very understanding neighbours and the walls of these buildings are very thick."

"But why? Does this great music give you release?"

"Yes. Music means everything to me when I'm here alone. And it's the best way of getting that bloody man Wilson out of my hair." He swept his fingers through his locks in illustration.

In effect, he was showing how bruised he was deep inside where no one could see; confessing that Wilson at the time was on top, almost conceding defeat. Because of his self doubts, he seemed unaware that *vis-à-vis* his Party he had an authority and integrity much greater than Wilson's.

When his morale was low he might have been cheered to know that Wilson, back at No. 10, was probably in an even more worried state as, at midnight, his "Kitchen Cabinet" sought to restore his badly shattered morale by telling him over an extra brandy how wonderful and commanding he was. Music uplifted Heath's morale, flattery Wilson's.

Surveying the Heath decade the question remains: did Fleet Street, particularly the parliamentary and political newspapermen, get him wrong or was he wrongly packaged from the start? When good public relations are a prerequisite for success the question is of importance for one side or the other. In this case I think it was Heath himself who blundered and the experience of Edward du Cann is relevant testimony. Du Cann had been appointed Party chairman by Douglas-Home but was rapidly unseated by the new-broom Heath despite the fact that he was a substantial figure in the City and an expert on finance and economics. Furthermore, he was cold-shouldered when Heath formed his Government and he was never included in any of the subsequent reconstructions. At the time there was considerable speculation to the effect that du Cann had somehow slighted Heath's sensitive feelings over his humble origins. It was not quite as simple as that, but the episode does illustrate how prickly Heath could be in human relations, even with close colleagues.

Edward du Cann explained to me:

> I stated in a newspaper article at the time that there was no personal difference between Heath and myself, no friction or anything like that. That's true. The only difference between us was in our conception of the role of the leader with his Party. I have always taken the view that the leader exists to serve his

Party; Ted alas takes the other view that the Party exists to serve the leader.

It's not quite true that I was sacked as chairman of the Party simply because Ted was angry with me for reminding him of his humble origins and how this could be put across to the Party's advantage. Not quite right. I suggested that we could build him up for the Press and TV as the new Conservative leader in one of two ways: as the epitome of the new generation, the abrasive, organisational man, success symbol, new horizons, the pacemaker; or the Party machine could build him up, project him, as an entirely new type of leader, making British history: the prospective Prime Minister who had risen from the most humble surroundings, the son of a small one-man jobbing builder with a wife of similar background. It isn't right that I said to him that we in the Party organisation would do a wonderful job on him for the election, in selling him as the son of a lady's maid. That's journalistic licence touching up history, I'm afraid. But I did tell him that we could project his personality as the son of a lower-middle-class family. I don't think he approved of my second alternative.

Ted prefers, I think, and finds it easier to do so, to identify with the more worldly side of power, public life and success.

His preference won the day, but the advertising experts were convinced that he could have beaten Wilson earlier if they had been allowed to project on the national screen a Conservative Party led by "the man of the people".

In the end it was the super-secrecy of his Government which brought his own downfall. He kept in his own hands all the levers of power and information and of the latter precious little was allowed to escape. When he became enmeshed in his confrontation with the National Union of Mineworkers in late 1973 the people were totally uninformed and confused. In his final months there was panic in the air. He made desperate efforts to get on terms with Fleet Street, issuing pressing invitations for urgent talks at No. 10 particularly after critical reports and editorials. When editors and journalists assembled, usually in small select groups, his opening gambit was that he wanted to create a better understanding of his policies. Yet his manner was still cold and commanding. Heath did not like general discussions, he preferred monologues, and many editors did not welcome what they saw as his efforts to manage the news and condition their opinions. To them it was clear that Heath was not interested in their views, only in the need for better understanding of his. The result was acute embarrassment on the part of the media men; because of his previous determination to treat Fleet Street as untouchables, he had never studied the art of dealing with its representatives.

Research confirms that the treatment of all senior Fleet Street executives followed the same pattern. The experience of Sydney Jacobson (later Lord Jacobson), editorial director and deputy chairman of Mirror Newspapers, may therefore be taken as typical. Heath telephoned Jacobson from Chequers one Saturday when events during the miners' pay crisis were reaching a peak and asked him to come to No. 10 on the Monday morning. There, in the drawing room, Jacobson found Heath anxious and depressed, his steely self-confidence lacking. He could not, he said, get on any terms with the miners' leaders, who were making the dispute more and more political. He explained that Mick McGahey, the Scottish Communist, had said to his face: "We want to see you out and we are going to get you out". As for Joe Gormley, the NUM President, every time he seemed to make progress with Heath he was turned down by his fellow negotiators and came back saying: "The lads upstairs won't wear it". What was Heath to do? How could he get his case across to the country? He was being pressed to declare a quick election, but did not wish to do so.

Jacobson said that all his experience was that Party leaders who tried to focus elections on one overriding issue had failed. If the Tories concentrated an election on the "Who Governs Britain?" issue, he thought they would fail, too. Jacobson suggested that the TUC offer to regard the miners as a special case, inapplicable to any other wage demand, should be taken more seriously. If the TUC subsequently failed to uphold this undertaking the Government's case would be stronger for having at least tried it out. However, having in mind Vic Feather's ineffective TUC pledge of restraint to Wilson in return for the dropping of "In Place of Strife" Heath replied that he was not prepared to accept yet another empty declaration of intent. In short, he did not believe that the TUC could deliver.

Jacobson then suggested that a report on wage comparabilities about to be issued, might provide a fresh basis for talks. At the time Heath did not appear to think much of this, and Jacobson subsequently found that some Ministers close to him, including at one stage William Whitelaw, were not keen on the report as a formula for political peace. (Indeed, when the report was issued, some industrial reporters were briefed by the Ministry of Employment not to make too much of its relevance to the miners.) Heath himself did later toy with the report, but made no progress.

167

As for the Prime Minister's inability to put his case across to the country, Jacobson offered to send over the *Mirror*'s political editor for a major question-and-answer interview and the offer was accepted with alacrity. The result was prominently displayed under the heading "My Case—by Edward Heath". The *Mirror*, on that day at least, appeared to please Downing Street.

As the crisis deepened and the miners balloted on a strike, it was clear that Heath had given up hope of a settlement and would go to the country. Shortly before the election was announced, Jacobson was again invited to No. 10. This time, the Prime Minister was far more ebullient. He had made his decision, his self-confidence was back. What line, he asked, would the *Mirror* take in a general election? He reminded Jacobson, fairly enough, that he had led Britain into Europe, for which the *Mirror* had campaigned over the years. He hoped the *Mirror* would be fair to him.

Jacobson informed him, without any blurring at the edges, that the Mirror Newspapers would give unequivocal and vigorous support to Labour throughout the campaign. Heath could scarcely fail to recognise the likely impact of this on popular public opinion. In previous elections the *Mirror* had often adopted a teasing "wait-for-it" pose until the final day when they predictably came out for Labour; this time they were to campaign from the very first moment. They were as good as Jacobson's word. When Heath announced that he was going to the country they declared in strident headlines: "Now he has the nerve to call an election". The leading article in the same issue made the crucial point that Heath, who had sincerely tried to unite the nation, had now divided it more bitterly than at any time since the General Strike.

When the campaign became more feverish, almost at the halfway mark, Ted Heath once again called for Jacobson. This time he was at his most official and cold. He told the editorial director that after their conversation at the start of the campaign he had expected fairer treatment than he had been getting, and once more reminded him of their previous harmony over the Common Market. It seemed that Heath was particularly irked by the *Mirror*'s "Now he has the nerve" blast, by a *Sunday Mirror* centre spread which showed a cross for every miner killed in the pits in a year, and by a moving *Daily Mirror* account of the funeral of the last miner to lose his life at the coal face before the pits were closed by the strike. A more pliable Fleet Street leader might have been susceptible to the pressures exerted from No. 10 but Jacobson insisted that the Mirror papers were completely fair: they were careful to be impartial in handling news reports of the election, while fully supporting Labour in their leader columns. There had been criticisms of policies, but no personal attacks on Mr Heath. Jacobson and his papers stood their ground, and according to the best researchers the *Daily Mirror*'s final editorial advice on polling morning, "For all our tomorrows vote Labour today", tilted the balance to give Wilson the verdict in the photo finish.

Not all pressures on the Press are exerted in such eyeball-to-eyeball confrontations. When political power is at stake—especially when the incumbent at No. 10 feels that it is slipping irrevocably from his grasp—stealthy flanking movements are also on the tactical agenda. A typical example from the first 1974 campaign concerned Anthony Bevins, later the political correspondent of the *Daily Mail*, but at the time a political correspondent of the *Sun*. During Heath's daily Press conferences at the Central Office Bevins used to fire penetrating and challenging questions on Tory policies, not at all the "feed" style which politicians prefer, and Heath was obviously nettled by them, especially since they were being picked up by radio and TV. Bevins was due to accompany Heath on his election tours. However, a Party aide hinted to one of the *Sun*'s editorial executives that in view of the fact that Heath regarded some of the questions "unfriendly and unhelpful" it might prove embarrassing if the Conservative leader found himself in Bevins's company too frequently. It was a clear wink-and-nod back-stage method of trying to remove an able young journalist from an assignment because he was successfully performing his primary duties in journalism—to discover the real facts.

The *Sun* kept Bevins in the Heath entourage throughout the campaign. Once more the lesson was emphatic: Press freedom, the independence of editors, and the public's right to know demand constant vigilance and courage.

Time did not quickly soften Heath's feelings. When in May 1974 Parliament was setting up the Royal Commission on the Press proposed by Harold Wilson, Heath, during the debate, singled out the *Daily Mirror* for attack. Despite his many previous friendly contacts with Jacobson and other executives and writers and his many invitations to go to No. 10 or Chequers to hear his interpretation of the crises threatening to overwhelm him, he was in no mood to forgive or forget the *Mirror*'s effect on his election chances. He said: "It seemed to me that it went to the depths not known since the *Daily Mirror*'s campaign against Churchill and 'Whose Finger on the Trigger?' ... I have never seen anything agreeable about myself."

His conviction that he would never get a good Press and that there must be a hidden motive behind most of what journalists wrote was exhibited again in unusual form many years later, after he had lost the Party leadership. In July 1975 the *Spectator* re-published an article by him which had first appeared in April 1940, when he was twenty-four. He was highly critical of the original plan to admit State schoolboys to the public schools on scholarships claiming that it would really make the boy from the State school "a pawn to be used if and when necessary for the continued existence of the public school system. Such an attitude, I am sure, can only bring harm to the rest of the educational system and pain and distress to many of the boys who would be involved in the proposed scheme . . . the secondary schoolboy has no desire to become a member of a privileged class, to be given advantages merely because he has been to a particular school." As a secondary schoolboy who by then had passed through Balliol and into the Army for front-line action, he argued vigorously that equality of opportunity could be created only by abolishing inequality of education. The article did Heath great credit for the strength of his convictions, his loyalty to the home and community which cradled him and to the educational system which shaped him.

But when the article was re-published twenty-five years later Heath was bitter in his comments and reactions. He saw it as a calculated move to discredit and embarrass him publicly in a Party then dedicated to campaign for the future success and expansion of the public schools. In particular, he convinced himself (wrongly) that Patrick Cosgrave, the paper's political commentator, was behind the "plot", because he had written biting anti-Heath and ecstatic pro-Thatcher articles during the Tory leadership election. When he saw Cosgrave at a social evening to honour a retiring Central Office official—a party attended largely by supporters of the overthrown leader—Heath snapped: "What on earth are *you* doing here? Spying again I suppose."

It was all a very far cry from the opening of the opaque windows and the "New Style of Government". Indeed both Heath and Wilson—despite their early hand-on-heart dedication to open government—presided over administrations which allowed less access to information than those of Attlee or Macmillan, neither of whom was basically interested in the day-to-day operation of the information and public relations processes—leaving them instead to Francis Williams and Harold Evans. What, for instance, happened to the open windows when it was rumoured that Edward du Cann and Heath had been in conflict and that the Party chairman was about to be kicked out? Heath described the reports as "damned lies". Two days later du Cann was succeeded by Anthony Barber. Such incidents explain why newsmen develop a cynicism over accepting briefings and denials on their face value.

If I were to choose I would have to say that Harold Wilson, notwithstanding his obsessional nightmares about the Press and his state of seige-warfare with the political correspondents, made more significant advances towards informed discussion than did Heath. After all, he did encourage Parliamentary specialist committees to investigate and report on particular subjects, and he introduced the valuable Green Papers which stimulate debate on alternative policies before they reach the finality of White Paper status, the embodiment of Government holy writ.

By comparison there was only one major reform proposed by Heath. He suggested through his Press aide, Sir Donald Maitland, later Ambassador at the Common Market Commission, that the traditional method of information being given to the Lobby through "Government sources" on a non-attributable basis, might be changed to an on-the-record quotable system, with sources of all information identified. Like many of my colleagues I was all for the reform on one condition: that journalists should have the major influence on the system and control of what was "on" and what was "off". We had no intention of dancing to the tune of the Government. Clearly it would be all too easy for the Government magnanimously to go on-the-record to suit its own book and then to slide back off-the-record when the going became rough. The Lobby having refused to swallow the bait whole, the fine print of the scheme's operation was never discussed. Nothing again was ever heard of the idea during the Heath Premiership.

Years later, with the relaxed hindsight of a man no longer Premier or even Party leader, Heath agreed that "on the whole the machinery of Government tends to be too secretive and to adopt a self-destructive posture". Furthermore, action had to be taken to "prevent the system developing into greater and greater secrecy". He also resurrected, with the confident air of a man who was in no imminent likelihood of having to implement it, the suggestion that all Lobby briefings should go on-the-record. For the first time in years he was in harmony with newsmen who have a vested interest in smashing the barriers of secrecy.

It is a pity that, as Heath himself had already so potently demonstrated, incoming Prime Ministers are so prone to memory blackouts.

12

JAMES CALLAGHAN

April 1976–

"His exploitation of trade union contacts and of the Press ...
were for the experienced observer a virtuous performance."
RICHARD CROSSMAN

In the exercise of power through the media James Callaghan is
probably the best example in my case-book of the ability to succeed
without appearing to try. Among his fellow post-war Labour
Premiers Wilson substantially over-rated the influence of newspapers,
radio and television while Attlee grossly underrated it, dismissing
the media as a circus. Callaghan got it right. He is a most adroit
wheeler-dealer, very much the master of political skills—but he is
a man who takes care never to get his hands dirty, let alone leave
his fingerprints around.

Richard Crossman, that remarkable combination of psychological
warrior, don, journalist and politician, was one of the shrewdest
judges of the sophisticated arts of public relations, news-
management, and the manipulation of real power at the top. His
admiration of Callaghan at the head of this chapter is therefore
tribute indeed. The virtuoso performance to which he refers concerns the methods of Party and news management through which
Gentleman Jim out-boxed and out-foxed the Wily Wilson over "In
Place of Strife".

He warned his Cabinet colleagues that the Wilson–Castle proposals would provoke an even more disastrous split than
MacDonald's decision to form a National Government in 1931.
Callaghan genuinely feared that the Party and the unions would go
their own separate ways—a prospect which concerned him deeply.
He himself came up through the trade union wing—the first leader
and Prime Minister to do so—and he saw the unions and constitu-
ency parties as integral partners in the movement as a whole. For
more than thirty years he commanded a much more formidable

Party power base than any of his contemporaries, pulling off the unusual double of always topping, or being near the top of, the elections for the National Executive and Shadow Cabinet, rival stables which normally breed totally different political animals. It was for this reason that, in the end, he easily routed the more fashionable rivals such as Jenkins, Healey, Crosland and Benn to become leader and Premier. It was for this reason also that during a meeting of the National Executive, a brief intervention by Callaghan aligning himself with the unions and warning the Government of the dangers of their "strife" policy, was sufficient to compel the Cabinet to drop the whole programme. Thus he imposed on his own Prime Minister a public humiliation and defeat. But worse to come for the Wilson faction, for immediately afterwards the most detailed stories appeared, reporting how "Big Jim" had masterminded the massive revolt. It was a leak operation completed with consummate skill, without Callaghan ever calling a briefing meeting or even being seen in casual conversation with a single newsman. Like all successful coups it had been conceived in secrecy and executed with ruthless daring.

Wilson was furious. Not only was he humbled nationally by one of his own Ministers, but he had been out-witted in the very sphere in which he had always claimed the highest professionalism, namely the managing and making of news. Furthermore, fearing a new conspiracy against him, he saw Callaghan's coup as the first move in a plot to overthrow him. At once, the Prime Minister and the No. 10 machine screeched into operation—not to rescue the policy, for "In Place of Strife" was beyond recall, but to denigrate Callaghan in the hour of victory which had made him the toast of the trade union movement. Callaghan was represented as disloyal and irresponsible, the big bully running wild, a man ready to destroy the Government. As part of this exercise, Wilson then decided to get into the business himself in a big way; he leaked Cabinet records to show that all Cabinet Ministers, including Callaghan, were totally committed to the tough new laws for the unions. It was a mistake. A percipient Conservative M.P. noticed the leaking of Cabinet decisions in a clear attempt to get the Wilson version into the papers and on to TV, and raised the question of official secrets and Cabinet confidentiality. Wilson was forced to go through an extraordinary performance in the House of Commons, confessing that he had been leaking his own Cabinet secrets in the national interest and with the authority of Cabinet to back him.

When it came to the defence of Government and Whitehall preserves

Jim Callaghan could prove as tough and dictatorial as anyone in my Premiers' gallery. The most illustrative incident occurred during his period as Chancellor of the Exchequer and concerned my Washington colleague, Henry Brandon, who had prepared a series of major articles for the *Sunday Times* on the theme of "How Sterling Came In From The Cold". The articles revealed much of the secret history of the Labour Government's handling of the financial crisis of November 1964, Wilson and Callaghan's first challenge, and were obviously based on much inside information furnished by numerous key officials and bankers in London, Washington and elsewhere. The articles were completed in February 1966—a sixteen-month time-lag which ought to have helped dispose of the usual obsessions over official secrets and to encourage a greater sense of Government detachment. However, life is seldom so simple. Unbeknown to Brandon and to the editor, Denis Hamilton, who had asked him to write the series in order to see to what extent Whitehall security could be breached, Wilson had resolved to hold a general election and seek a larger majority than the one to four on which he was surviving perilously. Both Wilson and Callaghan were aware that the articles were being completed— especially since Sir Derek Mitchell, Principal Private Secretary at No. 10, had negotiated with Brandon the previous December the terms of reference which should govern his contacts with Government and Whitehall figures—but when they learned in February that the draft articles were actually ready, they became excitably nervous, fearing that Brandon's disclosures before the imminent election might somehow injure the Government's reputation and harm their chances at the poll.

In constant tensions between Government and Press it is too often assumed that it is the mandarins of Whitehall who manipulate their political masters into pro-secrecy hunts. But in this case my researches confirm that all the initiatives came from the Government and primarily from Harold Wilson. For both Sir William Armstrong, permanent head of the Treasury, and Mitchell had been shown drafts of the articles and strongly advised Callaghan and Wilson, despite the fact that the election had now been announced, that their fears of possible repercussions were exaggerated.

The Downing Street and Treasury files—both of which are still Official Secrets—reveal a fascinating picture of the way in which the figures of real power and influence go into action when the alarm bells start ringing. At the Treasury, Armstrong read the Brandon articles and at once dictated a "Secret—Note for the Record" paper giving his immediate reactions and comments, especially in identifying the clues to the writer's sources inside the official network.

Sir William did not feel "that the article was so damaging that I must plead with him not to publish it". Next door at No. 10 Downing Street Derek Mitchell gave similar advice to Harold Wilson after having read Armstrong's note*.

Yet Callaghan and Wilson—by now in the throes of a conspiracy spasm in which his downfall was being plotted by the Press, the City and Bank establishments and the gnomes of Zurich—disregarded their officials' advice, and sought to suppress, censor or delay Brandon's articles for purely political reasons. Any remaining doubts that Wilson was the real power behind the pressures on the *Sunday Times* are removed by reading between the lines of a postscript to Mitchell's minute, added on 3 March: "PS—Since dictating this I have heard that following your talk with the Chancellor this afternoon he has asked Lord Thomson to defer (or cancel?) publication and will be seeing him and Denis Hamilton early tomorrow morning". And he again counselled caution over an attempt at suppression: "If the *Sunday Times* gives way all well and good. I would only emphasise the risk of a leak. A main purpose of my call on Brandon this afternoon was to take stock of plans for publication, and before he told me that the first article was to appear this Sunday I saw that he had galley proofs lying on the table. There are, therefore, many people in the Thomson Organisation who must know of the existence of the articles."

The crunch came on Friday, 4 March 1966—two days before the first article was scheduled to appear. In a desperate effort to render the articles electorally harmless, Callaghan pressed Lord Thomson of Fleet and Denis Hamilton to meet him not in the Treasury but in his private room at No. 11 Downing Street. With him were Sir William Armstrong and his principal private secretary, Ian Bancroft. Callaghan, in an uncertain and noticeably nervous state, argued that publication of the articles would be contrary to the national interest because they would injure sterling. In this taut atmosphere Roy Thomson again testified to his life-long discipline that as proprietor he never interfered with the independent judgment of his editors. "I leave the decision whether to publish or not with Denis, who has my complete confidence", he told Callaghan. "Whatever Denis decides will have my complete confidence and support, and he knows it." The only other intervention by Thomson was directed to Armstrong: "Do *you* think these articles will really *harm* the pound?" he asked. The Treasury chief parried with the comment that he did not think they would do any good.

* The full text of both the Armstrong and the Mitchell notes is printed for the first time in this book. *See* Appendix page 185.

Hamilton was not one to be overawed by the variety of appeals, arguments and fears paraded by the Chancellor. He told the Chancellor that as an experienced editor he would be the last man ever to allow anything to be published in his paper which might injure sterling in any way, at home or abroad. The articles were historical, dealing with events a year and a half before, and were unlikely, in his judgment, to harm the pound or British interests. Of course, he added, if there were any errors of facts he would gladly correct them. The final decision whether to publish or not was his and his alone, he stressed, but at no time did he suggest that he was likely to decide in favour of delay, amendment or suppression. It was at this point, when he realised that Hamilton, backed by Thomson, was unlikely to be influenced by words, that Callaghan started to tighten the screws. He threatened action; he would now seriously have to consider invoking the Official Secrets Act, he said, and supplemented this by intimidating hints that he might introduce the Judicial Tribunals machinery.

By these threats Callaghan came full circle. When Brandon was conducting his initial inquiries he arranged to see the Chancellor. When he arrived at the Treasury Callaghan issued an impossible ultimatum: before answering questions he must know the names of other people Brandon had already interviewed. Brandon retorted that this was a totally unacceptable, unethical demand he could not accept. Callaghan insisted on names, or else. . . . Brandon, refusing to be browbeaten, then got up and walked out on Callaghan in protest—splendid independence.

Callaghan obviously believed that by invoking the Act and Tribunal powers he might in due course compel Hamilton and Brandon to reveal their sources for the secret details of the rescue of the pound. But the threats had no effect. Thomson and Hamilton stood their ground in the face of the huffing and puffing and bluster. Finally, Armstrong, sensing that there was to be no conclusion, suggested that he might go over the Brandon drafts once again to identify any errors of fact which might be corrected. Hamilton responded in the same spirit; of course, he would co-operate with his old friends on cross-checking facts. It was a sensible peace-making formula, and helped to bring a highly charged confrontation to an end. But the final word went to Roy Thomson. As Callaghan was showing him out, he turned to the Chancellor, grasped him in a friendly fashion by the lapels, and with his unique ability to tell the truth without causing offence he said: "Jim, what really troubles you is that it might cause you to lose the election". Callaghan smiled, patted Roy on the shoulder, and added his friendly goodbyes.

Subsequently Hamilton went over every word of the long articles, satisfying himself that there were no words which could conceivably harm sterling, and paying particular attention to the headlines, since in his long experience he judged that headlines cause more genuine complaints than anything else in a newspaper. Finally he gave the all-clear for publication. In full.

As my own postscript to that tense interview at No. 11 I spoke recently to two of the principals. Armstrong (now Lord Armstrong and Chairman of the Midland Bank) commented:

> It is ridiculous to talk about the Official Secrets Act and possible Tribunals and imagine one could persuade the other side to be conciliatory. I had the feeling that there was a good deal of political sensitivity, that some people had been talking too much about secrets in the hope of embarrassing the Labour Government. I regarded the affair as part of Jim's education in that field—he was always a very quick learner.

And Sir Denis Hamilton, who would never discuss the interview until ten years later, regarding it as a private matter, saw one of his most difficult and sensitive editorial decisions like this:

> I am the last person ever to allow anything to be published which might conceivably injure the pound or the country's interests. It was a difficult question of judgment, with sterling in a delicate situation, with a lot of speculation going on about devaluation prospects. There were no reactions against the pound in the British and overseas markets the day after the *Sunday Times* disclosures. So the fears of the Prime Minister and Jim Callaghan proved groundless.

Hamilton retains a respect for Callaghan and at a Press lunch spoke with considerable warmth about him, and especially about his sensible media relations since becoming Premier.

Students of the complex exercise of power will find the Wilson–Callaghan case-book fertile ground. By setting up the Department of Economic Affairs as a rival to the Treasury the Prime Minister guaranteed that George Brown and James Callaghan would be always at each other's throats. An even more potent problem posed for Callaghan was that Wilson ostentatiously paraded the fact that he himself was the real Chancellor and Treasury overlord, even going to the length of announcing personally to the Commons a package of economic and fiscal policies in order to demonstrate that it was he who was the mastermind. Later on, when devaluation finally proved inevitable the boot was on the other foot; it was Chancellor Callaghan, having loyally carried out his master's policies, who was demoted, being moved from the Treasury to the Home Office. But, just as when he was ceremoniously excluded from the inner Cabinet following his stand over "In Place of Strife" Callaghan never uttered a single word of recrimination. He accepted such snubs with gusto and good humour. He did not seek to counter-attack through the media; he continued to keep communicators warily at a distance. With a few of us, perhaps, he could be chummy, relaxed and indiscreet but he was generally on his guard. Certainly he was never fashionable among the feature writers, opinion formers and editors in the sense that Jenkins, Crosland and others became. But then he knew that he had no need of such assistance. His Party power-base was all that mattered.

After devaluation had been announced on that Sunday morning of 18 November 1967 and after a formal news conference on devaluation mechanics, a few of us were invited to join the Prime Minister for a buffet lunch at No. 10. As one who could recall the setting in Whitehall on a Sunday some twenty years earlier when Sir Stafford Cripps announced the Attlee Government's devaluation I could savour the techniques and gradations of reality with which such decisions are announced. Wilson was no Crippsian realist, no hairshirt for him.

"I feel very very sorry for Ted Heath this morning", he said. "I'm glad I'm not in his shoes."

"Why so, Prime Minister?"

"Don't you see, devaluation has made me the most powerful Prime Minister since Walpole. I can do whatever I like now, my power is absolute in economic and financial policies. Poor Ted, I'm sorry for him. I like him, you know, and I'd like to ease things for him to help him a bit with his Tories. My announcement this morning is very very bad news for Ted."

One felt at the time that Wilson had genuinely convinced himself that he had worked tirelessly for devaluation ever since October 1964 and had finally succeeded in overwhelming the resistance of all his Cabinet colleagues, especially last-ditch obstruction by Callaghan and the Treasury, to bring off the greatest coup of statesmanship since Walpole. It was therefore less than astonishing that shortly afterward, when *The Times* disclosed the reality of Wilson's bunker-style defiance in preventing devaluation, he should lash himself into a temper demanding of top civil servants and law officers that they invoke the full rigour of the Official Secrets Act and other inquiry procedures to smash what he saw as a sinister Ministerial and Press conspiracy.

It was on 23 November, only five days after devaluation, that Peter Jay, economic editor of *The Times*, wrote the sharply critical article in question: "Devaluation—Who is to Blame?" He condemned Wilson as the man totally responsible for opposing and delaying devaluation for three years at a disastrous price for the country. Most telling of all was his revelation that in mid-1965 and then again in 1966 the Prime Minister had personally suppressed two reports from two separate groups of economic and financial advisers both of them strongly advocating devaluation. On the second occasion, wrote Jay, Wilson ordered all copies of the draft report to be destroyed, except one.

Jay had been a civil servant of great brilliance at the Treasury and had resigned only months earlier to join *The Times*. In the story of plot and counter-plot which follows, the most significant feature is that Wilson never once denied the accuracy of his revelations; indeed the Premier's very action substantiated the version of history made public. Nevertheless, he was furious and ordered the pursuit and, if possible, the humiliation of Jay. He provided two instant counts for the indictment. First, as Callaghan's son-in-law, Jay was being manipulated in a plot to make Callaghan Prime Minister with father-in-law providing the ammunition. Secondly, Jay had committed a crime under the Official Secrets Act by publishing information which had come into his possession as a career civil servant, the gravest conceivable offence against Whitehall's code of integrity.

The true explanation was that as a good investigative journalist Jay had acquired his facts from the independent economists who had been called in to advise the Government. It was surprising that this did not occur to the Prime Minister; his truly astonishing memory must have slipped up for once. In the case of Henry Brandon's sterling crisis articles one amendment suggested by Sir William Armstrong was that the names of four pro-devaluation economists might be omitted; if my Washington-based colleagues could discover their identities how much easier was it for Jay, a brilliant economist moving in the world of academic and professional economists, to discover the names for himself in London—the more so when the experts were indignant that their advice had been suppressed when they had been right.

Three relevant footnotes must be added to illuminate the world of power when Ministers lose their heads over secrets, leaks and injured reputations: first, on the day *The Times* report appeared Wilson blackballed Jay from a panel of four journalists due to question him the same evening in the "This Week" TV programme. He said: "It's not for me to comment on a very slanted article by a former civil servant". The ban was counter-productive: Jay was immediately invited to appear on the David Frost programme and enjoyed an audience three times greater than that of the Prime Minister.

Secondly, Sir Laurence Helsby, then head of the home Civil Service and Joint Permanent Secretary of the Treasury, telephoned William Rees-Mogg, editor of *The Times*, inviting him to visit the. Treasury to discuss the legal, official and professional issues involved in Jay's disclosure (splendid confirmation of their accuracy). The editor received the solicitous invitation with admirable coolness. He would, of course, be delighted to see Sir Laurence but alas, checking on his diary, he appeared to be fully committed for the next three weeks. Nevertheless, he would see what appointments might be rearranged in order to accommodate a trip to the Treasury. The meeting duly took place. "We had a very civilised and relaxed chat", the editor recalls.

> He understood my position on the right of *The Times* to disclose facts of major importance discovered by an able journalist and to publish them in the public interest. For my part I sympathised with the reasons why he invited me to see him and the Prime Ministerial pressures on him to do something. Our chat was marked by cordiality and mutual understanding, and we parted as always the very best of friends, with goodwill to each other.

With goodwill—but with nothing to pacify the wrath in high places.

Thirdly, Sir Elwyn Jones, the Attorney-General (later Lord Chancellor Elwyn-Jones) was brought into the act to see if the legal apparatus could be activated to nail Jay under the Official Secrets Act. The learned Attorney decided that no legal action was tenable.

Years later Jay told me that before writing his article he had cross-checked all his facts with four or five independent leading economists. He continued:

> I wanted to avoid the re-writing of history which I suspected would happen and I wanted to get the record straight at once, even though I knew that my disclosures of what really went on would cause political embarrassment to Jim because of the conspiracy nightmares of the period.

Jay and the rest of us did not have to wait all that long for confirmation of the way in which Callaghan was cast in the role of villain and why such strenuous efforts were made to put Jay in the dock. Richard Crossman, in the second volume of his Diaries, commented on the "astonishing" Jay article which

> gives a completely detailed and, as far as I know, truthful inside story of all the previous occasions on which the Treasury and Harold's advisers had pressed devaluation and he had turned them down. The point of the article is perfectly clear—to show that it was Jim who was flexible and Harold who was adamant—and that's all the more sinister because I'm told there's a very similar article by Sam Brittan in the *Financial Times*. It's clear that in the briefing of the Press Jim had come out number one and Harold number two. This was clear enough when Harold spoke to me on the telephone and asked me to do a certain amount of briefing about the Jay article, something I tried to do throughout the day.

After the Diaries had been published, however, Jay told me that Crossman's implication of family collusion was totally without foundation. He said: "I had no contact with Jim during my investigations or in writing my article. Indeed after my piece appeared in *The Times*, he left me in no doubt that he was very displeased with me over the embarrassment caused him."

In that golden age of intrigues, when Minister was afraid to be seen talking unto Minister, and least of all to be seen with political correspondents—Callaghan was involved involuntarily in yet another incident in the Government–Press minefield. This time it was the initiative of Jay's opposite number on the *Guardian*, William Davis, which triggered the explosion. In an article before devaluation on the economic situation, particularly tracing the Chancellor's record, he made the point that Callaghan would soon have to be moving on from the Treasury to escape from the exhaustions of the job. He concluded with the comment that in view of the tradition of status and seniority a Chancellor could move to one of two places: and failing No. 10, it could only be the Foreign Office for Jim.

When Harold Wilson read the report at one of his midnight sessions he by all accounts "hit the roof". Another ploy by Callaghan, this time using the Press to capture the Foreign Office. That settles it, then. No Foreign Office for Jim. As P.M. he'd see to that. It would be the Home Office—or nothing—for Callaghan; Wilson was convinced that the Chancellor was orchestrating another coup. It was no good the Chancellor trying to calm tempers by saying he knew nothing about the Davis article or for Davis letting it be known that it was his own idea to send Jim to the Foreign Office (based on many precedents); the Prime Minister remained convinced that sinister motives prevailed. And lo! After devaluation Callaghan did not get the Foreign Office, but was sent to the Home Office instead.

Davis himself was living dangerously, with the nerves of so many Ministers at breaking point. At an overseas conference of Western Powers George Brown headed the British delegation as the Secretary for Economic Affairs. At a private briefing Brown resented Davis's sharp questions and, shaking his fist angrily, he screeched: "I'll have you drummed out of the country, I'll have your new British passport withdrawn." Normally this might have been brushed aside as a melodramatic gesture of disapproval. But its cutting edge was that Davis, born in Germany of splendid stock, had only lately become a British citizen and been issued with a British passport. Brown was next morning full of contrition, but his remarks caused great offence at the time, especially amongst other journalists who were proud to welcome a colleague to British citizenship.

When Callaghan became Prime Minister himself he did not have to wait long before learning the hard way that leaks are an occupational hazard of Prime Ministers. In his case it was a more serious problem than usual; the magazine *New Society* published fully and accurately details of Cabinet discussions and Cabinet papers on child welfare benefits, and reproduced the text of the documents. The circumstances compelled Callaghan to take a sterner view than he might normally have preferred; but police inquiries and a Whitehall investigation by the permanent head of the Civil Service, Sir Douglas Allen, failed to discover the sources, though as a result of his report Whitehall security over the circulation and copying of documents was reinforced. Purely incidentally, however, the Prime Minister did reveal facts of great value to the Government–Press war on secrecy. He mentioned that in the course of his inquiries he had found that in the previous Heath Government there had been thirty-seven leaks and thirty official inquiries (inquiries are never mounted into canards or hoaxes). His figures confirm my impression of the par for the course over forty-three years.

Later when the *Daily Mail* published with great pride and fervour what turned out to be a forged document about slush-money payments by the State-owned British Leyland car company, with accompanying innuendoes concerning public figures and public departments, Callaghan—as with Baldwin, Attlee and Macmillan beforehand—received a welcome bonus. Events followed the pattern set by the three earlier instances of Press excesses and they are highly pertinent to the theme of this book. Callaghan moved in smartly to condemn the "contemptible display of political spite that has reduced journalism to a lower level than I can remember for many years" and made unflattering allegations about the motives of the editor, David English.

Sir Harold Wilson followed up by accusing the paper of being a "pedlar of forgeries", citing earlier reports, and demanding that the law should be altered so that editors who knowingly bought stolen documents should be treated criminally—in the same way as "fences" or resetters of stolen gems. Indeed the case was referred for comment to the sitting Royal Commission on the Press just before it completed its final report and went out of existence. In Parliament and outside demands multiplied for the Press Council to be equipped with tougher disciplinary powers to maintain standards and punish offenders—and for a majority of the Council to be independent lay members.

Once more, as happened under the three earlier Prime Ministers, the Government was on top, the Press in the dock. Callaghan punched home the lessons—and it could not have happened with timing more calamitous for the Press. Once again the tide of Press freedom and access to the centre of power and information was turned at the time there were high hopes of a series of major reforms to modernise the Official Secrets Act and the laws on de-famation, libel and privacy; advances which would have helped to weaken Whitehall's defences, contributing thereby to a climate of more open government. But the *Daily Mail* affair reinforced the strongly-held view of Whitehall and Government that the Press could not be trusted. Indeed, the elitist group of Permanent Secretaries were fortified in their view that reform of the Official Secrets laws should be so weighted as to make certain that behind a superficial picture of progress and concession, disclosure and access would really become more difficult.

My record of the manipulation between Downing Street and Fleet Street ends where it started all those years ago with yet another crisis focused on the role of the Lobby correspondents. On this occasion the tensions started innocently enough with the instant and inevitably critical reactions to the announcement in 1977 that Peter Jay was to become the new Ambassador to Washington on the recommendation of Dr David Owen, the new Foreign Secretary: Ho, ho!—cries of nepotism—Jay is Callaghan's son-in-law. But these conditioned reflexes would have proved transient had it not been for an unexpected diversion and extension. The day after the Jay announcement, when the initial ripples over family connections were disappearing across the waters of the Thames and the Potomac,

183

reports appeared in two London evening papers (with identical headlines) and several regional evenings, suggesting that Jay had been appointed to Washington because his predecessor, Sir Peter Ramsbotham, was a "fuddy-duddy" and "old-fashioned snob".

The widespread simultaneous quotation of the comments could not be dismissed as accidental. Only one conclusion was tenable: the comments about Sir Peter had been inspired by a common briefing —and whether or not he had been identified by name was academic if he could be easily identified as the target. The national reaction was that the briefing had come from the Press Office at No. 10 and the damaging inference clearly was that the Press had been used to make an anonymous smear against a distinguished public figure who was unable to answer back.

The incident played into the hands of the critics of the Lobby system, with its non-attributable off-the-record tradition, since it demonstrated the way in which a Government and its civil servants could exploit even distinguished and case-hardened political correspondents, enmeshed as they were in the rules of the game. In turn, however, the experience led to a major reform in the Lobby system—in theory if not in practice: the political correspondents agreed at a special meeting that for an experimental period there should be the *opportunity* for "on-the-record" exchanges between the Lobby on the one side and Ministers and officials on the other —as long as both sides agreed on the occasion. I have already expressed my doubts on the similar Heath-era proposals. Now that the idea has been put into practice it will be interesting to note whether it can indeed survive on a selective and limited basis rather than being compulsory and general. Political newsmen have never liked being cast as compulsory plagiarists by giving credence to others' opinions as their own, without attribution or acknowledgement of sources.

Of course, it is in principle an advance towards more open journalism. But it would be an illusion and a total misunderstanding of the seat of real power in the modern state to imagine that such a modest change will in itself lead to more open government. The stark fact is that Whitehall and the Executive have during this century—and before my very eyes—arrogated to themselves the supreme power and authority of Parliament. That being so, the struggle to break down the barriers of secrecy and confidentiality, to obtain significant access to sources of power, information and decision-making must continue unabated. Before there can be any sanguine talk of a free society many battles have to be won. The walls of the Forbidden City of Westminster—Whitehall still stand, and the people of Britain wait at the gates.

Appendix

The Treasury and Downing Street Notes on Henry Brandon's *Sunday Times* Articles

THE TREASURY

SECRET—NOTE FOR THE RECORD

HENRY BRANDON'S ARTICLES ON STERLING

I saw Henry Brandon on Monday February 21 and again on Monday February 28. In the course of these two interviews he showed me the whole of his article. It is about 25,000 words and will be divided into at least two and possibly three parts for publication. The proposed title is "How sterling was saved". It covers the period from the entry into office of Sir Alec Douglas-Home in October 1963 to the announcement of the "September arrangements" in September 1965. Mr Brandon admits that he is no financial expert and he had concentrated on the political aspects of the story; his treatment of some of the technical issues is at times naive. He seems to have made a serious attempt to be balanced. In general he is critical of the Conservative Government and Mr Maudling and quite critical of the present Government, especially in the parts relating to the early months of their office. The moral of the story as set out in the last paragraph is that "the pound should be taken out of politics".

2. The style and treatment are very like his celebrated articles on the Skybolt affair, that is to say he purports to take the reader behind the scenes giving the views of the various participants at various stages in the story. Thus he describes in general terms, but with fresh colour, to give the impression of an eye-witness account:

a. the meeting of Ministers at the beginning of the present Government's term of office when it was decided not to devalue sterling;

b. two interviews between the Governor of the Bank of England and the Prime Minister;

c. the meeting at Chequers when it was decided that Bank Rate should be increased;

d. a telephone call from the Prime Minister to President Johnson in Vietnam;

e. a meeting which the First Secretary held on August 26 with representatives of the C.B.I. and the T.U.C.;

f. the First Secretary's meeting with the T.U.C. on September 1.

3. He naturally was evasive about his sources, though he admitted to having got a good deal of it from Americans (there are strong suggestions that he has certainly got a good deal from Mr Roosa and Mr Bundy). He implied that he had got little or nothing from the First Secretary or the Chancellor of the Exchequer. He certainly had opportunities to get a good deal from the Governor of the Bank of England [Lord Cromer], though how much I do not know. For the most part, in answer to my questions, he said he simply could not remember where he had obtained particular bits of information.

4. I said that I could not give him any help at all on passages which purported to give the views of individual Ministers as expressed in private meetings, or on the advice given to the Government by their economic advisers or civil servants or by the Bank of England at particular moments in the story. I therefore confined myself to suggesting corrections on matters of fact where the events described were already public property or undeniable. The main items of this kind were:

a. He had got a good deal of the chronology wrong in relation to the events leading up to the increase in Bank Rate;

b. As part of that story described a telephone call between the Prime Minister and President Johnson and made this the occasion for quite a considerable digression on the President's reactions to being telephoned by the Prime Minister, I told him that we in the Treasury had no record of any such telephone call. (It was evident from the text that what he described as the Prime Minister saying on the telephone was the gist of the telegram which was sent on November 18, and what he described as the President's reply on the telephone was the gist of the reply received on November 19);

c. I pointed out to him that he had omitted altogether from his narrative the reduction in Bank Rate, together with the tightening on hire purchase terms which took place in June 1965.

5. Turning to the article as a whole, I said that I thought it gave an unfair impression of the Government being buffeted about by

events and the initiatives always being taken by somebody else—the Americans, the Governor of the Bank of England or the Continental Central Bankers. I pointed out to him a number of places where this wrong impression was created; he said that it was difficult for an outsider to get these things right and undertook to do what he could to rectify it.

6. At the opening of that part of the narrative relating to the present Government's term of office, he stated that Sir Donald MacDougall, Professor Kaldor, Mr Nield and Dr Balogh were known to be in favour of devaluation. I said that whatever the views of these people might have been before they came into Government service, it was wrong to create the impression that this was the advice they had given when they were in the Government service, and even more dangerous to let it be supposed that this was still the advice they were giving. Mr Brandon disclaimed any intention of doing this, but agreed to take the sentence out altogether.

7. He asked me whether I thought the article as a whole would do damage to sterling. I said that I found it very difficult to say. He had certainly done his best to avoid this by treating it all as past history, and in particular by ending on the note of success of September 1965. Nevertheless, the markets were very irrational and the mere reminder of past dangers overcome might make people feel more nervous. I did not feel myself, however, that the article was so damaging that I must plead with him not to publish it.

8. He then said that his editor was considering the timing of the publication given the announcement of the Election. He was inclined to think that it would be better for it to be published during the period of the Election campaign when it would attract less attention than if it came out afterwards. I said that this might well be so from the point of view of the effect of sterling, but no doubt his editor would also think of the effect on the campaign itself.

1 March 1966 *W.A.*

NO. 10 DOWNING STREET
TO: THE PRIME MINISTER
"THE GREAT STERLING RESCUE OPERATION"
FROM: (SIR) DEREK MITCHELL

The attached note by William Armstrong was given to me yesterday afternoon and submitted to the Chancellor at the same time. For reasons that will emerge I held it until today, though I gather that the Chancellor may already have raised the subject with you. Even so—though writing in ignorance of any conclusion you reached with the Chancellor—I suggest that you read on.

In December 1965, I negotiated a concordat with Brandon on help he might have from Ministers and Officials in writing his articles and the conditions to which that help was subject. I heard no more from him until early in February when he invited me to have dinner with him on February 18. We met at Ronnie Grierson's house, where he was staying, and conversation was quite general until he produced with the coffee the complete first draft running to some 22,000 words. He was nervous about it on the ground that the subject matter was a technical one in which he had no expertise, and he begged me to read it through quickly and give him my impressions on whether it was worth publication. Having taken his salt I could hardly refuse, and in any case my curiosity was too strong.

My reaction on a quick reading was much the same as William Armstrong's when he was given a sight of the article (though, strictly speaking, articles, since it is to be published in three parts). On this, see Paragraphs 1–3 of William's note attached.

As with William, Brandon was evasive on his sources, but it was quite clear that he had got a lot of information in Washington and rather less in London. He regarded his talks with the First Secretary and the Chancellor as quite useless (both had closed up like clams) and Thomas [Balogh] had refused to see him (not that he had expected otherwise). During my reading I limited myself to making mental notes of some potentially awkward passages, and otherwise offered corrections only of numerous typing and stylistic errors.

On the following Monday we went to Moscow, but as soon as we returned I contacted William and found that he had meanwhile had the first of his own talks with Brandon and had arranged another (for Monday of this week). Brandon telephoned on Tuesday of this week and asked me to see him again because he was anxious to check certain of his facts. After a further word with William I called on him in the afternoon. Some of the points he wanted to check were ones to which he had been alerted by William. Most of them concerned your various meetings with Mr Governor [Lord Cromer] and here he was hoping not only for confirmation of dates but help in getting the atmosphere right and checking the arguments used on both sides (William discovered that Brandon had been to the South of France earlier this week to stay with Lord Cromer, and it is pretty clear that I was being asked to help with points put to him by Cromer with insufficient circumstantial detail).

This morning I heard from the Treasury that the Chancellor's reaction to William's note dated March 1 was that (a) the *Sunday Times* should be asked to defer publication until after the Election and (b) he should discuss the whole matter with you. If you did discuss this with him this afternoon it was in ignorance of a vital fact which emerged when I saw Brandon today: that the first of the three articles is to appear in the *Sunday Times* this Sunday and the remaining parts on March 13 and 20.

So much for the facts and history; now for comments.

The articles have probably been revised substantially since I saw them, but unless they are very different I do not myself believe (nor does William) that they will have a damaging effect on confidence. On the contrary they may give the impression (which could be damaging from another point of view) that the Labour Government leant over a little too far backwards to appease foreign opinion, including, of course, American opinion: for the links between the support operation last summer and the tightening of the Prices and Incomes policy emerge clearly. But the first article, is, to my mind, even more damaging to the Opposition. The picture which emerges of the handling of economic policy by Sir Alec Douglas-Home and Mr Maudling is one of appalling weakness and ineptness (I can give you some examples).

While *overall* the account can be regarded as politically neutral in the sense that both Governments are criticised and the moral is drawn that the handling of sterling should be "removed from politics", some of your colleagues do not emerge unblemished. For example, there is a vivid account of the First Secretary's meeting with representatives of the C.B.I. and the T.U.C. at which he urged on them the need for a tighter incomes policy in order to satisfy the foreign bankers.

As far as your own image is concerned the general impression is pretty favourable; though even here there are some things that could be put better: for example, I do not think you will enjoy reading the account of the alleged fits and starts by which you brought your relations with L.B.J. to their present high peak.

What can be done? Two things, I suggest. One, which the Chancellor had in his mind, was to persuade Lord Thomson to withhold the articles at any rate until after the Election. On this I would only say that it would be highly damaging if it became known that the Chancellor had got the articles suppressed. Although it could be said that this had been done in the interests of sterling it would be assumed that it had been done in the interests of the Labour Party during an Election campaign. And, if the Chancellor were rebuffed by Lord Thomson, the *Sunday Times* with memories of Anthony Howard fresh in their minds) might well blow the whole thing up.

The second would be to see Henry Brandon yourself. Ostensibly this would be so that you could give him your own account of some critical events, including the meetings with the Governor on which at the moment his articles are confused, or at any rate imprecise. This would improve still more the presentation of your own role, though, inevitably at the expense of depressing that of the Chancellor and perhaps the First Secretary.

This is an awkward situation, but in retrospect I do not think that there is anything that could have been done by H.M.G. to avoid it (apart from strangling the project at birth, which would have been exceedingly difficult). I do not believe that Brandon has obtained any information of any significance from Ministers or officials. Unfortunately, it may be thought on some points that he has. For example, there is an account of advice given to Maudling by the Treasury. I drew William's attention to this and he was startled when he read it, but established that it had been given to Brandon by Maudling himself!

5 *March 1966*   *D.J.M.*

Index

Index

Lloyd George, David — *contd.*
Daily Herald, 20–1; pioneer of
Lobby system, 21; memoirs, 22
Lobby system, 5–6, 7; and Lloyd
George, 21; and MacDonald, 44–7;
and Chamberlain, 51, 52–3, 58–9;
and Harold Wilson, 51–2, 141,
145–6, 152, 153, 155; and Churchill,
66, 69; and Attlee government,
89–90, 95, 98–9; and Macmillan,
122; and Heath, 157, 171
Lothian, Lord, 54

McColl, Ian, 151
MacDonald, Ramsey, 1, 48–9, 63,
151, 172; press persecution of, 37–8;
and Daimler affair, 38–40; and case
of *Workers' Weekly*, 40–3; and
Zinoviev letter, 43–4; and leak on
India policy, 44–7, 176
McDonald, Iverach, 107
McGahey, Mick, 167
McLachlan, Donald, 106
Macleod, Ian, 51 and n, 131, 132
Macmillan, Harold, 1, 6, 7, 24, 48 and
n, 63, 85, 111, 128, 129, 130, 131,
136, 137, 155, 159, 170, 182; and
Radcliffe inquiry, 9–10; and "Eden
Group", 102; and Suez, 113; character as Prime Minister, 115–18; and
personal interviews, 118–19; attacks
on his economic policy, 121; and
Vassall spy scandal, 120, 122–3,
124–5; and Profumo affair, 120,
122, 123–5; and Conservative attack
on David Wood, 125–7; foreign pol-
icy, 138–9
Maitland, Sir Donald, 161, 171
Mallalieu, J. P., 97
Manchester Guardian, 5, 67, 69, 82, 83,
112
Margach, James, 51, 52, 61, 88, 93,
95, 110–11, 117–18, 119, 139; relations with Harold Wilson, 144, 147,
148, 153; and Edward Heath, 160,
162–3, 164–5
Marks, Derek, 127
Marlborough, 65
Marx, Karl, 138
Maxton, James, 139
Memoirs of a Conservative, 35n
Mirror Group, 7–8; and Churchill, 64,
72–84; and Edward Heath, 167–9

Mitchell, Derek, 143–4, 174, 175,
187–90
Monopolies Commission, 6, 145
Moran, Lord, 84, 85
Morning Post, 19, 20, 65
Morning Star, 104
Morrison, Herbert, 74, 75, 77, 78–80,
81, 82; and anti-Attlee press, 93–4,
97–8
Morrison, Colonel John, 126
Munich crisis, 5, 54, 60
Murray, George, 110
Mussolini, Benito, 5, 31, 33, 100, 112;
and Chamberlain, 51, 53, 55, 56, 58,
59, 60–1, 103; invasion of Abys-
sinia, 52; invasion of Albania, 52,
59, 61

Nasser, President, 100, 106, 108, 112,
113
National Government, the, 23, 172
National Opinion Polls, 134
National Union of Journalists, 94
National Union of Mineworkers, 166,
167
New Despotism, The, 12
New Empire Party, 23, 29
New Society, 182
New Statesman, 154
New York Times, 154
Newman, Frederick, 87
News Chronicle, 5, 44, 45, 176; and
Chamberlain, 50, 60–1; and Chur-
chill, 64, 83; and Eden, 109–10
News of the World, 6, 13, 14, 92, 152
Newspaper Proprietors' Association,
73, 74–5
1922 Committee, 125–7
Norman, R. C., 34
North, Lord, 105
Northcliffe, Lord, 15–16, 17, 135
Northumberland, Duke of, 14–15
Nye: The Beloved Patrician, 117n

Observer, the, 8, 107, 108, 129, 112;
and Harold Wilson, 147–50
*Off the Record, Political Interviews
1933–45*, 82n
Official Secrets Act, 2, 3, 4, 7, 10, 11,
19, 28, 183; and Ramsey Mac-
Donald, 44, 45, 46–8; and Callaghan, 176; and Harold Wilson,
178, 179, 180